THIS IS FOR THE MARA SALVATRUCHA

THIS IS FOR THE MARA SALVATRUCHA

INSIDE THE MS-13, AMERICA'S MOST VIOLENT GANG

SAMUEL LOGAN

HYPERION

NEW YORK

Library of Congress Cataloging-in-Publication Data is available upon request.

ISBN: 978-1-4013-2324-0

Hyperion books are available for special promotions and premiums. For details contact the HarperCollins Special Markets Department in the New York office at 212-207-7528, fax 212-207-7222, or email spsales@harpercollins.com.

FIRST EDITION

10 9 8 7 6 5 4 3 2 1

THIS LABEL APPLIES TO TEXT STOCK

We try to produce the most beautiful books possible, and we are also extremely concerned about the impact of our manufacturing process on the forests of the world and the environment as a whole. Accordingly, we've made sure that all of the paper we use has been certified as coming from forests that are managed to insure the protection of the people and wildlife dependent upon them.

For any kid tempted to join a street gang

ACKNOWLEDGMENTS

First and foremost, I would like to thank my wife for her unconditional support over this past year of work on my first book, and my daughter for her inspiration. I want to thank Stephanie Hanson and my agent, Rebecca Friedman, for realizing the potential in me. Kasey Gronau Ewing, my creative editor, guided me through the transition from journalist to storyteller. I can't thank her enough. Yvette Bennet, my transcriptionist, listened to countless hours of interview material, and was fundamental to bringing this book to life, thank you.

I want to thank the Paz and Calzada families for accepting me into their homes and treating me as a guest, despite my tough and painful questions. Finally, I want to thank the men and women with whom I conducted countless interviews. Without their help, this important story and powerful message would never have been told.

PART 1

arrollton, Texas, is a town with an identity and a presence normally not felt in the United States. It is a place where people use the sidewalks despite the weather and America's love for cars. There are always plenty of people waiting at the bus stops. Advertisements often read in Spanish, a constant reminder of the first language spoken by the people most likely to read them. Middle-aged men loiter around convenience stores, looking for work and avoiding the police.

Crime statistics are not high, but that's because many people in Carrollton never called the police. They silently absorb the criminals rather than deal with the law and possibly draw too much attention to themselves.

On a cold night just before Christmas in 2001, at a cantina in Carrollton, Brenda Paz was shooting pool with her friends on an ancient, rundown pool table. They listened to old ranchero music while the other patrons, with a dark past and no care for the future, sat at the bar trying to ignore them. Brenda's friends all had tattoos on their faces and necks, visible for all to see, despite the cold. Even though Brenda was underage, no one bothered her. No one was willing to cross her or her gang, who had a reputation for violence and spread fear everywhere they went.

Extortion was a daily activity for Brenda and her gang. They roamed the streets of Carrollton like a band of urban gypsies, looking for cash. They made regular stops with the owners of check-cashing stores, bars, and pool halls, prostitution joints, used-car lots, and other small businesses. The owners knew that if they didn't pay up, they would lose everything.

When Brenda leaned forward to take a shot, her shirtsleeve receded to reveal a large tattoo on the inside of her bicep. Another one decorated her elbow. Her boyfriend's name adorned the topside of her right wrist, and three equidistant dots in the skin between her thumb and forefinger completed her most visible gang signs. She was not a murderer, but she had been in the gang long enough to earn her stripes.

She wasn't very good at pool, but a sharp tongue and a quick wit kept her gangster friends at bay. Women in her gang rarely spoke back to the men, but Brenda could do so because she was the girlfriend of the group's leader, the only man who reserved the right to beat her. No one else could touch her. Her boyfriend's threat was always present.

The group played pool to pass the time. There would be a party later that night in the neighboring city of Grand Prairie, but no one was in a hurry. They had settled into a comfortable routine of shooting stick, drinking beer, and carelessly spending the money they regularly extorted from the hardworking men and women in their community.

Tonight, Brenda was impatient. She wanted to get going. She needed more action than this tired old cantina. Before the game was over, she walked to a public phone by the bar to call a new friend, a boy she had met only weeks earlier at a shopping mall. She wanted him to give her and her friend Flaca a ride to the party. The other guys could meet up with them later.

Options for friends outside Brenda's gang were limited. She knew that hanging out even for a short time with another boy might invite problems, especially because her boyfriend had no patience for outsiders. But Brenda was sometimes rebellious and defied his wishes. She liked making new friends outside the gang. They allowed her a moment to soften a little and act like a girl. Her charisma could quickly disarm anyone, and Brenda made friends easily. Thumbing the dirty blue receiver connected to the cantina's pay phone, Brenda filed through the numbers in her head, then settled on the cell phone of Javier Calzada.

He was a good-looking boy, the son of two Mexican immigrants. Brenda knew he was a proud young man who worked hard and enjoyed spending his money on nice things. He had told her all about his car the first time they'd met. It was a source of great pride. He had installed an enviable sound system, neon ground effects, and head-turning rims. Once, a guy he knew had stolen his ground effects; Javier had found the guy and confronted him about it. Brenda thought that took guts. Javier occasionally got into fights, but they were nothing like what Brenda's gang got involved in. He had seen some violence in his young life, but mostly he kept out of trouble.

Brenda admired him because he was respectful and well raised, not a common quality among the men and women in her circle. Many of them were the children of Latino immigrants who lived in the Carrollton area and were rough around the edges, or worse. Some were high school dropouts like Brenda. A few had never even made it that far.

Javier had met Brenda through a mutual friend at the local mall, and he had liked her immediately. Her smile lit up her face and immediately melted her hardened shell. That same smile had earned her the street name Smiley, but only her gangster friends called her that.

Javier thought Brenda was someone he wanted to get to know better. He had no idea she was in a street gang, let alone the gang leader's girl. In the brief moment they had spent together, there had been no space for talk of street gangs and who was dating whom. There was only a shared moment for small talk and the possibility of something more the next time they met.

When Brenda reached Javier on the phone, he was cruising at Bachman Lake Park, a local teen hangout. Javier was often at Bachman Lake because he enjoyed driving his car and showing it off, especially the rims. He didn't mind giving his friends a ride, and his parents were not strict. He had earned their trust, and they knew he never stayed out late.

Javier was happy to hear from Brenda again. It was his chance to get to know her better. When she asked for a ride, he was happy to oblige. As was his routine, he gave his mom a call to tell her he was going to give a friend a ride to Grand Prairie, then he would come straight home. When he arrived at the cantina, Brenda and her friend Flaca, a skinny young Latina, were waiting at the bar, apart from Brenda's tattooed friends. They didn't hang around, but walked quickly to Javier's green Chevrolet Malibu. Flaca got into the backseat on the passenger side and Brenda hopped in up front.

As they set off, Brenda asked Javier if he could just make one stop on the way. She wanted to pick up her boyfriend, Veto. Javier's heart sank when he realized Brenda had a boyfriend, but as he turned to her, she gave him that smile again. He was unable to say no. Javier didn't know anything about Veto, but the change in plans really wasn't a big deal to him. They were already driving to Grand Prairie. What was another five minutes out of their way?

On the way to Veto's apartment, Brenda talked freely with Javier, smiling and enjoying a rare moment away from her gang, where she was under constant pressure to be her "other self." They finally arrived and parked in front of Veto's apartment building. Brenda got out to get him. When Brenda returned to the car with Veto, Javier noticed she was a different person, reserved and quiet. Javier didn't like that. As she got in the front seat, she barely looked at him. Veto walked around the back of the car to get into the seat behind Javier.

As they all loaded up and Javier started the car, the mood had swung from friendly to something more serious. Javier wondered what Brenda was doing with a guy that seemed to make her so unhappy. Flaca was muted and stared timidly at the floor. Brenda didn't say a word. From behind Javier, Veto spoke up as soon as he was in the car with the door shut.

"Who you down with?" Veto asked loudly, shattering the awkward silence like a hammer hitting a glass table. Veto was in control now. As the leader of Brenda's gang, he had to know if the stranger was in a rival gang or not.

"No one," Javier told him, slightly unnerved by the rude confrontation.

Veto was considerably older than the other three in the car. He never backed away from a stare and challenged all strangers around him with the same edgy disposition. Those who knew Veto were well aware of what he could do. Javier didn't know him, but he could sense that this guy wasn't one to be messed with. He figured the faster he got them where they needed to go, the better. The night wasn't going as he had planned, and he was more than ready to just drop them off and go home. So he told Veto the truth. Javier was not a member of any gang.

As the Malibu merged onto Interstate 30, one of the highways that connected Grand Prairie with Carrollton, Veto was also thinking. He decided Javier wasn't telling the truth. Without a word to anyone in the car, Veto made another change to the night's plans: he sent a text message to his gangster friends at the cantina.

When the headlights of a car behind Javier's Malibu illuminated the interior, Veto took a quick look over his shoulder, mentally confirming that his friends were now following them. The moment had arrived to announce the change of plans. Veto pulled a chrome-plated revolver from his waistband and firmly pressed the barrel against the back of Javier's head.

Brenda's and Flaca's faces registered surprised, but Javier was stunned, still behind the wheel, as realization hit. He fought to control his fear, white-knuckling the steering wheel. His body tensed as he felt the cold metal press against the spot where the curve of the skull meets the top of the spinal cord. He became sensitive to every small movement of the pistol, every rustle in the car, as his body pumped full of adrenaline and his pulse began to pound. He fought to stay calm and make only the moves necessary to drive the car. He didn't look to Brenda for help, and she continued staring away from him. As much as she liked Javier, Brenda was in no position to persuade Veto to lower the pistol. Veto was her boyfriend and the leader of her gang. If he chose to pull a gun on Javier, she wasn't going to stop him.

Just as the two-car caravan crossed the line into Grand Prairie, Veto told Javier to take the next exit. Chaotic thoughts fought for space inside Javier's head as Veto kept the pistol pressed against it. Veto was calm and didn't act nervous or shout demands. He held Javier's life at the tip of his trigger finger, yet acted like he was giving directions to an old friend.

At the bottom of the exit ramp, the Malibu turned right onto MacArthur Boulevard and quickly veered left onto an open gravel parking lot across from a cement pipe factory. No cars passed on MacArthur Boulevard. The Malibu's headlights pierced through the slight drizzle to reveal an opening on the other side of the lot. Oh shit, Javier thought. It was a forgotten gravel access road that led to a pond that local fishermen visited on the weekends. Late at night on a Saturday in the cold rain, there would be no one at the end of that road.

Perfect, Veto thought.

He told Javier to drive toward the open gate, knowing the other car would follow. At the end of the access road, the Malibu's tires rolled to a stop in wet grass, gravel, and mud. The second car parked behind the first. Brenda was thinking steps ahead of the moment. She had seen this before. Veto enjoyed stealing cars, and he especially liked to steal cars with nice rims. She was almost sure that later that night, they would all be partying and laughing about how Veto had scared Javier and left him in Grand Prairie with no car.

"Get out," Veto told Javier before he opened his own door and, still pointing the gun at Javier, motioned for the others to join them. Javier was relieved to no longer have the gun pressed to the back of his head, but fear still gripped his chest. This was supposed to be a quick trip into Grand Prairie to take Brenda and her friend to a party. As he quickly assessed how isolated their location was, his mind was spinning with all the possible things that could happen to him. His brain was jumping from idea to idea, trying to come up with a flight plan. He quickly gave up any thoughts of passersby or cops. The only person who would be looking for him was his mom, who would soon begin to worry. Thinking about her didn't help.

No more time for thinking, though, as Veto and his friends circled Javier and pushed him toward a clearing in the woods, just off the access road and closer to the pond. Cars passing on the nearby highway occasionally interrupted the sound of the rain hitting tree branches and leaves on the forest floor. The brush was not thick, and the leafless trees did little to protect the gangsters and their victim from the rain and cold. Their feet pressed into the soft earth. Javier could hear the numerous feet trampling behind him breaking twigs and squishing on the forest floor. He could smell the crispness of the air, his senses on full alert.

Brenda and Flaca watched from the car as Veto shoved the pistol in his waistband and looked at Javier, then looked at the men in his gang. It was a silent signal. Someone kicked Javier, forcing him to the ground. He immediately tried to defend himself, but kicks to his head, groin, stomach, and back forced him into a tight ball. He instinctively used his arms to protect his head. His legs were drawn up into his torso to protect his stomach and chest. All his nerves became electrified with pain as they continued to pummel him, an onslaught of fists and feet. He couldn't feel the cold anymore, his brain seizing up, only able to focus on the overwhelming sense of pain. He fought to breathe. Brenda winced each time they kicked Javier in the head. She knew what that felt like. It would be over soon, she thought. Javier was tough. He could take it. The boys would soon grow tired of their fun and they would be off to the party.

By the time they finished beating Javier, Veto and the others were breathing hard. Their hot breath frosted in the night air as they stood over Javier, who lay on the ground in a mixture of mud, rotten leaves, and blood. He was still conscious, and when he was able to get past the buzzing in his ears, he realized they had stopped beating him. He was able to find relief in that thought as nausea clawed at his stomach. His vision was spotty. At least they were finished and would leave him alone. It was a pause in time just wide enough to allow Javier to hope. But Veto was not finished.

He motioned to another gangster, who helped him grab Javier and bring him to his knees. Javier swayed with little control over his broken body. He could barely hold himself up. His head fell forward as shards of glass seemed to shoot through his chest with every breath, and he wanted to fall back to the ground. But Veto's heavy grip with one hand on his shoulder kept him from falling over. The other hand, reaching for his gun, was quick. In one swift motion, Veto pulled the pistol from his waistband, pressed the short barrel against Javier's left temple, and pulled the trigger.

Rain continued to hit the windshield of Javier's car with a natural rhythm until Brenda heard the gunshot. Damp air had muffled the pistol's bark, but it reverberated inside the car and in Brenda's head with resounding clarity. She made a slight jump back against the seat when it went off. She took a deep breath, realizing that she felt a little sad. Most of the people Veto killed were nobodies to her, but she had liked Javier.

Through the rain-streaked passenger window, Brenda saw Veto release Javier from his grip. His body crumpled forward onto the forest floor. No one said a word. It had all happened so quickly, the men could still hear the noise of the kicking and punching and the final bark of the pistol in their ears as they stood in the rain. Their own blood pumped furiously; it took a moment for their instincts to die down and allow the calm of the evening to sink in. All of them knew why Veto had killed Javier. He had proved who was boss by killing a stranger in cold blood. It was their way.

Before they left, one of the boys squatted down and began to pull off Javier's shoes. Someone else took his wallet and searched his body for valuables. They left Javier there in the mud and returned to the cars. Before he got into the driver's seat of the Malibu, Veto wiped his prints from the door handle. He sat behind the wheel and made the sign of the cross. With a detached tone, he said, "Forgive me, Lord, for what I have done."

Veto's long, thin fingers twisted on the keys in the ignition and started Javier's car. He put the car in reverse, twisted his torso, and squinted into the headlights of the car behind them as he slowly backed down the access road. Once they were in the parking lot, Veto spun the car around with a sharp rotation of the wheel. Soon the small caravan was on its way to Dallas.

Brenda remained silent. Flaca was almost forgotten in the backseat. No one spoke during the twenty-minute ride back to Carrollton. Veto took an exit off Interstate 35, and headed toward Walnut Hill Lane, where he pulled Javier's car into a field near a go-cart park located near the old railroad line.

Veto, Brenda, and Flaca stepped out of the Malibu, careful not to leave prints. After wiping off the steering wheel and the inside of the driver's door, Veto ordered his crew to get to work on removing the Malibu's rims. Hands still swollen from beating Javier worked to strip off the lug nuts, one tire at a time. It was slow going. The rain-soaked earth couldn't support the weight of the car. The jack sunk into the mud before hitting solid ground. Cold, muddy hands fought to grip the slippery tire iron. Eventually the group was forced to abandon the Malibu, heedless of any consequence.

renda Paz had only been in Texas a few months before she met Vcto. Born in San Pcdro Sula, Honduras, she legally immigrated to the United States when she was three. Brenda grew up in El Monte, an immigrant community off the San Bernardino highway, east of downtown Los Angeles. She was a remarkable student and a well-behaved member of her loving family, one of sixteen children fathered by the same man with a number of different women. Despite having so many children, José Paz treated Brenda as if she were his only child. She was his youngest, and he worked hard for her. As a young teenager she had a pager and a cell phone. Brenda had two rooms to herself, while most of her cousins shared a single room with at least one other sibling.

Brenda's dad worked long hours as a diesel engine mechanic. He specialized in huge Caterpillar tractor engines. Short and stocky with weathered dark skin and close-cropped black hair, José Paz was the quintessential hardworking immigrant. He rose before dawn and returned home after sunset seven days a week. His gnarled hands were swollen and painful. Daily use of industrial solvent to remove grease dried his hands and fingers into a latticework of small cracks that itched constantly. After an accident at work smashed José's right foot, doctors inserted a metal rod to keep his toe straight. His whole foot hurt when it was cold, but no matter the weather José always wore the same outfit: shorts, a T-shirt, and flip-flops. He was a simple, humble man who wanted little more than to work hard and provide for his family, especially his baby girl.

Brenda's mom, Rosa, didn't work. She doted on Brenda, the only child she had with José, and picked her up from school every day, bringing her an extra umbrella when it rained. Brenda was very close to both of her parents and bathed in the affections of a close-knit family that included aunts, uncles, and cousins. During her childhood, Brenda had learned to depend upon her family's support and love.

In the early months of 2001, José and Rosa experienced marital problems. He worked long hours, and Rosa began a long downward spiral into the depths of a psychological disorder poorly understood by José, Brenda, and the rest of the family. It was something like schizophrenia, but no one knew for sure. Focused on supporting Rosa even as her sickness grew from a mild concern to a serious mental illness, José moved his family back to Honduras. There he purchased a house for them outside of San Pedro Sula, the country's industrial capital.

But José's solution wasn't enough. Rosa descended deeper into her mental sickness and could no longer take care of their daughter. Rosa required a daily dose of medicine to maintain a connection with reality. When she skipped her dose, she would wander through town, unsure of her surroundings or who she was. Brenda turned fifteen in Honduras. She had finished the eighth grade and needed to start high school, and José needed to get back to the United States to work. José was unable to depend on his wife. He wanted Brenda to start high school in the United States at the beginning of the regular school year, so he made a tough decision: he sent Brenda back to the United States at the end of the summer to live with his brother Rafael in Carrollton, Texas.

Brenda arrived in Texas with all the motivation of any curious teenager in a new environment, yet she was deeply saddened by her parents' separation and even more distraught over her mother's mental condition. For a fifteen-year-old girl, it was a heavy emotional burden to carry.

The separation was stressful, but her mother's sickness was the most acute cause for Brenda's distress. Brenda couldn't understand what was wrong with her. One day her mother was just as she'd always been; the next she was a complete stranger.

Living under her uncle's care in Texas, Brenda quickly discovered that her home life was going to be very different from what she was used to. Rafael Paz had two children and little time for Brenda. She shared a small apartment with four other people, a far cry from her privileged position as the only child in the house with two rooms to herself.

She felt like a burden, not a loved family member. No one picked her up from school. No one helped her with homework. Her life in Texas was an abrupt, dramatic change. She wasn't doted on, but was forced to adjust to life in a new town where she had no friends. The love and support she needed and had been so accustomed to simply weren't there.

A month after school started, classes became a secondary focus; making new friends became Brenda's primary goal. She craved attention and hated going home, where her sour uncle and his unwelcoming family offered little more than the bare minimum for coexistence.

With her naturally outgoing personality Brenda quickly gathered a large group of friends. Eventually her circle widened to include kids who were a little older than her and didn't go to school. Her friends at school only overlapped a little with the world of street kids, gangsters, and criminals, but it was enough to pull Brenda into a life very different from her old life in California.

One of her new friends was a Salvadoran of slight build, gaunt face, and burning determination. From the forehead down, he was covered in tattoos that proclaimed his very real power within a street gang. His world was all about survival and living on the street. He was edgy and tough, proud and powerful. But he was a man who looked her in the eye, listened when she spoke, and asked questions that showed he was really interested in what she had to say. He focused on Brenda and filled the part of her heart hollowed out by the distance from her extended family in California and the apathy in her uncle's home. When she met Veto, Brenda thought he was the love of her life.

For his part, Veto liked Brenda's smile, her saucy attitude, and her charismatic presence. They began dating only a few weeks after their first meeting. Veto enjoyed Brenda's presence. She made him laugh and showed heart. He respected her intellect and attitude. But because of Veto's position, he could only date female members of his own gang.

Brenda's disappointing home life made her an ideal target for any gang recruiter. She needed to belong and needed something to anchor her to her new life in Texas. Veto became that anchor as he evolved into an exciting love interest. After dating through the fall and into the winter, Veto convinced Brenda to join his gang.

CHAPTER 3

Women interested in joining Veto's gang had two options. In the first option they could be "sexed in." Gang members would force themselves on the female initiate, repeatedly raping her until all involved were satisfied. Women who joined the gang through sex were considered subhuman and had little or no respect among the other gangsters.

The other option was to endure a vicious beating; this was called "jumping in." For over ten seconds, five or six gang members punch and kick initiates, who are not allowed to fight back. One, one thousand, two, one thousand, three, one thousand . . .

Brenda chose to be jumped in. She was a young woman who always demanded respect, already a difficult proposition for female gang members. Gang banging was not an option.

On a cold winter night Brenda entered a circle of men and braced herself for a beating she couldn't have imagined. She was kicked in the head with vicious, full-strength blows. Fists rained all over her body. The men showed no mercy. Time slowed down and she felt every punch. The pain that racked her body was unlike anything she had ever experienced. Flying feet and fists attacked her ears, her ribs, her kidneys, her stomach, and then her face. The kicks were the worst. They made her head ring. She could no longer curl into a ball to defend herself. At the point when she couldn't take another blow, it ended. Brenda had endured the brutal beating like any male gang member. Veto and the others helped her to her feet. She was choky. Her fingertips tingled as adrenaline line still coursed through her body, but her mind told her it was over. She had made it. The group congratulated her with smiles as if they weren't the men who had just beaten her like she was a piñata. Though she was disoriented, she could see Veto pushing through the circle of men, the first to give her a hug.

After her jumping-in ceremony, Veto treated Brenda differently. He was able to open more of his life to her, tell her about his past days with the gang in Los Angeles, and share his plans for the gang in Texas. He was very proud of her. Everyone in Veto's gang knew she was his girlfriend. If she had cried out or shown weakness during the beating, it would have reflected poorly on him. But she took her beating like a man. There were no tears or girlish whimpering. She paid for the respect in bruises, blood clots, a black eye, and a nasty headache. They respected her all the more for it. She was now a homie, a term of endearment that she quickly learned gangsters used to address one another.

Once she was a member of the gang, Brenda resolved to live on the streets. She'd had enough of her uncle. He didn't want her around, and she didn't want to be there anyway. The gang could provide food and shelter for her and more support than she received from Rafael. School was boring and stupid. Hanging out with Veto and his friends was much more fun. Brenda thought she had chosen a life of freedom and fun and a new family that respected her. It was everything she'd been missing since she moved to Texas, all wrapped up into one experience. Being a gangster wasn't that bad at all. The decision to leave her uncle and stay with Veto and her new homies was an easy one to make.

They called her Smiley, and she loved it. But her honeymoon period only lasted a few days. Beyond the pain she endured from the jumping-in ceremony, there was a much steeper price to pay. Just days after her initiation, Veto forced her to go with him to a grocery store and rob the owner at gunpoint. She couldn't believe the rush she felt when Veto pulled a gun on the guy. She could feel him soak up the power, feeding off of fear. But she was also scared, and watched herself as a gangster going through the motions of the armed robbery as if she was watching a play. In the first few moments after the robbery, once Veto and Brenda were safe, she silently resolved to keep the scared Brenda somewhere locked up in her mind. Veto didn't like that part of her, so she would only show him the tough Brenda, the woman who had heart and who could take a beating.

Veto catapulted Brenda into a fast and furious life of crime, violence, and death. She loved the excitement of life on the street, but for all the fun and freedom that came with it, there was constant pressure to prove herself and her loyalty to the gang. The stakes constantly got higher.

CHAPTER 4

Smile now, cry later. Brenda learned the saying as she learned the true pains of her chosen gangster lifestyle. Don't look back at what you've seen or done—just focus on the moment and the future. There will be time for sorrow later. This is a common street gang philosophy, represented by the Greek masks for tragedy and comedy. Variations of these masks were a common gang tattoo, and one of the first Brenda received after having Veto's name inked onto her wrist.

As Brenda got to know Veto better and learned more about how the gang made money through extortion and prostitution, she realized that Veto's group of friends was obviously not a group of fun-loving teenagers, as she had thought at first. But once she had jumped in, there was no way out. She was always surrounded by her homies. Veto's constant presence reminded her of her place.

Her love affair with Veto, a source of happiness before she joined his gang, became a source of pain and fear. She could mask the fear but lashed out with strong words and attitude. It was the best way she knew to act like a gangster, but when Veto began to physically abuse Brenda to keep her saucy attitude in line, she learned when she could open her mouth and when she couldn't. Veto did not allow her to talk back to him around their homies.

In private, Veto respected her for her intelligence. He thought she had a memory like a video camera. Brenda could see something and never forget it, and for Veto, someone at the head of an ambitious group of Latino gangbangers in Texas, Brenda was a useful tool. Veto kept her close and showed her what the gang life was like from his point of view, through the lens of an old-school gangster at the peak of his game.

The gang that Brenda joined, and the one Veto was a high-ranking leader of, was the Mara Salvatrucha. The Mara Salvatrucha was a Latino street gang networked across the United States through smaller groups known as cliques. Some cliques, like Veto's, were large enough to have representation in multiple cities. Others were centralized around a single city or cluster of closely linked urban centers.

As the head of his clique in Dallas, the Normandie Locos Salvatrucha, Veto was a seasoned gangster from Los Angeles who originally moved from California to Texas to help establish his gang there. He eventually settled on the Dallas area as an ideal place to begin recruiting new members. The towns of Carrollton, Farmers Branch, Grand Prairie, and other towns that were part of the Dallas metropolitan area were full of troubled youth in search of something beyond their frustrating home life. Recruiters in Veto's gang focused on the schools in the area. They would approach groups of young Latinos at local parks, places where they worked, bars, and nightclubs.

The Normandie Locos was one of the larger cliques within the national Mara Salvatrucha network. Veto had given his life to the clique and his gang. He lived on the street and took his gang life very seriously. Brenda joined Veto's clique at a time when it already had strong representation in Los Angeles and a half-dozen other cities. Veto thought that once he had recruited enough MS members in Dallas, the city would be an ideal place to build on his favorite criminal enterprise: human smuggling.

Veto was from the San Miguel region of El Salvador, an impoverished area where entire village populations had been transplanted from Central America to neighborhoods in Los Angeles. His family had long been in the human smuggling business; Veto himself had crossed the border illegally a number of times and easily entered the United States to work, returning to El Salvador to visit his family from time to time.

As a young man living and working in Los Angeles, Veto knew that there was money to be made in human trafficking. But as a Salvadoran living near downtown Los Angeles in the early 1990s, he was part of a minority of immigrants who were constantly harassed by immigrants from Mexico. He needed protection, and the only protection around was with the Mara Salvatrucha. At the time, MS was nearly completely Salvadoran and limited to a small number of cliques inside Los Angeles. Veto joined the Normandie Locos clique, paid his dues, and from the early 1990s to 2001 rose through the gang's ranks. He reached the top because he was tough and ruthless, but more importantly, he had passion and pride in his gang and his country. When Veto met Brenda, he was in Dallas making business plans and slowly building his clique, one member at a time.

Brenda arrived in Texas in the late summer as a well-loved, innocent girl. Yet with every day marching toward the end of her first semester, Brenda met more MS members and men who gave her all the attention she could ever want. She became Veto's girl and thereby reaped the rewards of being in a position of importance. She sat next to the most respected man in the group at informal meetings. His friends who came to visit were also MS leaders. They adored Veto's girlfriend. They were strong, confident men who had no fear and enjoyed enormous respect. Brenda enjoyed this role, and though she had learned to fear the dark side of street life, she never thought that gang life would get as serious as it did the night Veto killed Javier Calzada.

CHAPTER 5

The city of Grand Prairie was unaccustomed to violent murder. In a community where burglary was considered a rare crime, murder was extraordinary. It was a small city with a small crime-fighting budget. When news of Javier Calzada's murder hit the local papers, it shook the sleepy community to its core.

Mr. and Mrs. Calzada were Latino immigrants who owned a two-bedroom home in a middle-class Latino neighborhood just south of Farmers Branch and north of Dallas Love Field Airport. Marisa was a short Mexican lady with a naturally kind face. She moved slowly, with deliberation and purpose. Her husband, Ben, was slightly taller. His forearms rippled with muscles developed by working long hours with his hands. He liked to wear a baseball cap and tilted it back slightly on his head in a relaxed way when he wiped his forehead with the back of his hand. Ben often carried an easy, half-parted grin. The Calzadas were a happy, well-matched couple who had emigrated from Mexico in the 1980s and met in the United States. They had two relatively well behaved sons, Luis and Javier. Dallas had been their home for years, and the family never had any street gang trouble or disciplinary problems with Javier or his older brother.

Before leaving for Grand Prairie on the night he was killed, Javier turned to his mom and said, "I'll be right back." A little while later, he called to let her know he was giving a couple of new friends a ride to

Grand Prairie, then he'd come straight home. No problem. Javier was in high school, but his mom was accustomed to him calling to give her regular updates, even if his friends gave him a hard time for being a mama's boy. He was a good kid. She did not expect Javier to take too long.

Midnight came and went. Marisa and Ben sat up in the living room, waiting for Javier to come home. They couldn't help but worry. Something was wrong. Javier was usually mindful of his mother, and he often called her, even when he was out cruising around with his friends. He didn't drink or smoke, nor did he stay out late. Normally he would come home at a decent hour, but he didn't come home that night.

The next morning, Marisa was distraught. Her red-rimmed eyes burned from a long night of waiting up for her son. When she left the house at first light to drive around and look for him, she hadn't taken the time to pull herself together. Her son was missing, and she knew nothing. With increasing anxiety, she visited all the hospitals in her neighborhood, all within miles of Bachman Lake Park. As she drove around, her eyes never stopped moving. Her heart leaped from her chest when she thought she saw him, but her eyes were tired, her vision blurred by the lack of sleep and the tears that were on the verge of falling.

That afternoon, she printed dozens of MISSING posters and put them up around the neighborhood and in areas where she knew her son hung out. All day she kept repeating the phrase "I'll be right back" in her mind even as she began to fear the worst. It was not like Javier to keep his mother worrying, and when he did, it was never for this long.

While his wife visited local hospitals and posted MISSING signs on lampposts, bus stops, and gas stations, Ben drove to the Dallas Police Department to file a missing-persons report. He was distrustful of the local police; he felt like they never came around when they were needed. When they did show up, the men in uniform wore smug expressions and never took off their sunglasses. They asked too many questions and harassed hardworking people. Ben was in the country legally and would never have trouble with the hard realities of deportation, but he still avoided the police. He didn't want to push his luck with local cops or the *federales* with immigration enforcement. Yet as much as he didn't want to engage the police, Ben had no choice. He needed their help.

Two days passed before a Dallas policeman found Javier's car in the mud off Walnut Hill Lane on December 19, less than ten miles from Ben and Marisa's home. That same day, a construction worker discovered Javier's wallet off Interstate 35, which ran north-south through Dallas. When Ben and Marisa received the news, it felt like a punch in the stomach. Reality crushed their hope: the odds were against finding Javier alive. But there was still no body. He might have been robbed, but he could still be alive somewhere, they thought. The Calzadas grasped at what hope remained.

Sleep was impossible. Marisa was in shambles. She cried continually. Each time they called the Dallas police, they found out there were no leads. Ben grew impatient. He couldn't just wait. Early one morning during the first week after Javier's disappearance, Ben went out to look for his son in the surrounding countryside. He took a backpack, food, and water. He was up before dawn and spent the whole day away from the house. When he returned home, Marisa was furious. She thought he had been out commiserating and drinking with his friends, but, no, he explained to his wife. With a tight hug he told her he had been looking for their lost boy.

By the end of the first week of Javier's disappearance, the Calzadas' natural joy and easygoing natures had been extinguished. With each night, the sorrow deepened. With each day, the weight of despair increased. Marisa's happiness was broken, but not her will to find out what had happened. He would be right back, her son had told her. She needed to know why he had never returned.

In the middle of a town awash with Christmas carols, candy canes, and Papá Noel, the family felt hollowed out with despair. As everyone around them drew together in groups of family and friends, the Calzadas felt drained and listless. They sang no carols. A sad, gray Christmas came and went. It was the first time Ben, Marisa, and Luis had spent the holidays without Javier. And they still didn't know what had happened.

CHAPTER 6

Early in the afternoon, two days after Christmas, a local fisherman parked his car in a gravel lot near the highway and next to a cement pipe factory off MacArthur Boulevard. He grabbed a pole and some tackle before setting off down the old access road toward Bluebonnet Lake, one of his favorite fishing holes. After a short walk, he noticed out of the corner of his eye a bundle of clothes and something that looked like bones in the bushes off the side of the road. Curious, he walked a little closer to the clothes and realized with a grimace that he was looking at decomposed human remains.

The skeleton was splayed at awkward angles on the ground, twisted in dried brush and leaves. White sport Polo socks clung to the partially fleshed feet. The shoes were missing. A blue fleece jacket and a navy blue shirt were twisted about the neck and shoulders. The words ALPHA CHI OMEGA, KAPPA SIGMA, SPRING 2000 were printed on the torn shirt.

The remains had been in the woods long enough for insects, stray dogs, and other animals to destroy recognizable features, ripping clothes off the skeleton and making the body all but unidentifiable. The midsection was empty of organs. Lungs, kidneys, heart, stomach, intestines, and liver had all been eaten. The flesh on the skull had eroded. The fingers on the left hand were missing, and some ribs had been torn from the torso. Those that remained were stripped clean, along with the spinal cord and pelvis. Flesh lingered on the arms and upper chest where the torn and muddy clothes had protected the skin, but there was little left to make any sense of what had happened or when.

The stunned fisherman called the Grand Prairie Police Department to describe the scene and the location. Within minutes, department personnel notified Sergeant Alan Patton, head of the Major Crimes Unit. Patton quickly grabbed his partner and drove out to the cement pipe factory.

Sergeant Patton was born and raised in Grand Prairie. He was a hometown cop who had the appearance of an old-school Texas Ranger, the kind who considered a horse his best friend and took pride in protecting the frontier. As a senior officer in Grand Prairie, Patton had served ten years as a major-crimes investigator and eight years as a detective.

Patton and his young partner arrived at the parking lot after a short drive and speculative conversation over what might have happened. Passing under the highway, Patton pulled off the road and stopped his car next to the police cruiser that was the first responder on the scene. He got out of the car and told his partner to stay close before walking down the access road toward a small group of men gathered by the body. The first two patrolmen on the scene were finishing up their interview with the fisherman who had found the remains. As Patton walked up to the group, the sight of the remains filled his vision. He furrowed his brow as his eyes swept across the scene. It was not pretty.

The gruesome sight was a first in Patton's long years working homicide. The accelerated body decomposition combined with the animal activity struck a chord he'd not felt since he was a rookie, experiencing everything for the first time. He thought he had seen everything, but a first look at the remains reminded him that he hadn't.

A moment later, Patton's sense of time and place returned. His partner and the other two cops stood nearby, patiently waiting for orders. Patton began running through the routine of securing the scene, ordering the two patrolmen to cordon off the area. Then he told everyone to stay put until the crime scene investigators arrived. While they waited, Patton took the fisherman aside and asked him some questions, but he didn't have much to add to what he'd already told the two patrolmen who had interviewed him, so Patton let him go and told the two patrol cops to make sure a detailed report was on his desk by the time he got back to the station. Patton was going to wait with his part-ncr until the crime scene investigators finished their work, and then head back to the station to sort out this mess. The investigators took their time collecting soil samples, taking pictures of the scene, and inspecting the remains. A van from the medical examiner's officer arrived. The scene technicians helped place the remains in a body bag and carry it back to the medical examiner's vehicle, which set off to transport the body to the Dallas County medical examiner's office for an autopsy. This was the beginning of a long investigation.

Patton was silent on the short drive back to the office. He needed to think. He knew the body had been there for some time, but there was no indication of the cause of death. Nothing at the scene suggested a crime, but he had to treat it that way, as any evidence the crime scene investigators recorded might be useful in the future. But the first task was to identify the body.

Back at the station, Patton walked quickly up the steps and toward his office, through a tightly packed group of cubicles, ignoring the usual chatter of patrolmen and investigators who were procrastinating in filing routine paperwork. He closed the door and sat down to punch out a press release. It was the first task he had to complete before moving forward with this case. Patton wanted to use the local newspapers to get the word out on the fisherman's discovery. It was the most logical step toward pulling together any information that might help him figure out who belonged to the remains.

Since Javier's disappearance on December 17, Ben Calzada had been scanning the news for anything that could even remotely connect with his son. When he saw the article about the body that had been discovered, he thought with some dread that it could be his son. He gathered his keys and coat and immediately drove out to the Grand Prairie police station. As Ben sped down the highway toward Grand Prairie, he allowed himself to hope for news, answers, or at least something more than nothing.

It had been two agonizing weeks since Ben and Marisa's son had gone missing. No one had responded to the posters. No one at the hospitals knew anything. No one had called. Ben had hiked miles of backcountry trails looking for his son. Marisa had spent countless hours driving around their neighborhood, looking for any signs of their son's presence. She had called everyone she knew, conducting her own investigation, but no one had any idea what had happened to Javier. The Calzadas couldn't think of any reason why Javier would run away, and they still couldn't bear the thought that he might have been kidnapped—or worse.

Ben swung his van into the parking lot and half walked, half jogged into the station's front hall. He headed straight for the reception and rang the bell, pacing until someone came to the front desk. Ben told the patrolman on duty why he was there. Before the patrolman responded, Ben began telling his story, speaking fast and passionately. The officer let him talk and silently took notes. When Ben finished, the patrolman said he couldn't comment on the John Doe case, but someone would be in touch with him soon. Ben took a pause to look the man in the eye. There had to be something else. But the patrolman spun on his heel and walked away. Deflated and powerless, Ben walked back to his van to return home. He still didn't have any answers.

That same day, Patton sat in his office and explored the theory that the remains might belong to a murder victim. The area where the fisherman had found the body was heavily wooded and relatively isolated. Was it possible that someone had dragged the victim there, knowing that no one would walk by and witness the murder? And there was a time issue: long years of investigation had taught Patton that the best time to catch a killer was within forty-eight hours of a crime. If he couldn't catch the murderer within that critical time frame, the chances of solving a case were cut in half.

The poor state of the remains made it obvious that well over forty-eight hours had passed. Without identifying the body, it would be nearly impossible to move forward with the investigation. Patton was also frustrated that his press release had generated so little activity, but he had to push ahead. Against his better judgment, Patton decided to move from words to images. He picked up the phone and began dialing local television stations. Then he called the medical examiner to request some photos of the clothes found with the remains. He would need them for the cameras.

Patton held a press conference just before the New Year and showed the photos of the clothes found with the body. Four local news stations carried the story. Standing in front of the reporters, Patton read his statement and looked directly into the cameras, hoping there was someone out there who would recognize the clothes and make the phone call he needed to move this case forward.

Home from work after another long day, Ben Calzada was watching the local news with his wife when he saw Sergeant Patton holding up pictures of his son's clothing. He nearly fell out of his chair, scrambling for the telephone in the kitchen. He called the station and in a shaky voice told the attendant that he had information on the clothes Sergeant Patton had held up before the cameras.

Patton had just sat down in his office at the end of a long day with still no leads when the switchboard operator passed him the call from Ben Calzada.

This name is vaguely familiar, Patton thought, before picking up the receiver. As Ben Calzada spoke, Patton realized he was the same man who had earlier filed a report about his missing son. Ben was speaking quickly, in broken English. He's nervous, Patton thought, as Ben insisted the clothes belonged to his son. Through all his nervousness and broken speech, Patton detected Calzada's sorrow and pain. This was a desperate man who clearly recognized the clothes. Patton allowed himself to consider that the body in the morgue might be Mr. Calzada's missing son.

As Ben talked to the sergeant, Marisa whispered that she had bought two identical shirts from a garage sale. The one she gave Javier, she said, was the same shirt that was on the news. Marisa felt her stomach constrict even as the words left her mouth. She was certain. What she had feared the most might actually be true.

Before he concluded the conversation, Patton asked the Calzadas to come in to the station. They wanted to come immediately, but Patton told them it would be best to wait until just after the holiday. They reluctantly agreed to visit the station on the second day of the New Year.

When Ben hung up the phone, he looked at his wife and knew what she was thinking. The saddened couple hugged each other and cried. Both felt their last strands of hope dissolve and their worst fear confirmed. Their baby boy was dead.

CHAPTER 7

etective Rick Oseguera of the Major Crimes Unit had just returned from vacation when Sergeant Patton slapped him and his partner with a new case. With a fresh cup of station coffee in hand, Oseguera sat down at his desk and looked at Patton's thin file. There was little information, but Patton's observations of the scene where the fisherman had found the remains and notes from the conversation with Ben Calzada told him enough. Nothing about this investigation was going to be easy. He picked up a case that Patton had only just begun to consider as the Javier Calzada murder investigation, weeks after the remains were first discovered. By any measure he was playing catch-up from his first moment back on the job.

Detective Oseguera's west Texas roots were buried somewhere not far from the border near El Paso. His light brown skin contrasted slightly with his graying moustache, which had been part of his personality for decades. Oseguera's first language was Spanish, but he spoke English fluently, with only a slight accent. He was a details-oriented, no-nonsense cop. His firm handshake and honest, steady gaze spoke of someone who worked with diligence, truly believed in justice, and took pride in his job. Oseguera was known among his peers as someone who chipped away at his cases until every last question had been answered, every shred of evidence discovered, and every connection made. He was called Bird Dog because he hounded after details like a dog on the hunt.

This investigation would immediately take Oseguera deep into the Latino community living in the greater Dallas area. He would need to interview individuals normally not comfortable with speaking with the police. This was a community where families preferred to keep a low profile and avoid the attention of local authorities. It was a barrier Oseguera himself had had to surmount, and his background and language skills were essential.

Oseguera looked at the open file on his desk. A note at the end said he was scheduled to speak to Ben and Marisa Calzada later that morning. Good, he thought. At least he had a starting point where he could learn as much as possible about their missing son. He would need all the information available to get this case moving. Weeks after the remains had been discovered, there was no confirmation it was a crime, and the body still hadn't been officially identified. Oseguera sighed as he sipped his coffee. What a way to return from vacation.

The detective's phone beeped. It was the officer at the front desk telling him that the Calzadas had arrived. He got up and walked down a flight of stairs to the reception area where the Calzadas were waiting. Their eyes darted in his direction when he entered the room. They immediately stood and made quick work of the introductions, but then they fell silent and didn't look him directly in the eye. These people are not used to dealing with police, Oseguera thought. In silence, the detective escorted them to a simple, stark interview room. There was nothing on the walls, door, or floor that could distract them. The only furnishing consisted of a round, white particleboard table and a few uncomfortable blue chairs.

The Calzadas had introduced themselves in Spanish, so Oseguera also spoke in Spanish. He asked them to tell him about Javier. Marisa sat in resigned silence as Ben began talking. Oseguera didn't have to ask many questions: Ben had been waiting a long time to finally tell someone everything he knew that could lead to some sort of conclusion to his pain. Picking through what he heard, Oseguera made note of Javier's cell phone number, the names of two of Javier's friends, and his girlfriend's name, address, and cell phone number. He also noted the two facts that Ben repeated, information that Oseguera knew already from Sergeant Patton's file: Javier Calzada drove the Malibu that was found in Dallas off Walnut Hill, and the boy's wallet had been discovered underneath an overpass off Interstate 35.

Oseguera continued to take notes as Ben told him that his son worked at a car dealership in Carrollton. He rarely got into fights, Ben stressed. Ben said Javier hung out around Bachman Lake Park in the evening and on weekends. Finally, when there was a pause in Ben's monologue, Oseguera quickly asked him for the name and address of Javier's dentist so he could obtain X-rays. That's when Marisa spoke up. She had the information with her and handed it over with the reluctance of someone who didn't want to know the truth but had to have it.

Oseguera completed the interview and escorted the Calzadas to the front lobby. They left arm in arm, walking through the cold, gray morning back to Ben's van in the parking lot. Oseguera returned to his office to start working the phone while the interview was still fresh in his memory. He had to double-check the information he'd just taken down.

His first call was with the Dallas Police Department's Criminal Intelligence Division. It was a clearinghouse for all information in the state, from birth dates and phone numbers to criminal records and last-known locations. In one call, he could verify the information of all the names Ben had given him. He hung up the phone with almost all his information verified, then he grabbed his coat and headed to the motor pool. He had to meet with the Dallas policemen who had been assigned the Javier Calzada missing-persons case, opened on December 18, the day after Javier failed to come home. They should have additional information and would likely want to ride along as he interviewed everyone associated with Javier.

Days later, Oseguera was at his desk reviewing the notes in the now much thicker case file when his phone rang. It was the Dallas medical examiner. The dental records confirmed that the remains were those of Javier Calzada. The ME also verified that Javier had been murdered, shot point-blank in his left temple. Only fragments of the bullet had been recovered, making ballistics tests impossible. Oseguera thanked the medical examiner for the information and hung up, thinking that at least the missing-persons case could be closed. His next phone call was to the Dallas patrolmen who had accompanied him to every interview he'd conducted over the past forty-eight hours. They agreed to close the case and send their files over to Oseguera's office so he could take control of the evidence they had gathered up to that point. He thanked the Dallas police for their help and cradled the phone.

Patton and the Calzadas have been right all along, Oseguera thought to himself. He had suspected that this was a murder case, but up until minutes ago, he didn't have the official confirmation. Now, sitting at his desk with the case file spread out in front of him, Oseguera looked it over and frowned. He still didn't have much to work with, and the stakes had just gotten much higher. This was now officially a murder investigation.

CHAPTER 8

By the end of the first week of 2002, Oseguera had contacted everyone on his list of names associated with Javier. He had spoken with the victim's two best friends, his girlfriend, his brother, and a number of other people loosely associated with Javier's peer group. Oseguera had already gathered all the information he could from interviews, so he decided next to focus on the physical evidence.

Oseguera left his office and headed to the car pound behind the station to pick through Javier's Malibu. He had arranged for it to be towed from the Dallas Police Department auto pound to Grand Prairie. The detective immediately noted that the car had low-profile tires with expensive chrome rims. Raising an eyebrow and thinking about how much each one of those rims cost, Oseguera concluded that they alone were reason enough to steal the car.

The detective knew that the crime scene investigators had lifted latent prints from the interior window trim of the backseat. They also found a cigarette butt and had collected soil samples from the floorboards in the car. Soil samples with red stains taken from the crime scene matched the soil samples in the car, placing it at the scene of the crime.

When the tow truck driver had picked up Javier's car from Walnut Hill, he had to move one lug nut from a front tire so he could secure a back tire that was missing all of its lug nuts. It was clear that someone had tried to remove them. Oseguera saw that the left front rim was missing two lug nuts and the left rear rim was missing three, consistent with the tow truck company's account. He spent another couple of hours picking over the car, making sure nothing had been left behind, undiscovered or unconsidered.

By midmorning Oseguera was exhausted and a little frustrated. He felt like he was spinning his wheels. There was nothing else in the car, nothing that generated a new lead. Back in his office, he had concluded that he was unable to draw a clear suspect from Javier's group of friends. Oseguera had gone over his notes from the bits and pieces of stories told to him by wary teenagers suspect of anyone asking questions. No one wanted to get arrested. Many were willing to talk, even visit Oseguera at the Grand Prairie police station, but few remembered all the details. Slowly, however, he was able to piece together some of the facts and rule out all of Javier's friends as suspects.

They don't call me Bird Dog for nothing, he thought as he poured another cup of coffee. Though he didn't have any real answers, Detective Oseguera knew that his diligence with the details would pay off. As he ruminated over the first two weeks' work, he ticked off in his mind the facts that he was dealing with. He was now certain that Javier was last seen at Bachman Lake Park, about 8:30 P.M., eight days before Christmas. Through eyewitness accounts, he knew that someone speaking English had called Javier later that night, and he had deduced that the caller wasn't a friend or acquaintance that he had interviewed. Someone had tried to steal the tires off Javier's car. Oseguera furrowed his brow in puzzlement as he tested a thought. Javier was not in a gang. He did hang out at Bachman Lake Park, but the area wasn't known as a hangout for gang members. Besides, gang activity in Grand Prairie was nearly nonexistent. But if none of Javier's friends or acquaintances killed him, then who did?

CHAPTER 9

Oseguera's murder investigation languished for another week until he got a surprise phone call from a detective with the Dallas Police Department's Gang Unit. Its primary role was to document and track gang activity within the city of Dallas, and the detective had stumbled across Oseguera's murder case during one of his investigations.

Oseguera stroked his graying moustache as he listened to the detective explain why he was calling: through colleagues in Virginia, they had tracked an out-of-state member of the Mara Salvatrucha gang. It was the first time Oseguera had heard of the gang. He had to repeat the name a couple of times in his head to get it straight. When Virginia cops had issued an arrest warrant for the gangster, he decided to get out of the state and lay low. He was hiding out with his homies in Dallas, where they took care of him and protected him from the police.

Oseguera listened closely and quietly took notes as the detective continued detailing the story. Apparently, the gangster's flight wasn't enough to shake off the Virginia cops, and they had succeeded in tracking the guy to Dallas. They had alerted the Dallas Gang Unit of his presence, possible whereabouts, and likely associates. By mid-January, members of the Dallas Gang Unit were searching for two suspects, the gangster on the run and Brenda Paz, someone they thought was hiding him from the law. When members of the Gang Unit, following up on intelligence from Virginia, visited a low-income apartment complex in north Dallas, they recovered a shoebox that belonged to Brenda. As he listened, Oseguera made a note of the new name: Brenda Paz. Not one of Javier's friends, he thought. The Dallas detective then told him that inside the weathered cardboard container was evidence related to Oseguera's case.

In this shoebox, Brenda had stored a number of items, including a receipt from Blockbuster video with Ben Calzada's name printed on it. Oseguera immediately made the connection. The detective explained that they had followed up on the address they had obtained from the Blockbuster membership file, hoping to find Brenda and the runaway gangster she was hiding. Ben Calzada had answered the door when the Gang Unit detectives arrived. Mr. Calzada had explained to the officers that his son was recently murdered in Grand Prairie. They showed Ben some of the contents of the box that allegedly belonged to Brenda Paz, and he had identified some cassette tapes that belonged to his son.

Along with the tapes, they found a pair of white Adidas tennis shoes stained with mud, a blue bandanna with MS13 stitched on it, a notebook, and a few letters addressed to Brenda Paz. Wrapping up his story, the detective told him they had left the shoebox with the attending officer at his police station.

Oseguera thanked the detective and hung up, then walked downstairs to take possession of the shoebox, with the intention of examining the contents in more detail later. At that moment, he didn't want to focus on the contents of the shoebox. Maybe they held some clues, but this inspection would have to wait, Oseguera thought as he walked from the lobby to the evidence locker to drop off the shoebox before heading to the motor pool. He was headed to Dallas to follow up on a hunch, something he thought might be connected to the Calzada murder. He drove to the Dallas County Jail to dig a little deeper into a suspect he wanted to question in connection with an armed robbery in Grand Prairie. His investigation had revealed that there were two suspects, a young woman and a man. During the phone call with the detective from the Dallas Gang Unit, Oseguera had begun to realize that his armed-robbery suspects might be connected to the Calzada murder. He knew from Dallas Intelligence that his male suspect had been arrested on Christmas Day and was in prison in Dallas County.

He checked in with the attendant and passed through security before rounding the corner to the holding pen where they had placed his suspect. Oseguera looked at him and saw something he had never encountered as a veteran police officer in Texas. The skinny Latino man had MS tattooed across his forehead in bold, three-inch gothic script. Its placement shocked the detective. There was a tattooed teardrop under his left eye, and the name VETO was tattooed in a vertical line up one side of his neck. Tattoos snaked up and down his arms, forming a crude canvas of body art. He was looking at Brenda's boyfriend, Veto.

Oseguera didn't know at the time, but the MS on Veto's forehead and the teardrop tattoo were hard-earned symbols of status and power in the Mara Salvatrucha. The teardrop was a common street gang symbol that meant one thing: at some point the wearer had killed in the name of his gang. Within the MS, a teardrop symbolized murder, but it took more than one murder to earn the right to tattoo the name of the gang above the neckline. This was no wannabe. Oseguera was looking at his first true-to-the-death gang member. The gang life was his reality, and he was willing to die and kill for it.

Veto exuded an extraordinary confidence—too much for a man of slight build dressed in a prison jumpsuit and slippers. Yet his eyes were dark and void of emotion. Despite Veto's manner, Oseguera thought he was probably the kind of man who didn't have the courage to stand up to someone else on his own. Oseguera got over the shocking tattoos before he cuffed Veto and signed him out for the seventeen-mile trip back to Grand Prairie. His suspect didn't say a word the whole ride. Oseguera escorted Veto into the Grand Prairie police station, where he was read his rights in Spanish, fingerprinted, and photographed.

"Quiero un abogado," Veto said. "I want a lawyer."

Veto clearly knew his rights. He appeared to be a hardened gang member and had said nothing on the ride. He'd obviously been in a similar situation before. Oseguera concluded that Veto would never talk, so he submitted Veto's prints and photo to the Grand Prairie police database for comparison, but little more could be done. After only fifteen minutes at the Grand Prairie police station, Oseguera drove Veto back to the Dallas County Jail. His hunch hadn't panned out. But it was something he had to check. Leave nothing unturned, Oseguera thought as he got out of the car back in Grand Prairie. He stopped by the evidence locker to grab the shoebox and tucked it under his arm for the quick walk back to his office. He placed the box on his desk, pulled the top, and removed the contents, carefully spreading them out before he started sifting through the evidence.

The white Adidas shoes were too small to be Javier's, but the mud was useful. He logged the shoes and took a sample of the mud to have it compared to the mud removed from the floorboards of the car. The blue bandanna with MS13 stitched on it might be interesting, but he didn't focus on it. What caught his attention was a letter addressed to Brenda Paz. In the upper left-hand corner of the envelope was a Dallas County prison inmate ID number, 01098008. With the letter in front of him Oseguera grabbed the phone to call the Dallas Sheriff's Department to confirm the number. He was surprised to learn it was assigned to the same inmate he had just returned to the Dallas County Jail.

Oseguera smiled as he hung up the phone. He now had a link between Veto and Brenda Paz. He could also connect this Brenda Paz with Javier Calzada because of the Blockbuster receipt found in her shoebox. Together, it was enough to arrest Brenda for her connection with the Calzada murder and to seriously consider Veto as a second suspect. Oseguera called Dallas Intelligence and learned that Brenda had a local address in Carrollton, Texas, and was listed as a runaway. She was now a prime suspect.

CHAPTER 10

Oseguera's arrest warrant for Brenda Paz sat in police stations across the greater Dallas area by the end of January. Policemen all over the region now knew that she was wanted for capital murder in connection with the death of Javier Calzada. If any of them picked her up for anything, Oseguera would know about it within the hour. He was pleased with himself. This case was on firm footing, even though he had begun with next to nothing. It was the first arrest warrant he issued for the Calzada murder, just under a month since the fisherman had discovered Javier's remains. But he didn't stop there. Oseguera considered it a stretch, but Brenda could leave the area, maybe head back to California and hide out at one of three addresses he had found in the journal in her shoebox. Before he was content to let the system do its job, Oseguera called the police departments in El Monte, Monrovia, and Bell Flowers, California, to ask them to post his warrant.

For two weeks, Oseguera kept busy with other cases while he waited for someone to serve the arrest warrant on Brenda Paz. She was a runaway and a street kid who was likely to get into some kind of trouble, perhaps by being in the wrong place at the wrong time. Oseguera was content to wait.

On Valentine's Day, Oseguera's cell phone brought him good news. It was a call from the Dallas Police Department. An attendant on duty had seen the arrest warrant issued for Brenda Paz and informed

Oseguera that she was in custody at a hospital in Carrollton. The occasional arrest for small-time offenses was a way of life for gang members, but this time it was different. Brenda was in the hospital with one of her homies who had been hospitalized after a brutal fight with a rival gang member. He was somewhere beyond the reception area, where Brenda waited in a bad mood. She scowled at anyone who looked at her too long. The staff at the hospital's front desk alerted law enforcement, saying there was a problem at the reception. When the police showed up, they questioned Brenda and called in her information. The attendant notified the officers at the hospital of Brenda's arrest warrant, and then called Oseguera. Brenda was eventually fingered as a runaway and taken into custody. But because she was a minor, she had to be released after twenty-four hours had passed.

"You come and get her now, or we're letting her go," the attendant told Oseguera. He agreed to go get her, and drove the forty-mile stretch to pick her up and bring her back to the Grand Prairie Police Department before taking her to the interview room for questioning.

His first impression of Brenda was positive, despite the circumstances. She acted like there was nothing to worry about. Her wide smile accentuated high, rosy cheeks that stood out against the light brown tone of her face. She was a little overweight, but obviously comfortable in her skin. Dressed in jeans, tennis shoes, and a loose-fitting shirt, Brenda didn't appear malnourished or addicted to drugs. To Oseguera, she looked like a normal, well-adjusted teenager. He wondered what she was doing corresponding with someone like Veto.

While Brenda was in custody at the Grand Prairie PD, her disposition was confident, with a slightly hardened outer shell. She's lively, Oseguera thought, with some attitude. Brenda had not been with her gang long, but she knew the first rule: Mara Salvatrucha do not rat. She would not break that sacred rule by speaking to this cop. When Oseguera began to question Brenda, he quickly learned two things. She was very smart. And she wasn't going to tell him anything that would incriminate her or anyone she knew. Seated at the round table, across from Oseguera, Brenda remained relaxed despite her surroundings and the fact she was being questioned about a murder.

"So where are your belongings?" Oseguera asked, knowing she was picked up as a runaway.

Brenda replied she had been at a friend's apartment for two days before moving on.

"Do you know [his] name?" Oseguera asked.

"No," Brenda said.

That much was true. Within her gang, there were no real names, only street names. It was a habit among gang members to use one another's street name and never use given names. The result was often an added level of confusion for detectives trying to unravel a case laced with street names. This was really only the beginning of the gang's code.

Oseguera pulled out a stack of photos and flipped through them, asking Brenda if she recognized anyone. She easily identified the gangster Dallas Police were chasing down for their Virginia colleagues. Brenda knew that pointing out this guy to the cop wasn't a big deal. He was long gone anyway.

Once he was through the stack, Oseguera put the photos away and opened a new line of questions about the items he found in the shoebox. He also asked about the muddy shoes.

"The stuff is mine, but the shoes you're talking about are not," Brenda said. "They're Jessica's."

"Can you describe the shoes?" Oseguera asked.

"No," Brenda said with a huff.

Oseguera then asked her about Javier Calzada. He asked her about Bachman Lake Park and where she was on the Monday Javier disappeared. He didn't mention that he knew Javier was dead. And he left out information about the young man's green Malibu and the other details of the case.

Brenda began recounting her story. She didn't miss a beat. "That Monday I was home when Flaca came over in a green car around ten thirty," Brenda recalled with surprising precision. "It was raining that night and very cold," she added, becoming more animated. "I got in the car and asked Flaca if it was hers. She didn't say, but later my homie Spooky told me that Flaca had killed some boy and stole his car."

Oseguera carefully noted the names Flaca and Spooky.

"So we went over to Rio Loco, smoked some pot, and hung out. Then I went home," Brenda continued, bored and slouching in her chair. "The next day, I called Flaca and asked her why she killed that guy and stole his car. She told me she took the guy out to the boondocks and shot him to make rank in our gang, the MS. I've been a member for two months," she admitted proudly before sitting up again.

Brenda's pride in her gang compelled her to declare her association with the Mara Salvatrucha even if she had to lie about what she remembered the night of Javier's murder. She believed it was her obligation to tell the cops about her membership with MS. Brenda considered the MS as her family. She was close to her homies, and her life with the gang was the only life she cared to know in that moment.

"I think Flaca's boyfriend was involved somehow because he had a gun that night at Rio Loco. And Flaca stole the car 'cause she wanted to steal the tires to sell them and make money to travel to El Salvador," Brenda explained. She was lying through her teeth.

"Do you know where I can find Flaca?" Oseguera asked.

"I don't know, but I think she's in Houston. She should be passing through Dallas on her way to Maryland."

This time she was telling the truth. It would be to her advantage to have Flaca arrested and throw Oseguera off her trail so she could escape before he found out too much.

Oseguera decided that talking more about Flaca was a dead end, but he wanted to see if Brenda would identify Veto, his aggravated robbery suspect and the man who had written Brenda a letter from the Dallas County Jail.

"Do you know Veto?" Oseguera questioned, carefully looking at Brenda.

"Yeah, he's my boyfriend," she admitted without hesitation, looking directly at him, but that's where she stopped.

There was no way she was going to sell out Veto to this cop. She knew he was already in prison, so she was willing to point him out when Oseguera showed her his mug shot after she admitted to knowing him. But Veto terrified her, and she wasn't going to tell Oseguera anything about the night Javier was killed, nor was she going to formalize what she told him during the interview. At the end of the interview, Brenda refused when Oseguera asked her to sign a statement. She knew exactly how far she could take this cop down the line. She knew where and when to lie and where to tell the truth. Veto had taught her a few things about how to deal with cops, but Brenda was smart enough to figure out the rest.

Oseguera closed his notebook and escorted Brenda to booking, where he took her prints and a photo. Then they walked out to his service vehicle. The drive to the Dallas County Juvenile Detention Center was silent. There was nothing else to say. Along the way, Brenda simply stared out the window. It was her first time under so much police pressure. She was determined to keep her cool. So far, she had done well, but she didn't know what would happen when they got to Dallas.

Oseguera took her inside and booked her. He knew he had other questions for her and wanted to prevent her from leaving town, but he didn't have enough evidence to hold her. A juvenile court judge in Dallas issued her release the next day. Brenda was ecstatic. She was free! Brenda had danced with the police, lied, dropped a smoke screen, and was free to go soon after. She had beat a capital murder rap and pushed Oseguera's focus to Flaca. For a rookie in the criminal underworld, Brenda had made a slick getaway.

Following Brenda's questioning, Oseguera issued a capital murder warrant for Flaca's arrest, the second warrant he'd put out for the Calzada murder. If she did pass through Dallas and was stupid enough to get picked up, Brenda reasoned, he would be able to question her.

Back in his office after dropping off Brenda, Oseguera returned to the contents of her shoebox. Veto had sent her a number of letters. In one, he told Brenda he thought the cops had found out he was the perpetrator in a separate robbery, one Oseguera suspected was the aggravated robbery at the local grocery store he was working. In the letter, Veto told Brenda to be careful. When he thought about it, Veto's mention of the robbery in the letter made her an accessory to the crime. He thought Veto was the male suspect reported by the store owner, but the detective had never nailed down the female suspect. He now believed that suspect was Brenda.

Oseguera needed confirmation. He hopped in his vehicle and drove over to the grocery store to speak with the owner who had originally filed the armed robbery report. Oseguera explained that there was a lead in the investigation and showed him a number of female mug shots, including one of Brenda Paz.

The store owner took a moment to look through the mug shots and narrowed the selection down to two photos, including Brenda's. Gotcha, Oseguera thought. Based on the owner's confirmation, Oseguera issued a probable-cause warrant for the arrest of Brenda in connection with his armed robbery case. He was almost sure Brenda and Veto had knocked off the grocery store together two days before Javier was killed, but he knew it would take some time to find Brenda again after the judge had set her free. That kid was smart: she wasn't going to just sit around and let him arrest her again.

CHAPTER 11

Oseguera returned to the station, resigned to actively pursue Brenda across north Dallas. He started by contacting Brenda's uncle. It was a quick conversation. Rafael told him she had run away and he hadn't seen her in days. Great, this isn't going to be fun, Oseguera thought as he dropped the phone into the cradle. She was a teenage runaway with possible gang ties and potentially enough money to leave the state. The hunt was on. He had to catch her before she left Texas.

He had to beat the streets. Before he left the station, Oseguera gathered his notes and made a mental list of all her possible whereabouts. His plan was to drive to each of these places and ask if anyone had seen Brenda. He was careful not to forget her photo.

Days passed as Oseguera doggedly followed Brenda's trail. Each time he got close, he learned from one person or another, usually an apartment building supervisor or tenant, that Brenda and a group of Latino males had been run off.

Brenda ran with her homies in a leaderless pattern, squatting and taking care of Veto's various businesses. Their leader was in jail and no one had stepped up to take his place. Brenda's clique was disorganized; it had abandoned all the routine and habit the leader had enforced upon its members. They would crash in an apartment for two or three days, until they were kicked out. Then they would move on to another squat or rent a hotel room for the night. This random movement made it very hard for Oseguera to draw a bead on Brenda's location.

After days of searching, as Oseguera sat at his desk, mapping Brenda's movements and searching for a pattern, he got a call from Gutierrez, the same Dallas Gang Unit detective who had passed him Brenda's shoebox weeks before. The detective told Oseguera that he had some information that suggested Brenda was hiding out in the Colony, another small town within the greater Dallas–Forth Worth area. But Oseguera was tired of chasing Brenda. He was now less worried about her leaving Texas and preferred to get smart about catching her. There has to be a pattern to her movements, he thought. Oseguera asked Gutierrez to give him a call if she was picked up. He didn't want to chase after her, but he wasn't going to pass up a second opportunity to arrest her.

Detective Gutierrez called back just hours before sunrise to confirm that Brenda was in a holding cell at the Colony Police Department. They'd caught her, but they wouldn't hold her for long because she was a minor. Oseguera didn't waste time. He headed out immediately, driving as fast as he could in predawn darkness. He arrived an hour later, just in time to take Brenda into custody.

Oseguera was considerably more relaxed on the way back—he had her now and could take his time. He drove to the Grand Prairie Police Department and led Brenda up the steps and into his office. He sat her in a chair in front of his desk and rounded the corner to the opposite side. Before he took a seat, Oseguera reached over to the corner of his desk in front of Brenda and turned the photographs of his wife and kids facedown. He considered Brenda a dangerous person and didn't want her to be a threat to his family.

Oseguera smoothed his moustache and leveled his gaze on Brenda. She looked a little nervous. Good, he thought. Maybe now she would talk. First he asked if she wanted to talk about the aggravated robbery case. She did not. Brenda crossed her arms and looked away. This was a decidedly different person from the Brenda he had first met. There was no smile, no bright eyes or bouncy attitude. This Brenda looked like a tough punk. She exuded bad attitude and disrespect. Unlike at their first interview, Brenda was not going to risk playing any games. Someone had gotten to her. Whoever it was, he scared her. She clammed up and waited.

Oseguera realized he wasn't going to get anything from her. He fought to maintain professional composure as he stood up, rounded the desk, and grabbed Brenda under one arm to walk her down the ~~ɯɫɐ̣ɯıʊɯɫ lɯɯ k ɯɯɫ ɯɯ ɫɦɯ ɯɯɯɯɯɯ pɯɯɯɫ ʹ́ʺíʹ̈ ɫ ɯɯ ɯɯɯ ɯı͡ ɫɫ́ɯ́ɯ, ʺɱɫ́ɯuɯıɯ̈~~ thought. He was resigned to driving her over to the Dallas County Juvenile Detention Center. Maybe this time they would hold her.

After they arrived, Oseguera booked her and took custody of her tennis shoes. They were white Sketchers with a light blue trim. He wanted to take a cast of the shoes to compare them to the ones in the shoebox. He also scraped out soil samples from her Sketchers so he could compare them to the soil samples taken from Javier's car.

Oseguera returned to Grand Prairie with some new evidence but little more than a headache. This girl's a pain in the ass, Oseguera thought as he slowly trudged up the steps to his office. He sat in the chair with a sigh and straightened the photos on his desk. It was still early in the morning, but he was accustomed to working the red-eye shift. With a sip of his coffee, Oseguera settled in behind his desk to focus on processing all the evidence gathered from his case. He wanted to look over everything and see if he could draw any conclusions from the evidence.

Throughout the whole investigation, the letters MS kept popping up. The letters stood for Mara Salvatrucha, which meant, loosely translated from Spanish, "street-smart Salvadoran group." Oseguera had first seen them tattooed on Veto's forehead—a striking sight he would never forget. MS13 was printed on the blue bandanna in Brenda's shoebox. While looking for Brenda, he had interviewed a few people who claimed they were members of this gang. He had learned from the Dallas Gang Unit that there were a number of MS members across Dallas, and they all seemed to be loosely affiliated with each other. It was the first encounter Oseguera had with this street gang, but he had learned enough to realize that the gang was organized and violent, and that its influence wasn't limited to Dallas.

He knew Veto was an MS member. Brenda had confirmed it, and it was possible the other men arrested with Veto were also MS members. The gangster on the run from Virginia was also an MS member, which meant the MS likely had a presence in that state as well. He thought Flaca, the girl Brenda said had killed Javier and stolen his car, was also an MS member. To Oseguera, it looked more and more likely that Javier's murder was gang-related.

It took weeks to test the soil samples and shoe casts: Oseguera had sent everything to the FBI, and the lab technicians there took their time. When he finally learned that the soil samples were a match, thus placing her in the vehicle and possibly at the scene of the crime, he knew that Brenda had probably lied during their first interview. Oseguera now believed that Brenda was present when Javier Calzada was killed. This made it even more important for him to persuade Brenda to open up.

But Brenda spent only one night in the juvenile detention center before officers there released her. Soon after, she left Texas, taking with her any chance for Oseguera to arrest her a third time.

CHAPTER 12

L ike a good gangster, Brenda had remained tough and collected under Oseguera's questioning during both interviews, but she still had doubts about being an MS member. She had been a member for less than a month when she witnessed Javier's murder. After less than four months in the gang and just weeks before she turned sixteen, Brenda had become a prime suspect for capital murder in Texas. This was not what she had signed up for. The time span between her two radically different lives, from beloved daughter to gangster wanted for murder, had passed too quickly, but she didn't have time to dwell on it.

After her second meeting with Oseguera, Brenda realized that she had to run. She couldn't trust the cop, and she couldn't go to her family in California—the MS might follow her and harm them. She couldn't go back to her sour uncle, Rafael, or to Honduras. Her only option was to do what Veto had told her to do in a letter from prison: go to Virginia and find Denis Rivera, a trusted homie Brenda had met briefly when he came down to Dallas to help Veto take care of a rival gang member. Veto was in prison, and the other guys at Calzada's murder were leaving the state. Without Veto, she had no direction, no stability in Texas. She needed another anchor to keep her street life stable, so she placed Denis in her sights and traveled to Virginia to find him.

On March 23, 2002, Brenda turned sixteen. It was a lonely birthday. When she'd turned fifteen in Honduras, she had been surrounded by friends and family. This time, she was on the run from a murder rap in Texas and a member of a violent street gang. What a turn her life had taken.

Through the spring, Brenda traveled with some of her homies from Texas throughout the Southeast and connected with other MS cliques in Tennessee and North Carolina. They traveled by day and squatted in hotels, living rooms, and garages by night. Brenda began to understand that her gang had a real presence all over the country. She had no problem finding a place to stay or making money. There were many parties, new faces, and stories to tell. She reveled in the experience, the good side of gang life, yet she continued to feel very conflicted about being a member of the Mara Salvatrucha. Javier's murder weighed heavily on her conscience. On the outside, Brenda had permanently affixed the mask of a gangster, but she needed something more to harden herself against the fearful possibility that she would let the mask slip at the wrong time, in front of the wrong person. This gang was serious. There was no room for maybes or doubt. She was hanging with true-to-life gangsters. If she didn't match their fervor, there would be serious consequences, so she lied to protect herself.

She told new acquaintances on the road that her dad was an MS member and that she was jumped in when she was thirteen in Los Angeles. She knew enough about MS history and Los Angeles to back up the story. Each lie boosted her credit among the MS members she met. Brenda was still a second-class member simply because she was female in a macho gang world, but her affiliation with the Normandie Locos, combined with her lies about her MS origins, generated respect everywhere she went. Doors opened for her.

The combination of real power and street credit were heady drugs for a girl her age. They kept her alive and propelled her forward, away from Texas and toward an unknown future. Surrounded by gangsters and protected by her lies and a tough outer shell, Brenda kept the doubts and fears of a normal adolescent girl away from the men. She learned more than she should have, and remembered everything she saw and heard, just like a video recording.

Once Brenda decided to head toward Virginia, she knew exactly where to go. Through Veto, she had strong connections with gang leaders in northern Virginia, particularly with Denis Rivera. Denis and Brenda had met in passing before her arrival in Virginia. Veto knew he wasn't getting out of prison anytime soon, so he wrote in a coded let-

ter to Denis that he wanted Denis to take care of her. It was a relationship sparked by an order from a senior gang member to ensure Brenda's
protection and companionship.

Denis was not the typical MS member. He was respected by members of the Normandie Locos, as well as a number of other cliques in
the area, including the Silva Locos and the Centrales Locos—both Los
Angeles "13" cliques that were well established on the East Coast. At
eighteen, Denis was the leader of his own clique, the Biggie Gangster
Locos, and was as respected as any leader solely because of his willingness to kill.

When Brenda met Denis after her trek from Texas, his reputation
as a cold-blooded killer didn't turn her off. She'd already been desensi-
tized by Veto's stories and his penchant for using murder as a solution.
Just as she had been attracted to Veto, Brenda found Denis's power and
confidence alluring. Denis found in Brenda a smart and charming girl.

Brenda arrived in Arlington, Virginia, after many weeks on the road.
She was tired of moving and looked forward to getting to know a new
place where no one knew her, especially the local cops. Her reputation,
built partly on lies and partly on Veto's letters, had preceded her, and
Denis and many of the other MS homies in northern Virginia accepted
her with open arms. They treated her as family. This was the part she
most loved about being MS. Anywhere she went, people took her in as
family.

Brenda was the only member of the Normandie Locos in Virginia,
so she spent time hanging out with homies from different local cliques.
Denis introduced her to the men who operated at his level, the leaders.
Veto had taught Brenda when to be respectful and when to be sassy.
She knew the rules, but found the MS members in Virginia to be a little
less serious. Compared to Veto, these guys are easy to deal with, Brenda
thought. With Denis at her side, she easily made new friends and settled into her new life on the streets of Fairfax, Arlington, and Alexandria. It took some time, but after a few days, she felt safe from Detective
Oseguera, far away in Texas.

Brenda hadn't yet spent a year in the gang, but after the initial days
of meeting important MS local leaders, she relaxed a little. She started
to smile again. One by one, she easily won over Denis and the others.
They slowly began to trust Brenda. She was privy to all but the gang's
most secret information, which set her apart from all other female
members and many males. As she went from party to party at night

and from one job to another during the day, Brenda's mind never stopped working. It took snapshots of everything she saw. She recorded names, places, faces, numbers, and addresses.

Most of what she recorded was unimportant and didn't bother her, but disturbing scenes from Texas began to creep into her dreams. In Virginia, she learned information that burned away her innocence. Javier's murder was one scene she'd never forget, but she was especially disturbed when Denis told her about the time he killed someone he thought was a member of a rival gang. Denis had said that cutting out the guy's throat was like cutting through raw chicken. She'd cut raw chicken before and knew what that felt like. Brenda had fought hard to control her emotions. Denis wasn't kidding. He had a disturbing dark side, and he'd shown Brenda only a peek. For days after that moment, Brenda couldn't shake the image of Denis sawing through someone's neck. It was too gruesome and entirely too real. She knew Denis had killed this guy. Like Javier's murder, it was another horrible scene that played in her mind constantly.

CHAPTER 13

Denis Rivera's youthful, handsome features and smooth, light brown skin veiled well what was simmering underneath, a desire to control everyone around him through fear, violence, and even murder. His good looks were not marred by gang tattoos of rank or reputation. His face was clean. In another life, Denis could have passed for a pretty boy, except for one thing: his dark eyes held no remorse.

When Denis told Brenda about the time he cut out a kid's throat, he began by explaining that it had happened in the fall of 2001, when he had planned the murder of Joaquin Diaz, a twenty-year-old Latino who he believed was a *chavala*, a rival gang member. Joaquin hadn't seen it coming, Denis said. As was customary among street gang members, those targeted for death were lulled into a false sense of confidence. It was a tactic they called "rocking the cradle," and it has been employed by organized crime for decades.

Joaquin sold marijuana from time to time, and Denis thought asking to buy some would be a legitimate reason for them to meet up. The two met on a chilly evening in Alexandria, Virginia, at a fast-food restaurant where Joaquin's girlfriend worked. Denis and another friend sat in a booth, with Joaquin on the other side. After a few minutes of idle conversation, Denis began to tease Joaquin, jokingly acting like he was going to punch him, threatening to jump him and deliver a beatdown. It was a macho act Denis liked to do in jest. But Joaquin didn't think it was funny and got up and left. I don't need Denis's money that bad, Joaquin thought as he hurried out the door. Shouting for him to stop, Denis got up and followed him outside. Joaquin was startled and broke into a run.

Denis ran after him, shouting that he was just kidding, that everything was cool. He kept shouting as he followed Joaquin across the parking lot. Joaquin decided that maybe Denis was kidding after all, so he slowed down to a walk and turned around. Denis caught up with Joaquin and calmed him down. Denis tried to convince him that he just wanted to hang out and invited Joaquin to a nearby house party. Reassured, Joaquin agreed to hang out, but he wasn't going to stick around that long. Just enough time for Denis to get too drunk or stoned to care. Then he would leave.

Joaquin and Denis talked casually as they walked a half mile to the apartment of a local leader from Denis's street gang. They walked up the stairwell, and as they approached the door, the sound of people talking and laughing mixed with thumping music and the smell of marijuana and cigarettes. When they entered the living room, where a number of his friends were hanging out, Denis introduced Joaquin to his homies in the room, asked someone to get him a beer, then told Joaquin to sit tight. Denis turned and walked down the short hall to a back room, where he knew the leader, known as Fiel, would be hanging out. He needed Fiels's support to kill Joaquin.

In the back room, far out of earshot from an unsuspecting but slightly nervous Joaquin, Denis explained to Fiel that he had a *chavala* he wanted to kill. Fiel said it was cool but suggested Denis take some help. He knew the young killer could handle it, but didn't want the murder to get out of control.

He left the room and headed back toward the living room to round up his crew. Denis was getting excited. He had received backing to make a hit in the name of his gang—a *luz verde*, or green light. All gang members considered a *luz verde* serious business, but most tried to avoid being the one to pull the trigger. Fewer than two in ten actually request a *luz verde* on someone. It meant taking the life of a specified target. If they were assigned the task, a member either killed the target or received serious discipline for not carrying out the hit.

When asked if they would kill for the gang, most homies puff up and give a resounding affirmative, but secretly they hope they don't have to follow through. Denis was different from most members in his gang. Fiel knew that Denis was a seasoned hit man. He would carry out the hit and come back to celebrate the next day. The willingness to kill was what separated Denis and a limited number of hard-core members in his gang from the rest, who tried to avoid violence.

Denis stepped into the living room and spoke discreetly to the men he wanted to join him that night, one by one. One was the largest guy in the house; Denis wanted him to come along to add muscle. Another went along for fun. A third grabbed a knife from the kitchen and agreed to help Denis kill Joaquin; he was another of the gang's seasoned killers. The fourth homie offered to drive and be the lookout. The owner of a green Toyota Camry offered to let Denis use his car. Denis had pushed through the crowded living room to speak to each homie he wanted in on the plan. He had whispered under the loud music, planning his murder in the very apartment where the victim sat waiting on a couch.

With the plans in place, Denis and the other four prepared to leave. Denis invited Joaquin to come with them to pick up some marijuana for the party. Maybe on the way back they will drop me off, Joaquin thought, so he agreed. They all left the apartment and in the chilly fall night, piled into the Toyota Camry and headed for an address in northeast Washington, D.C. On the way, they decided to make a stop at Daingerfield Island.

Daingerfield Island was a national park just off of the George Washington Memorial Parkway, a couple of miles north of Old Town in Alexandria. It was close enough to Reagan National Airport to hear the constant drone of plane engines during takeoff and the screeching of rubber tires as they landed.

But between flights, the natural sounds of a wooded area in Virginia prevailed. During the day, birdsong mixed with car tires crunching over gravel as visitors came and went. Like many park areas along the river, Daingerfield was a known meeting spot for clandestine lunch encounters among gay men and illegal nighttime activity for local teens. At dusk, crickets were in song. Otherwise the park was quiet and empty. Later in the evening the park was silent, save for the noise from the airport and the gurgle of water lapping against the muddy slopes and tree roots along the banks of the Potomac. While major crime in these parks was fairly uncommon, the density of the forest and the confusing number of footpaths that meandered through the overgrown underbrush made it a perfect place for murder.

Denis told the driver they would just make a quick stop by Daingerfield Island to see if any of their friends were hanging out by the river. If so, they could get more money for the marijuana. Everyone thought it was a good idea except for Joaquin, who was silent and stuffed in the back of the Camry. He just wanted to go home, but he decided it was best to keep his mouth shut and just go along with Denis's plans. It was nearly dark when they arrived at the park. The small group wasted no time in piling out of the car to head toward the water.

Denis offered to let Joaquin start down the path first. It was a single track, a winding trail thick with the thorny green branches of blackberry bushes and the creeping tendrils of vines crisscrossing the forest floor. Woody tree roots rose from the earth, daring visitors to run and not trip. Denis followed close behind Joaquin, with another homie just behind Denis. Two more homies followed in case Joaquin tried to run back up the path. The driver stayed with the car.

The narrow footpath led from the back of the parking lot to the river. They walked in silence for a few minutes, marching farther away from the parking lot and any chance for discovery with each step. When the small group was two hundred yards from the river, Denis silently removed a knife from under his shirt. He then quickly reached over Joaquin's shoulder and stabbed him in the chest.

Suddenly frenzied with pain and adrenaline, Joaquin ran, wrenching the imbedded blade from Denis's grip before it fell to the ground. I've been stabbed! Joaquin's mind screamed with disbelief. The reality of the moment flooded in. If they caught him, he would die in that park. How stupid he was to trust Denis! Fear flooded Joaquin's senses. The pain in his chest was sharply focused on the point where Denis's knife had ripped through his skin. It hurt to breathe and even more to run. Adrenaline took over. He had to escape.

Denis and his homies pursued. Crazed with fright, Joaquin began screaming. Maybe someone would hear him.

Denis caught up with Joaquin only moments later, after he tripped on an unseen root. Sprawled out on the ground, Joaquin fought the pain in his chest and tried to get up, but it was too late. Denis jumped on top of Joaquin and held him down. Joaquin bucked and fought to get Denis off of him, but when another one of Denis's friends ran up and kicked Joaquin in the head, the world spun. His ears were ringing and his vision was blurred. He was on his back on the cold ground with Denis straddled on top. Still he fought to get Denis off him. A second homie arrived and passed Denis the knife he had grabbed from Fiel's kitchen. Denis gripped the knife and attacked Joaquin with powerful downward strokes, slashing his raised forearms and hands and stabbing him repeatedly in the chest and stomach. Before Joaquin stopped trying to defend himself, Denis had stabbed him thirteen times, a macabre salute to his gang. Still on top of Joaquin, Denis breathed heavily from the exertion. Joaquin's body was still, but his chest still rose and fell with shallow breaths. Joaquin still wasn't dead, and Denis wasn't finished.

As the others watched, Denis sawed at Joaquin's neck, cutting deeply to the spinal cord before cursing, frustrated with the inadequate steak knife. It wasn't sharp enough to cut off the head. Denis settled for what he could do with the dull blade: he cut out his victim's larynx, esophagus, and windpipe. Finally done with his grisly task, Denis threw the body parts aside, stood up, and stepped over Joaquin's body to begin the walk back to the car. The others followed in silence, stupefied by what they had just witnessed. But no one dared to say a word. As calmly as they had arrived, the group drove back to an apartment in Alexandria, where Denis washed off the blood.

Early the next morning, two fishermen nearly stumbled over Joaquin's remains while walking to the river. They were sickened by the sight of a nearly decapitated body and immediately called 911. The next day, news of Joaquin's murder hit the papers. Denis loved it when the press picked up on his work. As word of the crime spread through the ranks of his street gang, Denis once again enjoyed a swell in his reputation as a heavy hitter and a man who had no problem committing grisly murder.

Many months later, in the summer of 2002, as Denis got to know Brenda, he readily shared his story of killing Joaquin. He respected her as someone he thought was a hardened homie who was jumped in at age thirteen, and he wanted to boast. Denis's story represented everything she hated about her gang. His story pushed her to the edge of what she thought she could handle. Smile now, cry later—it was a mantra she found harder and harder to follow. Brenda wanted to cry now and smile later, but she maintained her façade. After Denis told her about Joaquin, Brenda had to focus on what she liked about Denis. She didn't dare allow herself to think about what he had told her.

Brenda longed for a moment alone, but after Denis confided in her, he was more watchful, careful to see how she carried the weight of this information. Now she knew about two cold-blooded murders. These two murders settled heavily on her conscience, mixed in with all the other images and experiences she had endured as a member of the MS-13. As much as she loved the gang, and some of the men she had met during her time as a gangster, Brenda felt like she needed a break. A small part of her even wanted out. This gang life was too intense, a small voice in her head began to repeat softly. Her inner feelings of disquiet and desire to leave the gang sat dormant until a fateful day when the Arlington police finally separated her from Denis and the Mara Salvatrucha world. That break she longed for set her on a path to becoming something she never thought possible: an informant.

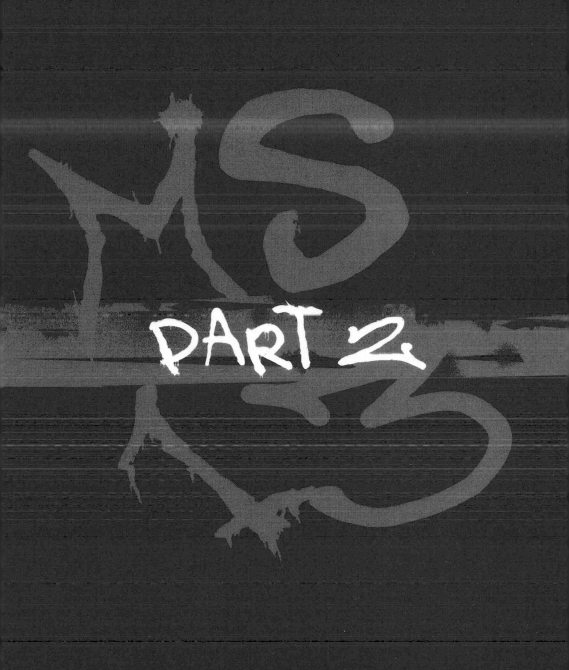

PART 2

CHAPTER 14

Fairfax and Arlington counties, the city of Alexandria, and the surrounding region of northern Virginia became a collage of international culture as wave after wave of immigrants settled within commuting distance of Washington, D.C. Immigrants from Vietnam, Africa, Eastern Europe, and Central America, especially El Salvador, flocked to the region in the last quarter of the twentieth century.

Hundreds of Salvadoran immigrants fled the civil war that raged across their country in the 1980s, settling in Culmore, a six-block area near Bailey's Crossroads in Fairfax County: Culmore had become a hub for the refugees, where Spanish was the first language, housing costs were low, and groups of day laborers could almost always find work.

Pioneering immigrants served as anchors in the United States for a long line of relatives and friends who would follow them there, seeking a better life. It was a simple pattern: Once established, the pioneers sent word that they had arrived and where they were situated; others followed. Soon the lack of space in small apartments became a problem.

If someone was not already sleeping on the balcony, it was used as outdoor storage space. Couches and tables were exiled from the living room to make room for more beds. Hot cots, they called them. The sleeping rotation was so tight, the beds never had enough time to dissipate heat. Adults had priority for mattresses, and the kids fought over any that remained. The middle was a coveted spot. Those who didn't have a bed slept on the floor wherever there was space—in the bathroom or on the linoleum under the kitchen table. There were so many inhabitants in these one-bedroom apartments that they slept in shifts and ate meals on the run.

For new arrivals, life was about keeping a low profile and earning as much money as possible to send home. Fathers left behind their families. Married couples left their children with grandparents. The parents always left home with a promise: we will send for you when the time is right.

Years might pass, sometimes ten or more. More children were born in the United States. When reunion was finally possible, the older children who traveled to the United States experienced the severe culture shock of their new home, their parents' new reality, and a biting truth: American-born children were always placed above the others. They were U.S. citizens. They could speak English and they had a future. In many cases, the children born in Central America were an afterthought, little more than a fulfilled promise made during a desperate time.

The displaced kids, by the nature of their situation, triggered a crisis for each family. The parents were unable to devote much time to work through their family problems. Mom and Dad each worked two jobs. Earning money was paramount. The American-born siblings resented the newly arrived foreign siblings they had never met. The new arrivals didn't even speak English and found further humiliation at school, where they were often held back a grade.

When Denis was four or five, his parents left him and his sister with their grandparents and didn't return for years. Denis had little contact with his parents, just the occasional phone call or letter. When his parents finally did send for him, the new home life he found in the United States was not a happy affair. He shared the house with two younger brothers. To him, they were strangers who also called his mother Mamá. Both were born in the United States, which gave them an unspoken level of status above him and his sister.

There was also a whole new set of rules. English was the language at school and a constant source of frustration. Denis was in class with black and white kids, adding to the novelty of his experience. It was stressful. Culture shock and difficulty with the language was enough to keep Denis quiet for years.

Denis was a decent kid who came from a troubled family. There were many kids from his community in the same situation. Some of them were punks and bullies. Others were quiet and didn't bother to interact with anyone. Like Denis, they were all the result of dysfunctional family situations, one born by the breakup and reunification process many immigrant families endured. But most didn't turn into killers.

Once Denis joined the Mara Salvatrucha, he was in a world where he could speak Spanish and be understood. He was surrounded by respect, and as he grew older and did work for the gang, he gathered power. His power and rank in the gang also won him Brenda's attention and loyalty.

CHAPTER 15

On a hazy summer day in mid-June, only days after Denis had shared his story of Joaquin's murder with Brenda, they roamed the streets of Alexandria on the lookout for a car to steal.

"I want a black Honda Accord," Brenda told Denis.

Hondas were Denis's specialty and one of the MS's favorite cars to steal—they had a number of compartments to hide guns. Lucky for Brenda, Denis had Honda master lock keys, obtained through another MS member. With one key he could get into any door, and with the other, he could start up just about any model. Stealing a Honda for him was as easy as walking up to his own car, getting in, and driving off.

He had to be careful. Denis was wanted in Virginia for a number of different crimes, and there was talk on the streets that he was a prime suspect in the Joaquin Diaz murder. MS leaders thought Denis was too valuable to be arrested for driving a stolen car, but he didn't care. Stealing a Honda was too easy.

Near downtown Alexandria, Brenda spotted her new Honda, and the two quickly moved to break in and drive away. But when she looked inside, Brenda said to Denis, "No, not this one." It had a baby seat in the back, and Brenda didn't want to steal from a family. Denis shrugged and continued on. They would find another Honda soon.

Denis started up the next Honda Accord they found with no problem, but the joy ride in the stolen car didn't last long. As they rounded a corner in Arlington, not miles from where they had stolen the car in the first place, local police pulled them over for rolling through a stop sign. Arrest was not an option. Before the cop even got out of her car to ask for license and registration, Brenda and Denis jumped out and began running.

The cop and her partner immediately ran after the two, shouting at them to stop. With the police in hot pursuit, Brenda and Denis dove into a building to hide in a janitor's closet until the cops ran by. The cops, however, saw them enter the building and decided to wait.

Brenda and Denis crept out of the building a short while later, sure of their escape, when the police, with guns drawn, shouted for the two to get on the ground. Swiftly, Denis and Brenda found themselves arrested, cuffed, and seated together in the back of an Arlington County cruiser. On the short trip to the station, Denis told Brenda in hushed tones, "Do what you have to do to take care of yourself." He made a quick glance to make sure that the cops didn't hear. "With my rap, I know I'm fucked, but you've still got a chance to get out," he whispered.

At the station, the cops separated Brenda and Denis to interview them. Then they were seated together again in the same room and were able to speak to each other. Denis quickly indicated that they should speak only in Spanish. He'd caught on that the officers couldn't work out what they were saying.

When they had fingerprinted Denis and scanned his sheet, not only had they confirmed that he was an MS leader, they had also discovered that he was wanted for a number of car thefts, a long list of misdemeanors, and a malicious-wounding charge, and that he was a key suspect in the Joaquin Diaz murder. The officers were worried that Denis was conveying important information to Brenda, information that they'd simply miss because they didn't speak Spanish. They were forced to call in a Spanish-speaking officer, Detective Rick Rodriguez, to help them gather intelligence from Denis's conversation with Brenda.

Detective Rodriguez was Puerto Rican. He had seen many gangsters come and go over his extended beat as a street gang investigator. He had earned a reputation for tackling some of the toughest police work in Arlington County and had worked hard to earn the trust of the Latino community most afflicted by the MS and other gangs in his jurisdiction.

Rodriguez's tall stature, light-colored skin, and Anglo-American

looks belied his Latino roots and closeness with the local Latino community. His charisma and hard-nosed approach to detective work perplexed and maddened gang members in the area, who had often dealt
with his straight-shooter style of questioning and dry sense of humor.
One minute he would bully suspects with his fast-forward personality
and get them laughing with him the next, just before slapping on the
cuffs. His squinty blue eyes missed nothing. Through his diligent work,
Rodriguez had arrested a number of MS members, enough to place
him on their radar.

When Rodriguez arrived, he listened carefully to the officers' problem. In the interrogation room, Denis and Brenda kept saying "Simon," like the name Simon, but not quite. It sounded more like
something said in Jamaica, as in "Ya-mon." The officers couldn't make
heads or tails of it.

As Rodriguez listened to the tapes, he began laughing.

"What's so funny?" one of the officers asked.

"There is no 'Simon.' They're saying 'Si-món,'" Rodriguez revealed.

"Yeah, but isn't 'Si-món' the name Simon?" one of the officers asked,
still confused.

"Yes, but in the context of this conversation 'Si-món' is like you
and I in police jargon saying 'Ten-four' or 'Yes, I agree, I got it.' So if I
say to you, you know, 'You want to go and have dinner at McDonald's?'
you reply, 'Si-món,' it means yes. There is no one named Simon,"
Rodriguez concluded with a chuckle.

"Damn it, we wasted hours trying to figure that out."

As his amusement at the ease of his little translating job wore off,
Rodriguez reflected on what the officers had stumbled upon here. When
he had heard that Denis Rivera had been arrested, he immediately
knew it was a lucky capture for all of them. The detective was familiar
with various strategies and ideas to break up the MS in Arlington. One
of the most useful, placing an informant inside the gang, was also extremely difficult. Rick was determined to take advantage of this arrest.
It was an opportunity to flip Denis, convince him the weight of the law
was on his shoulders, and gain that informant. Denis would have to
cooperate or face many years behind bars. The only problem was that
Denis was a hard-core killer. It would take more than a couple of
hours in an interrogation room and a line of hard questions to soften
up Denis Rivera—even harder to get him to the point where he would
consider becoming an informant. But Rodriguez had to try. With this

in mind, he made a call to Victor Ignacio, the one detective who had known Denis since he was a kid.

Detective Ignacio looked every part of his name. Dark-skinned, with a well-trimmed moustache and a determined disposition, he was from the Dominican Republic, bilingual, a workaholic, and an excellent policeman. He volunteered to work undercover straight out of the police academy. Throughout a decade of investigative police work, Detective Ignacio had seen many kids come and go. A stoic expression was his default setting, broken up on rare occasion by a broad grin that never stayed long. Like Rodriguez, Detective Ignacio was a street gang expert and known among the MS as trouble, not someone to cross.

In fact, Ignacio had worked with the National Park police for months to solve the Joaquin Diaz murder on Daingerfield Island. The nature of the murder and the evidence that had been found led investigators to believe it was a gang hit, so the Park police asked for Ignacio's assistance with the investigation. With his help, the lead investigator had pinpointed Denis Rivera as a primary suspect.

When Ignacio took Rodriguez's call, as soon as he heard that Denis Rivera was in custody, he made arrangements for a special interview. Back at the Arlington Police Department, Rodriguez received a page from Ignacio, telling him he was in place. Rodriguez then walked over to the holding cell, signed Denis out, and took him to an interrogation room. Ignacio was waiting in the hall. Denis's mother and aunt waited in a sitting room in another part of the building. When he rounded the corner, Denis took one look at Ignacio. He remembered the cop from years ago, knocking on his door as a rookie, coming to ask his mom some questions when his older sister ran away.

How times have changed, mused Ignacio as he watched Rodriguez lead Denis down the hall in handcuffs. When Denis was in middle school, Ignacio had been called in to investigate a fight. Denis had been threatening kids with a machete. Ignacio couldn't believe it at the time. He suspected Denis had developed a powerful need for attention. With both parents working, it hadn't taken long for Denis and his sister to start acting out. Denis had started getting into fights and was caught trespassing on private property. Worse, he went after people who talked to the cops, people who got him into trouble. This type of vendetta separated Denis from the rest of the kids, thought Ignacio. As young as fourteen, Denis would start fights with just about anyone. He dared people to take him on simply out of spite or just because someone looked at him for too long. He had quickly become a very angry kid. His street name was Conejo, the Spanish word for rabbit. Small and compact, Denis was quick and could take a beating. At fifteen, he had all the toughness of any gang member. Though not in the MS at the time, he had all the makings.

Ignacio had seen all the signs of a kid headed for gang life. As the boy grew and Ignacio kept his thumb on local issues, the one thing that remained true about Denis was his strong love for his mother. Yet there was simply not enough love and attention to go around. A combination of different factors created a growing gap between Denis and his family. And the wider the gap grew, the more he sought to fill the emptiness in his heart and his life with something outside the home. Like so many kids who had chosen to join street gangs, Denis decided to look for acceptance somewhere on the street. Ignacio thought that he had been a good kid to begin with, but things had changed. Denis was a changed man, wanted for murder, no longer just an angry boy. Denis was a gangster, no longer scared of him or any other cop. Ignacio wanted to try using Denis's mother and aunt to soften him up and make the right decision to talk. That approach might have worked on the boy. He wasn't sure it was going to work on the man.

CHAPTER 16

Rodriguez sat Denis in the interrogation room and left him to await Ignacio's arrival. The room was a tight space with a metal table bolted to the floor, flush against a wall. One side had a handcuff chained to the table and a small metal stool affixed to the floor. An identical stool stood opposite the first.

Ignacio entered the room with the National Park police investigator and got straight to the point. He told Denis he was looking at many years in prison, and the best thing he could do was cooperate. Ignacio was angling for information on the Daingerfield Island murder. He needed Denis to open up and tell them about what happened, but it was a long shot. Denis didn't say a word. He was determined to hold out.

Rodriguez detected silence and peeked through the small window in the door. He rapped his knucles on the glass and motioned for Ignacio to come out. Rodriguez was getting antsy and frustrated with Denis.

He wanted to have a go at Denis but needed to run it by his colleague first. Denis had known Ignacio for a long time, so Rodriguez thought he could use that to their advantage. The plan sounded almost too simple, standard good cop, bad cop, but Rodriguez had found in his many years of investigating that a gang member's anger was usually his number one weakness. He intended to tap into that anger full force.

As the plan went, once Denis was good and fed up with Rodriguez, Rodriguez would leave the room and allow Denis to tell Ignacio whatever he wanted to say. Denis didn't like Ignacio, but he knew him. The two had a long history, and a plausible foundation for trust. Rodriguez was counting on this.

After hearing Rodriguez's plan, Ignacio argued to hold off a little longer. He still had his own angle, with Denis's mom and aunt waiting in another room. Ignacio was still betting on them. Both women were determined to talk to Denis, convinced they could get through to him as family, as blood. Ignacio was willing to give it a shot.

First, Denis's mother entered the room, her expression pained. She sat on the stool facing her son leaning forward, but she dared not reach out to caress his face. This was not the time or place to be soft. Denis would resent any physical act of emotion, she thought. Still, Denis's mom looked at her son longingly, willing him to come clean—to become the young man she always wanted him to be.

"Talk to the police," she pleaded. "Tell them what you know."

Denis only stared forward. His silence pushed her further. It was a mother's last chance to save her child from the possibility of life behind bars.

"Don't take the blame for things that you're not to be blamed for. Please, my son, help yourself," she begged in a terse whisper.

Still, Denis didn't bat an eyelash. They sat in silence for a long moment before his mother heaved a sigh and looked at the ceiling, trying not to cry. She rose to leave, realizing with resignation that she had gotten nowhere. As she stood, Denis also rose and reached out to give her a hug, as if acknowledging that it would be his last opportunity.

As Denis's mom left, deflated, Ignacio ushered his aunt into the cramped interview room. She was tough and direct.

"If you don't talk to the police, they're going to mess you up," she said. Her voice was like a taut wire, high-strung but strong. "You're gonna be put in prison. They're gonna put everything on you and you're going to pay the price," she warned. Nothing she said fazed Denis. He knew the stakes. He wasn't going to talk for anyone, not for his mom, not for his aunt, or for anyone else. This was child's play.

Rodriguez, watching through the glass, turned to Ignacio.

"Why don't I go in there," Rodriguez offered. "Let me get under his skin so maybe he feels it's better off for him to speak to you or somebody else," he said.

Ignacio finally agreed. Rodriguez pushed the door open and entered the interview room looking directly at Denis. He sat on the metal stool and stretched out his long legs, crossed his arms, and leaned against the wall. He was relaxed on the outside, but inside he was ready to rip into this kid.

Rodriguez started slowly. After a few easy questions, he folded his legs under the stool and shifted his weight to the front of his seat, so he was just a foot away from Denis's face. Rodriguez got louder with each question, closer to Denis's personal space, until they were nearly nose to nose. He wanted to know names, places, dates, plans, everything, and was using all the verbal force he had to squeeze information out of Denis.

Still, nothing seemed to faze Denis. He looked right through Rodriguez, who couldn't help but remind himself that Denis was a killer. He had stared death in the face and wasn't afraid of cops. Defeated, Rodriguez left the room to consult with Ignacio.

In the silent little room, Denis sat, knowing time was on his side. He was aware that the cops would come back and try something else. He didn't care about what he'd done or what the cops were going to do to him. He knew he was in serious trouble, but he felt confident that these two cops would have a hard time putting anything on him. He knew no one would rat him out or testify against him. He hunkered down and resigned himself to sitting out the interview, acting tough, then waiting to see what would happen. He breathed a sigh as he wondered what Rodriguez would come up with next.

Speak of the devil, he thought, as Rodriguez walked back into the room and sat down, adjusted his weight, and leaned forward onto his forearms, resting on the edge of the small table. His blue eyes stared from behind his glasses into Denis's dark pupils. He was calm and ready for a new approach. Hit Denis with the truth, Rodriguez thought. Maybe Denis hadn't thought through what prison was really like.

"Denis, you're eighteen years old," Rodriguez said, staring at him. "What would you normally be doing on a Friday evening?" he asked.

Denis didn't answer.

"I'll tell you what you would be doing on a Friday evening, more than likely," Rodriguez continued, leaning forward another inch, getting a little louder. "You'd be out somewhere with your homeboys, you might be at somebody's house watching TV. You might be at somebody's house playing a video game. You might be out roaming the streets, driving around, maybe sitting at McDonald's. You might be at a mall just walking around checking out the girls. You might be at a motel having a good time, drinking, smoking pot—who knows what you'd be doing? But you would be doing things that typical kids your age involved in gang activity would be doing. You might be driving around looking to steal a car. You might be driving around in a stolen car."

Rodriguez gained momentum. He had filled Denis's mind with images of freedom, of life as a happy teenager with not a care in the world. He knew the truth of his next words would stack in Denis's consciousness with the weight of facing life behind bars. It would only be a matter of moments before the kid broke, he thought.

"But here's the bad point, and you need to realize this. You are not going to be set free. Chances are, you're not going to see the light of day anymore. And as an eighteen-year-old kid you need to start wondering. What is your life expectancy? Let's say you live to be seventy-five. Do the math. How many years are you going to spend behind bars only because you don't want to talk and you don't want to cooperate?"

Denis didn't care.

"Okay," Rodriguez said, "let's take it to another level." He got right in Denis's face, nose to nose, and with a forceful tone enunciated bitingly. "Do you realize that you will never—if this continues the way it's going and you're convicted of these crimes"—and here he amped up the decibels of his voice even louder—"you will *never, ever, ever* ride again in a car with your homeboys. You will never go to the beach. You will never go see a movie. You will never sit down at a food court. You will never walk at a mall. You will never enjoy another Corona. You might never enjoy another soda. You may not even get a chance to enjoy a marijuana cigarette. I don't know, you may get that in prison, I don't know. But you're not going to enjoy another Christmas, New Year's, or birthday."

Rodriguez was counting off each "never" with his hands. As he moved ahead, Rodriguez remembered that after the interview with his mother, Denis had hugged her.

"This could be the last time that you ever embrace your mother," he said with no note of sympathy in his voice, only cold, hard truth. "You will never hug her the way you hugged her tonight. There might be a partition between you two from now on. You will never smell her perfume. You will never feel her tears. You will see them, but you will never feel the actual tear."

Still nothing. Rodriguez knew he hadn't hit a weak spot yet. He hadn't seen the flicker he was looking for that signaled that he'd tapped into that all-important anger. He knew there must be another approach. He thought he understood the mind of a teenage gangster, but he was running out of ideas. He looked past Denis at the back wall, going through his mental files on teenage gangsters. Then it hit him. Go after the girlfriend. With that flash of insight, he decided to focus on another female in Denis's life. He backed off a bit before starting on his new angle of attack.

"Denis, do you realize you will never, ever make love to another woman or girl again?" He registered a flicker of anger as he repeated, "Again . . . never, ever!" Rodriguez continued, focused on winning another flicker of anger, "You will never touch another female again. It's just not going to happen. If this continues, you will not. Which means that if you have a girlfriend, who do you think is gonna make love to her from now on? As a matter of fact, while you and I are sitting here, somebody in your clique may be hitting it. Somebody's balls deep in your girl."

That made him flinch.

"Why you gotta go there?" Denis asked, looking at Rodriguez, visibly perturbed.

Rodriguez drove his point home, probing the weak spot. "You're not going to please her. She's not going to wait around for you. She's eighteen, she's seventeen, whatever age she happens to be, she's not going to wait for you, and you know it. You know how this thing works. You know one of your homeboys is going to take care of her. And you know why I gotta go there, Denis?" Rodriguez asked, softening his voice a little and backing away from Denis's face.

"You know why I'm gonna go there? Because nothing else seems to get to you. We are trying to talk to you; we're trying to figure things out. Whether you look at it as if we're trying to help you or trying to harm you, legally, I don't know. But you heard your mother plead with you. She pleaded with you. Your *own mother*, the one that gave birth to you and brought you into this world, who cares for you. She has pleaded with you and you have ignored her pleas. Your aunt came in here and she laid down the law to you. She told you exactly what she thought was going to happen to you—it didn't seem to matter. Your mother's tears did not affect you. And I'm sitting here as a detective watching an eighteen-year-old, and I can't help think that when I was your age, what were some of the things I enjoyed doing in life?

"Nobody's perfect. But even if you chose to continue down a path of crime, you will not enjoy the things that I just mentioned to you *ever again*. You are going to be confined to a small room with bars. You'll be fed certain meals a day. Your freedom will be gone. And you may not think that that's a possibility, but it *is* a possibility, Denis. Your girlfriend is not going to be faithful to you. She's not going to wait around until you turn fifty and get out, if you get out. She's not going to wait around for you at all. While you're sitting in here thinking everything's cool and you'll be out soon, some homeboy is just tapping it and probably mentioning your name, like, 'Aww, poor Denis.' "

Denis still didn't say much, but he had reacted to Rodriguez's dig. Rodriguez could see it was a hook in him. He knew that whoever this girlfriend was, it was important to reach out to her.

Rodriguez didn't know at the time, but that girlfriend was Brenda Paz.

CHAPTER 17

When Brenda left Texas, she knew she would probably never see Veto again. His name was tattooed on her wrist, but she no longer considered him the love of her life. Veto's presence in her mind receded even further when she hooked up with Denis in Virginia. Veto was strong and confident, but so was Denis, and *bonito* too. He was good-looking and he gave Brenda all the attention and respect she was used to in the gang. During the weeks before their arrest, the two spent every day together. It was not long after Brenda's arrival that they began dating.

After her arrest and joint interview with Denis, Brenda was separated from her boyfriend, classified as a runaway, and placed in a holding pen at the Arlington County court. Before any papers could be filed or her parents contacted, the court required a lawyer, appointed by a judge, to act as Brenda's advocate, or guardian ad litem, on behalf of the state.

As Brenda awaited her fate, a judge began the process of deciding what to do with her. "Look out in the hall and tell me who's there," the judge told his deputy. After sticking his head out the door, the deputy quickly returned.

"Hunter's out there."

"Call him in," the judge said, not even looking up from his papers.

Brenda's case was classified as a child in need of services, or CHINS. She ultimately was just another piece of paperwork, one step in a process repeated every day as the court's bureaucracy ground out its daily tasks. But for Greg Hunter, a rookie lawyer, the day was anything but routine.

Greg Hunter's tendency toward proper manners might have classified him as a southern gentleman, but those manners were just a fine veneer covering an underlying fervor and competitiveness. Greg was driven and ambitious, and he had no problem stepping on people in his way. At six feet, six inches, and three hundred pounds, Greg was easily the biggest lawyer in the courtroom. His towering bulk and swagger clashed with a youthful face that masked a sharp intellect.

Greg's easygoing nature and appreciation of humor seemed to mix well enough with his profession, one that required a measured amount of levity to deal with courtroom politics and the grinding nature of bureaucracy. As a criminal defense lawyer, Greg dealt with some of the stupidest criminals in northern Virginia. "Evil is rare, but stupid is everyday," he liked to joke.

Because of his relatively minor position at the time, and his fateful location in the hall when the judge needed a lawyer, Greg was called upon to serve as Brenda's guardian ad litem. For all legal purposes, he was to serve the court as a parental representative for Brenda until she was free of her legal entanglements and could be returned to her real parents. It was a relationship that eventually brought Greg in close contact with more evil than stupidity.

Entering the chambers, Greg stood before the judge.

"You've been appointed as the guardian for this young girl," the judge said, indicating a stack of papers on this desk. "Here's the file; go talk to her," he told Greg in his authoritative, matter-of-fact tone.

Quickly reviewing the case file as he walked to Brenda's holding cell, Greg surmised it would be an easy case. She seemed just like a lot of the other runaways who came through the system. He quickly estimated investing about fifteen minutes in a conversation with the girl and then some paperwork. As he opened the door, he mentally calculated that within sixteen hours, maybe less, the case would be filed, and he'd bill the county for his time—easy money.

He smiled as he sat down with Brenda and began to walk her through the details of her case.

"Where are you from, Brenda?" Greg began. "And why did you run away?"

Brenda quickly glossed over her story about running away from her uncle's house in Texas. She told Greg as little as possible, hoping she wouldn't be sent back to Texas, but not willing to give this lawyer anything. She certainly wasn't going to tell him the truth about her family in California. It was the best possible place for her to go. She would be with her father, aunt and uncle, and cousins, but it was the last place she would take her gang affiliation. The last thing Brenda wanted was to hurt her family in California.

Moving from the basics, Greg delved into more important questions concerning her past and possible gang connections.

"Look," Brenda began, "I'm not gang-involved." She was tough and unrelenting.

Brenda dodged most of the other questions. Greg focused on her uncle in Texas. One way or another, Greg thought, this girl's going back to Texas.

For the moment, Brenda's story was believable. Greg did not know she had been arrested with Denis Rivera. Nor did he see her gang tattoos. Feeling that he'd covered everything, Greg made his exit. Just as he stepped out of his interview with Brenda, Greg ran into the youth probation officer assigned to Brenda's case. She was a short Latina woman who was very pushy and direct, likable but not one to sugarcoat anything. The officer had spoken with Brenda before Greg arrived. She took the opportunity now to share her findings with Greg.

"Did she tell you she's with MS?" she asked.

"*What?*" Greg was shocked, instantly realizing his slam-dunk legal guardian case had just become a little more complicated. He was a young lawyer, just turned thirty, but he'd been around long enough to know that the MS was one of the nastiest street gangs in the country. News of a near decapitation on Daingerfield Island just south of Reagan National Airport had made the Mara Salvatrucha a familiar name in Virginia's law enforcement community. A number of violent crimes associated with the MS crossed his desk monthly.

The officer repeated herself. "Did she tell you she was with MS?"

"No," Greg replied, his mental wheels spinning, thinking about how he would get out of this case and recalling everything he knew about the gang.

"She's got a bunch of warrants. They're coming in right now," the officer told him matter-of-factly, almost as if she enjoyed watching the big man squirm.

"Oh, *fuck*. Okay," Greg said, his mind racing. He'd better think quickly about his next move.

CHAPTER 18

In the span of minutes, Greg's case went from boring to exciting, from simple to a considerable challenge, possibly even life-threatening. Greg felt like he was in over his head. He had practiced criminal defense for just over eight months, hardly the expert counsel Brenda needed.

As he stood in the hall and turned the possibilities of Brenda's gang affiliation over in his mind, Greg realized he needed to talk to her again and try to get to the truth. He walked back to the holding cell where Brenda sat with the probation officer for another chat. Greg started firing away as soon as he walked in the door.

"Look, you can play it straight with me or not," he started. "I don't really care. But it's a lot easier for me to do this thing, to help you, if I know what's going on. Tell me what's going on," Greg said, looking down at Brenda, trying to read her.

Brenda still didn't say much, so the probation officer helped her out.

"She's Denis Rivera's girlfriend," the officer said, pushing Brenda to speak. The officer turned to Brenda and offered her a bit of advice. "Don't bullshit him, honey."

Before Brenda could react, the officer reached forward and pushed Brenda's T-shirt low enough on her chest to reveal a large M tattooed above Brenda's right breast and an s tattooed above the left. Greg was now convinced. Brenda was definitely MS.

"This is going to be a fun case," Greg said with biting sarcasm. "I'll see you in court in the morning," he told Brenda before turning on his heel and walking back to the judge's chambers.

On the way, Greg bumped into an Arlington County detective who was eager to speak to Brenda. In Grand Prairie, Detective Rick Oseguera had put out a national alert on Brenda Paz and the capital arrest warrant waiting for her in Texas. The detective had seen the bulletin on Brenda Paz, and when he had heard that she was in custody in Arlington County, he set out to find her and see about sending her back to Texas. Oseguera would be happy to know a Virginia colleague had served his warrant.

Greg cut the detective off before he got too excited. "Look, she isn't talking about anything because you can't make her. She's got Fifth Amendment rights, and I understand that as of right now you've got nothing."

Take that, Greg thought. He was right—the detective had nothing. Greg was a fierce advocate, even as he struggled to get his head around this bomb of a case that had just landed in his lap. In that moment, though, Greg was more interested in putting the detective in his place than protecting Brenda. This was a matter of professional pride. Greg's first impression of Brenda as a smart-ass runaway soon changed, but at that moment he didn't have time to think about where Brenda's case would take him. There were more immediate concerns, and at the top of the list was keeping Brenda in Virginia until he could get a handle on her case.

Still reeling, Greg speed-walked the rest of the way to the judge's chambers.

"This case is way more complicated," Greg said when he walked into the judge's chambers. "I know you were expecting to sign an order sending her back to Texas, but it's not going to be that way," he continued. "There are warrants coming in," daring to point out the obvious, but in need of buttressing his position before pressing on.

"Look, I don't think I'm qualified to do this. You know, she's definitely going to need criminal defense counsel help on that side because it's an ethical thing."

The roles of a defense counsel and a guardian ad litem are naturally in conflict. What's best for a client from a legal point of view is not always what a parent would want for the child. Greg wasn't comfortable working as both Brenda's guardian and her defense counsel.

"All right," the judge said. "Tell you what, here's a list of who's going to be here tomorrow. Pick someone on this list you'd like to help you out," the judge offered, only letting Greg off the hook slightly. Greg would remain Brenda's guardian. He chose a young lawyer and friend named Jason Rucker to be her defense counsel.

The next morning, Greg visited Brenda with Jason before her court case to give her the reality check she needed to make a hard decision.

"Look, you've got a capital murder warrant coming from Texas and a list of other stuff. You can help and get out, or you can not help and, you know, go to prison for what somebody else did."

The warrant from Texas was for the murder of Javier Calzada. Brenda absolutely did not want to go back to Texas and deal with Rick Oseguera again. As she thought about her options, Brenda remembered what Denis had told her in the car right after they were cuffed.

"Get out. Tell your story. Do what you gotta do to save yourself because I'm going to prison." They were words Brenda had taken to heart. She didn't want to go to prison. And she knew Denis could take care of himself. She had to do the same.

Minutes dragged by as Brenda considered her options and weighed her decision. Brenda was torn. She was a smart girl, and the pragmatic side of her knew talking to the cops was the best way to save herself from what she truly thought of as a dead-end lifestyle. For all her time on the street and experience as a member of the MS, she had had a good childhood and had not yet spent even a year running full-time with the MS. But how could she betray her homies? Since arriving in Virginia, she had become very close to the group that ran with Denis. If she became an informant, could she prevent them from finding out?

Greg had worked Brenda's case for less than a day and already knew it would be a challenge. As a child in need of services, Brenda had been assigned a guardian. From Arlington County's point of view, the guardian could resolve any legal hurdles with enough paperwork and time in court. In neighboring Fairfax County there were at least two other charges against Brenda. One was a false-identity charge: she had given an officer a false name a while back when she was questioned after the police broke up a party. The other charge was accessory after the fact to a malicious wounding. The Fairfax charges were a little trickier to resolve, but Greg was confident he could have them dropped. As her legal guardian, Greg's priority was to resolve Brenda's legal issues and get her back to her last known address, which was with her uncle in Texas. From his position, Greg's top concern was the capital arrest warrant in Texas. He didn't know the first thing about what Brenda had seen and done in Texas, but he was damn sure she wasn't going to leave his care until the issue was resolved.

Greg thought the best strategy was to try to obtain immunity for his client from the district attorney in Dallas County, where Rick Oseguera had filed the warrant. They might go for it in exchange for her information on the MS, Greg thought. He had never done an immunity deal before, and thus far had seen little indication from Brenda that she was interested in talking. He looked down at her now and wondered where on earth this was going to take him.

As Brenda met the stare of the hulking giant who called himself her guardian, the loyal gangster in her was aware that Mara Salvatrucha members do not rat, no matter what. That was rule number one. She felt cornered. Brenda shivered as she thought of her most important tattoo, the symbol of three dots arranged in a triangle that represented the three places that gang life would take you: a hospital, a prison, or the grave.

None were inviting.

CHAPTER 19

Brenda had seen so much death, pain, and suffering. Still, she knew there were options. Others, like Veto and Denis, were too far gone. There could still be a silver lining to her story. *Maybe Greg can help me find it,* she thought, still sitting there under his gaze. The allure of a future free of the gang life pulled her in one direction. The love she felt for her gang family and her addiction to the power of being a respected gangster pulled her in another.

Brenda knew the cops would be looking for information. Before her arrest with Denis, she had spent many hours wrestling with her loyalty to her MS family and her desire for a way out. She had finally come up with a number of people she wouldn't mind giving up. At the top of that list was Little Zico, one of the homies who had brutally attacked Javier that night in Texas. It still haunted her dreams. Little Zico scared her, and she knew he'd be valuable to the cops.

Two strong arguments formed in Brenda's mind. She settled on standing between the two. It was then in the crisp morning hours on the day after she was arrested that Brenda Paz decided to let down her guard, but only a little. She looked up at her towering legal guardian and told him she was willing to talk. Brenda had decided to give Greg Hunter and Jason Rucker general information, but to be very careful about specifics.

After her initial court case to resolve the CHINS placed on Brenda in Arlington County, Greg began to move forward slowly. He was confident Brenda felt comfortable with her decision to talk. Back at his office, Greg made a few phone calls to gang detectives in Arlington and Fairfax, testing the water to see if there were any detectives in the area who were willing to take a chance with a potentially valuable informant. He would offer up the opportunity of speaking with Brenda on the basis that she would not sign any statement or be arrested and forced to give up information about ongoing cases. If he could establish Brenda as a reliable source of information on the Mara Salvatrucha in Virginia, he could build a case for keeping her there and ultimately argue that the charges against her in Texas should be dropped.

Mike Porter, a gang unit detective with the Fairfax County Police Department, was the only one who returned Greg's call. Stout and professional, he was a pragmatic policeman, and his normally laid-back style and stature balanced well with his sharp focus and powers of observation. He was also a fixer—he believed in justice and sought to make everything right in his world. Porter was immediately interested in Brenda. Greg ran it by Brenda, and she agreed to talk to him.

Greg arranged a meeting with Brenda, himself, Porter, and Jason Rucker in a classroom at the Landmark Juvenile Detention Facility in Arlington, where Brenda had been held since her arrest. It was a dank, underserviced room with concrete walls, a chalkboard, and a worn table made of pressed-wood chips with thin metal legs. The plastic chairs were tired and cracked at the corners.

Porter was decidedly respectful at the meeting. He didn't try a tough-cop routine with Brenda, seeing in her some potential as a valuable source of information. By now, word had spread among local detectives that Brenda was Denis Rivera's girlfriend. Given Denis's high rank within the MS, Porter assumed that Brenda would know something about a number of open investigations he was working that allegedly involved MS gang members.

She did.

Porter was just one of many cops looking for Little Zico. Along with a number of other gang members, after Calzada's murder Little Zico had fled Texas with his girlfriend, Flaca, the same girl Brenda had described to Oseguera. Little Zico and Flaca had hidden out in North Carolina. When he finally came out of hiding, he headed up to Virginia, where he committed a string of crimes, including an alleged point-blank shooting of a Washington area taxi driver. By the time Porter met

Brenda, Little Zico was off the radar again. Brenda knew where he was hiding in North Carolina, and she thought that if she told the cops, they could arrest him and get him off the streets. He was a bad, angry man, and she didn't have any respect for him or his girlfriend, Flaca.

Brenda readily divulged to Porter the information about the specific interstate highway, the exit, the exact turns to take, and even a description of the house where Little Zico lived. She recounted the information as if watching a movie in her mind. It was always like that for her, clear images, as if any scene could happen over and over again in her mind. Her memory was both her greatest asset and her worst enemy. In this instance, it came in handy. Not long after that initial meeting, cops in North Carolina used Brenda's information to arrest Little Zico.

Over the four-and-a-half-hour meeting, Brenda told Porter everything she knew about Little Zico's location. She detailed statements made by over a dozen different MS members, implicating many of them in ongoing investigations in the area. Brenda also pointed out the location of an MS meeting spot previously unknown to police. Porter was impressed. So were Greg and Jason. From their point of view, Brenda was willing to share credible information and seemed to have intelligence on a number of cases. For Brenda, it was acceptable to sell out a member of the MS not close to her and give the police information she considered to be of little consequence. So far, she hadn't ratted on her friends in Virginia.

Gang member loyalty was one of the greatest challenges for law enforcement. If arrested, members never talked to the cops; nor could cops easily insert an informant because gang leaders were savvy enough to investigate new members. Discipline within the gang was nearly as ruthless as the gang's treatment of its enemies, further discouraging dissension within the ranks. Any would-be undercover officer had to think twice before getting involved in what could be construed as a suicide mission. The Mara Salvatrucha hated cops, and its members hated anyone who worked with the cops, especially a rat. Treason was the worst sin within the gang, one punishable only by death. This reality made Brenda's decision to cooperate with the police more valuable and more dangerous.

Only a few hours after the successful first meeting with Mike Porter, Greg's home phone rang. It was almost midnight. Greg recognized Victor Ignacio's voice.

"I hear you've got Brenda Paz. I know she knows Denis Rivera, and I know the Mara Salvatrucha is talking about killing cops," Ignacio began with little greeting or acknowledgment that it was late at night. "And if she's talking, whatever you all know about is very important to me. So I want to know right now," Ignacio demanded.

Ignacio had information the MS planned to kill two cops in the area. He didn't know who, but he suspected he could be one of them, as he was known among the MS for having busted a number of their gang members. If Brenda knew something, Ignacio wasn't going to wait around to hear about it tomorrow.

"Well, you can't talk to her now, it's late," Greg replied, somewhat perturbed that Ignacio had called him at home. He never gave out his home number.

"She's in my juvenile detention center, and I'm talking to her right now," Ignacio said, reminding Greg that as a cop with the Alexandria Police Department, he had the right to speak to anyone at the Landmark Juvenile Detention Center. It was located in the city of Alexandria.

Greg had little choice. "Okay, I'm coming down now," he said. Then he hung up and set out for a late-night rendezvous to see if Brenda knew anything about MS plans to kill cops.

Brenda did know of Ignacio. His gang-busting reputation had placed him at the top of her gang's hit list. Before she met Ignacio, she had thought he was the bogeyman.

Ignacio was waiting for Greg when he arrived. The two men, along with a third detective, entered the building, asked an attendant to get Brenda out of bed, and then escorted her to an interview room, where they began asking her about cop killers. Brenda, still sleepy and a little groggy, talked to Ignacio and was forthcoming with enough information over the two-hour meeting to put Ignacio's mind at ease.

"They want to kill you and another cop, but I can't remember his name." Brenda had nothing to hide about plans to kill cops. The truth was, she didn't know much.

Women in the Mara Salvatrucha held a second-class stature. Jumped-in women could hang with the homies at the same level, but they could not talk back or show any disrespect. And most women were not allowed into the *misas*, the clique's weekly meetings. Brenda's closeness with some of her gang's top leaders had opened doors most other women never considered walking through. Although she didn't attend the meetings, she had heard almost everything that had transpired, everything save the most secret plans. During the interview, Ignacio received enough information to close a couple of cases and decided he liked Brenda. He left the detention center satisfied.

Porter, Ignacio, Greg, and Jason decided to meet with Brenda again. It had been a week since her arrest with Denis. Though Brenda didn't know it, the police had given her some time to see if any of her facts had developed holes. Over a five-hour meeting, Porter and Ignacio asked her many of the same questions as at the first long meeting, checking for consistency. By the end of the meeting, both Porter and Ignacio were convinced that Brenda Paz was a legitimate informant and a wealth of information. It was in their best interests to protect her. They knew what would happen if the MS found out Brenda was talking to the cops. The MS would show no mercy. Any death for a traitor MS member was slow, committed with knives or a machete, and sometimes even meant decapitation.

CHAPTER 20

Brenda's continued separation from the gang reduced her craving for street life. Her already weak loyalty to the MS waned, gradually allowing Brenda to focus more on her own future and less on her gang. The cloud in her mind formed by the intoxicating feeling of respect and power receded enough for her to remember that she wanted to eventually get back to California. She began to dismantle her mask and act like the bright and curious teenage girl she was before she had learned to fear Veto.

Policemen she met while in custody told her she could make a great detective. Brenda began to feel real hope for a future beyond her gang. She thought someday she could get through this process and maybe even take care of her mom. Maybe she could get her mom from Honduras, move to Puerto Rico, and take care of her there. That fantasy and the appealing reality of a future away from the Mara Salvatrucha excited her enough to tell Greg and the cops more than she had originally thought prudent.

Greg's first few weeks with Brenda crawled forward, but he did make progress. He slowly opened her mind to the possibilities of finishing high school and attending college, and he gave her intellectually stimulating books to read from his personal library. *Crime and Punishment*, *Catcher in the Rye*, and *Don Quixote* were her favorites. Greg's continual attempts to make Brenda focus on her future was a steady process that moved Brenda forward into the role she began to play as one of the most important and charismatic MS informants run by U.S. law enforcement.

As the summer passed, Brenda's notoriety grew. Greg fielded calls from law enforcement in various states. Interview after interview ensued. They all occurred in a controlled environment. Greg and Jason always secured the necessary assurances that no cops would file an arrest warrant for Brenda, and none ever did. Her information was specific and highly detailed. The detectives who met Brenda immediately liked her and couldn't believe that she knew what she told them. Most of the information checked out. Sometimes Brenda spoke for less than fifteen minutes. Other meetings went on for hours.

Greg learned more about the MS as Brenda distanced herself from gang life and grew comfortable with talking to the police. She still didn't talk about details of her relationship with Denis and the Normandie Locos, her clique. Nor did she talk about Veto and the night he killed Javier Calzada. Veto terrified her. So did the other men present that rainy, cold night in Grand Prairie. But she knew so much about the MS and could remember so many names, places, and dates that most of the cops who interviewed Brenda could not know she was still holding back.

Greg observed and listened to Brenda as she slowly evolved into a storyteller. She wasn't recounting tall tales about boys, hanging out at the mall, or the pair of shoes she just bought. Her stories were about pain and death, especially when she spoke to him in private. The first time Brenda really opened up to Greg, just before Independence Day, he took a call from her on his cell phone while driving to pick up party supplies. Greg had to pull over to focus on the conversation. Brenda was clearly upset and prepared to get some heavy information off her chest.

She told Greg about Veto, her relationship with this old-school gang member, and how he had physically abused her. She told him Veto took her to Meridian, Idaho, once to dispose of the bodies of two prostitutes he had killed.

Brenda explained more about her gang's disciplinary action, called yellow-lighting. Gang members who required some discipline but had not been marked for death were beaten by a group, then stabbed and dumped in front of a hospital. She recalled for Greg a time when someone in Texas was yellow-lighted and stabbed in the neck.

"Blood was everywhere," Brenda said, obviously disturbed by the memory. They dumped the kid at the hospital. Brenda wasn't sure if he even lived.

Greg watched traffic fly by on the road as Brenda described the night Veto killed Javier Calzada, and how Veto shot him in the head. She could still hear the sound the pistol had made in the rain. She told Greg about when Denis described what it felt like to cut out Joaquin Diaz's throat. Greg listened to Brenda tell him about the evil she had encountered.

As Brenda continued telling Greg about her life with the MS, he became more worried about her safety. Her characters were real, and what she revealed about the MS was horrifying. When Brenda finished her monologue, Greg said he would see her soon, and she quickly hung up. Greg stayed in his car for a few moments, still absorbing what she had told him. He spent that Fourth of July distracted and concerned.

A foundation of trust was built between Brenda and Greg after that phone call. Greg was more convinced than ever that Brenda could take a step forward and away from her gang life. She now trusted him to guide her through the painfully long process.

In private with Greg, Brenda let her guard down and allowed herself to become more vulnerable. She trusted Greg as a friend and even as a father figure. He was her new anchor in this world of courts, judges, lawyers, and cops. While talking to the cops, she showed pride and confidence and took the opportunity to recount her days with the MS. She would speak with animation, sometimes adding to her story by displaying gang signs with her hands. Brenda was clearly proud of the MS. It was the toughest gang on the street.

She had seen enough to know the gang was serious and well entrenched in a number of money-making endeavors. Extortion, prostitution, and fencing stolen cars were the most common criminal activities across the nation. But human smuggling was on the rise, and by the time Brenda began speaking to the police about her gang, the Mara Salvatrucha had earned a reputation as a reliable group of assassins, prepared to kill targets in the United States or Mexico. Brenda had only been a member for a short time, but she knew enough to tell Greg about the roots of the gang, going back as far as the early 1980s. What she told him was enough to spur him on to many days' worth of research and investigation into the history of the Mara Salvatrucha.

Brenda told him that long before the gang grew to the strength and stature it enjoyed in 2002, it had struggled for survival on the streets of Los Angeles. In the early 1980s, the Mara Salvatrucha was a group of Salvadoran males looking for a social space where they could express their own culture and manner of speaking in a world where many Latino cultures were forced to live in close proximity. They initially called themselves the Mara Salvatrucha Stoners, wore long hair, listened to heavy metal, and wore Ozzy Osbourne T-shirts. These were little-known facts. Greg realized that the gang had come a long way from sitting around and head banging, moving on to extortion, fencing, stealing cars, and even killing people.

As the MS gained numbers, Brenda explained, its presence in Los Angeles pushed against other local cliques in the Pico Union area of Los Angeles. Sometimes there were street fights, Brenda had heard. Members used bats and chains against their neighborhood rivals. They would beat them into submission, stripping their rivals of their shirt as trophies. But when a Mara Salvatrucha founder named Black Sabbath died in the mid-1980s, the nature of the gang changed. This was a turning point for the gang: what could have been a peaceful group of friends turned into something much more sinister.

Black Sabbath's death might have been forgiven. But then another member, Rockie, was killed with a shotgun after a woman had lured him into an ambush. His attackers left him to bleed out on the street. The Mara Salvatrucha Stoners declared war. They asked some of the other men in the Salvadoran community for help. These men were war veterans who considered gangbanging to be child's play. But the murders of their countrymen represented a level of disrespect that was far beyond street fighting and stealing T-shirts for trophies. It was a knock against their pride in their country in a world where pride was one of the few things they had.

They were the ones who brought the machete to the streets. As Brenda explained to Greg, in Central America, the machete was a tool of daily life used to harvest fruit, cut weeds, or maintain paths that snaked through the jungle. It was common to see men playing dominos with their machetes leaning against one leg. Greg surmised that the men who had joined the MS Stoners to avenge the death of Black Sabbath and Rockie had learned to use machetes to kill their enemies in El Salvador. A little research confirmed that they didn't think twice about using their machetes to kill their enemies on the streets of Los Angeles.

The war veterans' violent tactics helped the Mara Salvatrucha capture turf in the area of Los Angeles near MacArthur Park and Pico Union, where many Salvadorans lived. Brenda told Greg how some of these communities were literally carved out with pure violence within miles of downtown Los Angeles and the palm tree–lined boulevards of Hollywood.

But well-established Latino gangs in the same area were not about to be pushed around by the Salvadorans. Greg talked to cops about the early days of the Mara Salvatrucha and learned that in the mid-1980s, a call went out among all the allied Latino gangs in Los Angeles to target and kill anyone in the Mara Salvatrucha. It was an order, Greg considered, that extended beyond gang members and deep into the Salvadoran community.

Gangs had to represent. Latino machismo and pride bred violence, and natural gang rivalries were born. The early members of the Mara Salvatrucha were more violent and willing to deal more death. Their low-technology brutality could not be matched. Turf controlled by rival Latino gangs eroded under the Mara Salvatrucha's widening footprint. They showed no mercy, and after too many lives were lost, an older, more established gang sought to bring about peace.

Greg already knew about the Mexican Mafia, a Mexican gang formed in California prisons in the 1950s. But he didn't realize that it was at the top of the Latino gang pyramid in southern California. For decades, the Mexican Mafia had carved out a niche in the California prison system by treating its members with love and respect and its enemies with gruesome and unabashed death. By the late 1980s, the gang wielded unparalleled authority on the streets because it completely controlled the prisons in southern California. Like many prison gangs around the country, the leadership of the Mexican Mafia influenced activity outside the prison walls; any Latino gangster locked up in southern California had to answer to the Mexican Mafia once in prison.

A quick call to a police contact in Los Angeles confirmed for Greg that most Latino gangs in southern California were aligned with the Mexican Mafia. It was a system that primarily prevented infighting among Latino gangs. It also allowed for smooth business transactions, mostly drug smuggling and wholesale drug dealing, between Mexican organized crime operating south of the border, and the Latino street gangs that operated in southern California.

From Veto, Brenda had heard that the men who ran the Mexican

Mafia in the late 1980s decided the rivalry between the Latino gangs and the Mara Salvatrucha was bad for business. They sought to force a truce by offering the Mara Salvatrucha membership within the Mexican Mafia's street gang network. It would afford members of the MS more protection in prison and on the streets and create space for a truce with other Latino gangs. But the Mara Salvatrucha had to provide a regular tribute of cash or some sort of other valuable commodity to maintain membership. It was the same deal the Mexican Mafia offered every street gang that operated under its fiefdom. The leaders of the Mara Salvatrucha were not willing to pay the price.

The Mexican Mafia knew it was better off with the MS as an ally, so the leaders made another offer. It was an offer focused on killing, something the members of the Mara Salvatrucha did better than most other gangs in the city. The MS could join the Mexican Mafia if they were willing to share their best hit men when the Mexican Mafia needed someone killed on the streets.

Wrapping up her story, Brenda revealed that when the Mara Salvatrucha leaders agreed, the MS became a *sureño* gang, part of the southern California alliance. It became La Mara Salvatrucha Trece, or MS-13. The number 13 was the position of the letter *m* in the alphabet, and was added to show respect for the Mexican Mafia, often referred to as simply The M, or *La Eme* in Spanish. That makes sense, Greg thought. He had always wondered where the number 13 had come from.

For a short while, the truce between the Mara Salvatrucha and the other Latino street gangs held, but old rivalries flared up, especially with a gang called the 18th Street. The bloodshed never reached previous levels, so the Mexican Mafia was content to let the rivalry continue with little oversight. Brenda said that so many MS members had been killed by 18th Street members, who in turn died at the hands of vengeful MS members, that a cycle of violence had become ingrained within the Mara Salvatrucha. Its violent posture toward any rival gang members in black, white, or Asian gangs extended to any rival MS members who were crossed. *Chavalas,* or members of rival gangs, were always ridiculed, beaten up if possible, or killed if necessary.

Unilateral aggression created cycles of hate that kept gangbanging violence alive as new generations of recruits learned to hate any rival, providing members with a well-founded and socially acceptable reason for what most would see as senseless violence.

As a *sureño* street gang, the MS-13 could rely on a solid foundation of authority and remain relatively safe within Los Angeles. From that foundation point the gang spread its influence throughout the United States, which is why Brenda first encountered the Mara Salvatrucha in Texas. By the time she met Greg, the Mara Salvatrucha counted over ten thousand members across the United States, with a presence in over forty states. Beyond the cities, the MS penetrated deep into rural towns and those one-blinking-light communities where local cops rarely patrolled in pairs and none spoke Spanish. The gang was as fluid as the labor market that attracted Latino immigrants. Wherever there was a Latino community, the MS burrowed in and thrived.

"One day," Brenda often said, "the Mara Salvatrucha will take over the United States."

CHAPTER 21

Full of confidence, Brenda was happy about being the center of such attention. It was a position that thoroughly satisfied her extroverted nature. And her vast knowledge of the gang never ceased to amaze Greg or anyone listening to her. She had told Ignacio he was the target of an MS plot to kill two policemen in Virginia. The other targeted cop had a physical description that matched Rick Rodriguez. That cop was in the most danger. And Brenda saved his life.

When Rodriguez had helped his colleagues figure out what Denis was saying to Brenda soon after their arrest, he already knew MS members planned on killing two cops, but he didn't know which ones. If Rodriguez had seen Denis that day when he listened to the tapes, Denis might have recognized him. Denis knew the MS wanted Ignacio dead, but he didn't know the other cop's name, only a physical description. Word had spread out among the MS that Ignacio and another cop, a bald guy who looked like a gringo but spoke Spanish, needed to die. That physical description could only fit one man: Detective Rick Rodriguez.

Like Detective Ignacio, Rodriguez had worked gang-related crimes for years. He was the first detective in Arlington County to focus on gangs, and for many years he was the only detective in the county's gang unit. Rodriguez made gangs and gang members, especially the Mara Salvatrucha, a priority.

Rodriguez was a gang expert. In the summer of 2002, his fellow officers considered Rodriguez a walking dictionary of gang information. But there was a time when he didn't know so much.

In the early 1990s, Rodriguez was a young police officer working a normal beat in northern Virginia. Because he was a native Spanish speaker, he gravitated toward the Latinos who lived in the immigrant communities in Arlington County near Columbia Heights West. He sometimes worked in Latino communities in neighboring Fairfax County—the heart of the Salvadoran population in northern Virginia.

Rodriguez dealt with the crimes that festered in these communities. There was little gang activity when he first started, not nearly enough to warrant any special attention to street gangs over any other type of crime, such as spousal abuse, robbery, or traffic violations. But by the early 1990s, reunified Salvadoran families became common in Culmore. The ostracized children reached out to anyone who accepted them, showed them love, and allowed them to love in return.

Rodriguez knew that in El Salvador, the word *mara* didn't always have a gang connotation. It meant a bunch of friends. In the United States, the Salvadoran kids looked for other young people in their same situation. Misery loved company. Cliques were formed. These groups were not violent street gangs. They were a crew of friends. They were *maras* in the original sense of the word. The informal cliques were a source of love and a place to be accepted, not judged. Invariably, however, some of these groups grew violent.

Street gangs in immigrant populations were, of course, nothing new in the United States. Dating back to the Irish street gangs in New York's Five Points area, gangs have formed where there has been a need for acceptance and a large enough group of like-minded people. The Culmore area of Fairfax County was no exception. And with such a large Latino immigrant community, it was a place where groups of friends could easily evolve into street gangs where the combination of teenage recklessness and rebellious desires clashed with the laws of the land.

Rodriguez remembered the old days, when it started with simple tagging. The *maras* in Culmore evolved into two memorable groups, the Mara Queens and the Mara Locos Intocables, or "untouchable crazies." Members of these groups spray-painted clumsy symbols of their gang, usually just the first letters of their gang's name, in random public spaces. They vandalized public walls, lampposts, and the large green Dumpsters near where they lived, went to school, or worked. Tagging was normal activity for these kids, nothing more sinister than meeting up at the park to drink beer or hang out on a street corner just to stay out of the house and away from their parents, the primary source of frustration in their new lives in the United States.

At times there were fights. Rodriguez could understand the motives of the early *maras*. No one liked to constantly look over his shoulder or worry about safety when hanging out near home or school. There was a sense of turf and protecting that turf, but this sense of needing protection had little to do with controlling an area used for criminal enterprise, as it did in Los Angeles. The formation of Virginia's street gangs was more about making sure everyone was safe in a part of town known to be dangerous.

Culmore was a focal point for crime. Poverty and unemployment fed armed robberies and sometimes murder. It was necessary for clique members to look out for one another. Knives added a level of enforcement, but they were rarely used. To combat rising crime levels, the police departments from Fairfax, Arlington, and Alexandria initiated community-policing programs and placed patrol officers on walking beats in direct contact with the communities that needed the most attention. Members of the immigrant communities slowly grew to trust the cops they always saw walking around, talking with shop owners, garage mechanics, people at the bus stop, just about anyone. It was an added level of protection that, for a short time, prevented any serious street gang activity from taking root in Fairfax County.

Then Snoopy arrived. Rodriguez had chuckled when he'd heard the street name. He quickly learned it was no laughing matter.

Snoopy was an old-school MS-13 member from Los Angeles. He was the first of a wave of MS members who targeted the second-largest Salvadoran community in the United States.

The Salvadorans and other Latinos who immigrated to northern Virginia were a gold mine of opportunity for MS-13 members who dealt with a level of law enforcement in California they wanted to avoid. Virginia police in the early 1990s had little idea what the MS-13 was all about. When Snoopy arrived, he was very open about being a Mara Salvatrucha. He was proud and handed out business cards printed with his phone number and street name, and some of the most com-

mon symbols used by the MS in Los Angeles, like MSX3, another way
to spell out MS-13, replacing the one with a Roman numeral. A gangster who handed out business cards had mystified Rodriguez and his
colleagues. This simply was not normal.

The pioneering gangster quickly set out recruiting new MS members. He offered the backing of a much larger, national-level gang.
Compared to the Mara Queens or the Mara Locos Intocables, the
Mara Salvatrucha was a serious and organized street gang. Snoopy's
arrival in 1993 signified the beginning of a higher level of gangbanging
in the Culmore area. The established *maras* in the area, however, were
not about to let the MS just come in and disrespect them.

Snoopy had his work cut out for him. For many months, his fledg-
ling MS group was a punching bag for the other, better-established
gangs in the area. But their numbers quickly grew. Dozens of MS
members were let out of California prisons in 1995 and 1996. Many
members who were not deported decided to leave Los Angeles, where
they were marked and well known by the cops. Many left for Texas
and Nashville, but a significant number decided to travel to Virginia.
Some MS cliques from LA took root in Virginia. The Normandie Locos, Brenda's clique, was among them. The Centrales Locos was another prominent MS clique that had originated in Los Angeles.

The native *maras* learned quickly that Snoopy brought from Los
Angeles a new level of competition. Rodriguez realized that this was a
street gang culture that thrived on violence, the strict enforcement of
turf, and the use of fear to control victims and earn money from a
number of illegal business practices. Snoopy recruited Virginia's new
MS members into an organization that was willing to kill with knives
and machetes to make a point. Discipline within the gang was strict.
New recruits quickly learned that the MS was the real deal from LA. If
you broke the rules as an MS member, they didn't kick you out. You
were severely beaten, maimed, stabbed, or killed.

Not surprisingly, Virginia's street gangs became a serious problem
by 1996, only three years after Snoopy first arrived in Fairfax County.
It was a banner year. President Clinton pointed to Fairfax County as a
model for how other counties in the country should work to absorb
divergent cultures. But a deeper look revealed colorful gang graffiti spray-
painted on walls, buildings, lampposts, trash cans, and just about any-
place gang members could get their message out loud and clear.

What started in the early 1990s as tagging became spray-painted warnings from one gang to another. The message was simple: This is our turf. Stay out or face the consequences. The MS had established enemies from LA, and it knew how to deal with *chavalas*.

Virginia's other *maras* didn't adopt this type of proactive aggression and violence until the MS arrived. But once the violence started, it didn't stop. One act of disrespect had to be answered by a show of strength. That show of strength was another act of disrespect. This cycle of violence continued until one gang became dominant. Supremacy was always the goal of the MS in Virginia. They were against everyone. And it didn't take them long to establish control. As the cops in the region struggled to react, the MS cut through the local gangs, forcing them to bend to their will and be absorbed or disband.

The Mara Salvatrucha's growing presence in northern Virginia caused a spike in violence during the summer months of 1996. The worst case occurred when a sixteen-year-old was stabbed in front of a middle school in Alexandria, just down the road from Culmore. Months later, in the Columbia Heights West section of Arlington, a Molotov cocktail was thrown into one family's living room.

Assigned as one of the community cops at the time, Rick Rodriguez responded to the call. He was sure it was gang-related, but the parents, who had a mattress propped against their living room window to prevent further damage to their apartment, denied their child was involved in a gang.

Rodriguez left the apartment and drove to a nearby corner popular with young MS members and found the kid he was looking for. Their child, while at home, acted appropriately and wore clothes that suggested good study habits and a well-mannered lifestyle. Once he was out on the street, gangland clothes came out of the backpack and the attitude changed. Mom and Dad never knew.

Rodriguez grabbed the kid, took him back to his parents' apartment dressed in his street gang clothes. Around cops the bad attitude was hard to mask. With the clothes and bad attitude still in place, Rodriguez revealed the boy's other life to his bewildered parents. Lifting up the kid's shirtsleeves, Rodriguez showed the parents their child's gang tattoos.

To Rodriguez, these tattoos were a brand and a constant reminder of the permanency of the MS influence on any kid's life. When Rodriguez explained all this to the unsuspecting parents, they were speechless. Rodriguez thought the kid was on the fringe of the MS. He wasn't yet a hard-core member. "The parents are the last ones to know," the kid's mom lamented before Rodriguez left the apartment.

For many immigrant families, the gap between their lower-class existence and the middle class always seemed to grow wider, making it impossible for them to pull themselves up and out of the hole they had tried to escape back home in Central America. They were constantly chasing an American dream that could be seen everywhere but was never obtainable at home. The only way to keep the family afloat was to work constantly. Keeping up with the Perezes—the Latino version of the Joneses—was never supposed to be this hard.

Three years after Rodriguez and others inaugurated their community policing program, the Mara Salvatrucha firmly established itself in the Culmore neighborhood of Fairfax County. Columbia Heights West and the Arlandria section of Alexandria were also MS-13 hot spots. It was a growing problem, one the local police had still not been able to completely control. Prevention programs, desperately needed to keep kids from joining gangs, were meager in the face of such need.

Rodriguez remembered that MS-style violence finally splashed across local media in the summer of 2000, when a fourteen-year-old was arrested for the stabbing death of a twenty-two-year-old man in the Falls Church section of Fairfax County. José Rodriguez, along with two other minors, pushed, kicked, and stabbed their victim outside the Culmore Shopping Center on Leesburg Pike. José had been jumped in when he was thirteen, having fallen under the influence of his older sister's boyfriend, an MS member who, like Veto in Texas, had MS tattooed across his forehead and numerous other tattoos across his neck, arms, and upper chest. José received fourteen staples in his head after his jumping-in ceremony. He had been beaten with a crowbar.

Before killing his victim, José met fifty other MS members in the woods behind a restaurant where he requested judgment and punishment for excessive drug use. It was rare for an MS member to request to be judged by his fellow gang members. Normally, MS members tried to avoid it. But José was adamant and he was found guilty. After the beating, he set out to find a victim to prove his loyalty to the gang and bolster his position within the group. José was still in elementary school when he was arrested.

At the time of José's arrest, Rodriguez had become familiar with twenty to thirty gangs in the northern Virginia area through police training. All except the Mara Salvatrucha had fewer than a hundred members. The Mara Salvatrucha boasted at least six hundred members in Fairfax County alone.

José Rodriguez was found guilty of second-degree murder. He was the youngest person in Fairfax County to be tried as an adult, and even after receiving twenty-two years for secondary murder, the young gangster didn't recant his loyalty to the MS. His sister started hanging around the MS when she was ten. His parents were never home. The MS had become his family, and even in prison, he was not about to let it go.

In August 2001, the brutal rape and murder of Diana Garcia, a young mother and not a member of the MS, hit the papers. Not a month later, the murder of Joaquin Diaz shocked Rodriguez and his colleagues, as well as federal authorities. They realized that there was a growing gang problem across northern Virginia. But the Mara Salvatrucha was a nebulous, fluid group, one that blended in perfectly with the Latino immigrant communities and, like these communities, was always flying under the radar of state and federal law enforcement.

Like the Latinos around them, members of the MS followed the labor market. They took jobs hanging dry wall, cleaning carpets, nailing down shingles, or building wood frame houses. Their daily interaction with other Spanish-speaking immigrants during lunch or after work was always laced with the allure of the money a criminal life could bring. The more MS gang members, the greater its power and presence. Power meant dominance. Once its rule was established in any Latino community, the MS could run a number of criminal rackets and enforce its position with the threat of violence. Drive-by shootings, stabbings, armed robberies, and other violent crimes were on the rise. More and more, hardworking mothers and fathers in the Latino communities found their children lost to a fast-moving world of crime, drugs, money, and sometimes death.

When Denis Rivera killed Joaquin Diaz, the MS was thoroughly entrenched across the mid-Atlantic region between Maryland, Washington, D.C., and Virginia. Nearly eight years had passed since Snoopy arrived, and the Mara Salvatrucha had control over most of the Latino communities across three states. The toughest hurdle for Rodriguez and others trying to combat the MS was the gang's ability to hide inside immigrant communities.

Immigrants, documented and undocumented alike, were afraid to talk to the cops. They were afraid of what the MS would do if word got out that they had shared information with the police. Worse than gang retribution, however, was deportation. Most members of the Latino communities where the MS thrived just wanted to work hard, send money home, and live a quiet, simple life. They wanted nothing to do with the MS or with the cops.

But the MS wanted something from them, something more than silence. The MS wanted their kids, specifically, their American-born sons. Many of these kids saw the MS as something cool, a source of pride in their Latino heritage, and a way to get ahead in life. The parents, ever fearful of deportation, could do little to prevent their children from entering a life of crime. They were forced into silence and remained at a distance from the local police. Immigrant parents could not share information that men like Rodriguez needed to rid Latino immigrant communities of predatory gang members.

Rodriguez worked hard to win the community's trust, reassuring people that he couldn't deport them. Only if they were arrested could federal agents put them in detention and have them deported. All he asked for was some information and a little trust. He needed them to help him make their communities safer and protect their kids. Rodriguez, and other local cops who spoke Spanish, could make some headway in these communities, but their numbers were limited. Most cops didn't speak Spanish.

Despite the surging MS presence in his jurisdiction and the general sense of trepidation among Latinos in the communities where the MS thrived, Rodriguez did manage to make some impact. It was enough to earn him a *luz verde*.

CHAPTER 22

I t was a hot day in mid-July, but Rick Rodriguez was determined to enjoy his son's baseball game despite the heat. It was the weekend, and Rodriguez was off duty, a rare break when he could enjoy himself and not worry about his law enforcement duties. He was in a part of Maryland where his police beeper didn't pick up a signal. I don't mind at all, he thought with a smile. He didn't know yet that he was a marked man. A short drive away, in Arlington County, Detective Mike Porter had learned from Brenda's description that Rodriguez was probably the other cop who was given a *luz verde* by local MS leaders. Porter couldn't get in touch with Rodriguez.

The marked detective was driving home after the game when his beeper began vibrating as page after page registered. He had at least a dozen calls from Porter, who was frantically trying to get hold of him before some MS member put a bullet in his head. Rodriguez called Porter immediately, curious to know what all the frantic paging was about. Porter quickly told him that he had a credible informant who knew something about the MS wanting to kill cops. The informant had accurately described Rodriguez.

"Well, Porter, I don't know what to tell you, but how do we know she doesn't know me?" Rodriguez asked. "I know we're not supposed to ask for names, but if you want me to know, you'll tell me. So in light of all this, can you tell me who this person is?" Rodriguez asked with some caution. He knew he was pushing professional boundaries by asking for the name of Porter's informant, but it was his life at stake here.

"Yeah, no problem. Her name is Brenda Paz," Porter replied.

Brenda Paz, Brenda Paz, Rodriguez swiftly mouthed, testing the name against his memory, but it didn't register. "The name doesn't do anything for me," Rodriguez responded. He had always suspected that he was a marked man, but it had been weeks since he had deciphered Brenda and Denis's conversation, and he had never heard Brenda's name. He would have to get to the bottom of this information and determine if Porter's informant was truly credible.

"Well, she knows you well," Porter said, explaining to Rodriguez that he needed to make it a priority to see her.

"Can I come by?" Rodriguez asked, looking at his watch while driving, guessing it would take him about an hour from Maryland to get there.

"No problem," Porter said.

Rodriguez wanted to be sure Brenda wasn't playing any games. "Okay, I'm headed your way now. Do not tell her I'm coming." Rodriguez emphasized that last part. If this informant knew who he was, he wanted to judge her reaction to him when he stepped through the door unannounced.

When he finally did walk through the door in the classroom at the juvenile detention center, Brenda was seated next to Porter and Greg. He looked at Brenda and didn't recognize her. So he turned to Porter, waiting to be introduced.

"Brenda, do you know who this is?" Porter prodded.

"No. Should I?" Brenda asked, not catching on.

"Well, you don't know him?"

"No."

"I don't know her either," Rodriguez added.

"This is Detective Rodriguez. He speaks Spanish," Porter said, looking for some sort of reaction from Brenda.

"Oh my God! You! I, I'm trying to save your life!" Brenda shouted, with a sudden burst of energy and recognition. Rodriguez was skeptical. She could have been faking the outburst.

Considerably more composed, Rodriguez said, "I appreciate it, Brenda, I really do appreciate it."

Rodriguez had his doubts. He was aware that Porter's informant could be setting him up in some way for a hit, rather than trying to save his life.

"Tell me about this," Rodriguez began as he sat down in front of Brenda, seeking to dig further into the matter.

"No, I'm trying to . . . I'm trying to save your life. They really want to kill you," Brenda said, still excited.

"Just me?"

"No, there's another guy named Ignacio."

"Oh, I see, and where does this information come from?" Rodriguez asked, curious to know how Brenda knew he and Ignacio were given a *luz verde*.

"You don't believe me?" Brenda asked, beginning to see that Rodriguez was going to be hard to convince.

"I didn't say, 'I don't believe you.' I'm asking you questions because I don't know who you are, and you apparently know me," Rodriguez explained. "If you've never seen me, how do you know what I look like, what I drive, where I work?"

"The meetings," Brenda said with a confident tone. She knew what she was talking about. "At *la misa*, they discussed you. They discussed you going after them, you locking up the leaders. How you're not giving them respect. You're always in their business. You know too much about them and they don't like it," Brenda explained. "And the same thing for that other cop in Alexandria. They say you two work together."

"Well, we do work together because we are police officers and we share information," Rodriguez responded, still cautious. "And that's a reason to kill a cop?" Rodriguez asked, still probing Brenda.

"Do you want me to prove it?" Brenda was obviously bothered that Rodriguez didn't believe her. "I can make a phone call right now," Brenda offered.

"You can make a phone call right now and do what," Rodriguez challenged.

Brenda had found a way to win Rodriguez's confidence. "I can get them to talk about it," she declared.

"Really? Well, as long as Detective Porter doesn't mind me using one of their phones, I don't mind sitting in. And I can listen to the conversation because I speak Spanish," Rodriguez said.

Porter arranged for Brenda to make some phone calls while Rodriguez listened, but it didn't work. None of the MS homies that Brenda called were willing to talk about killing a cop. They were cautious and suspicious, with reason. Brenda had been off the streets for just over a month. Suddenly she called asking about their plans to kill cops. It made Rodriguez nervous. Even though she pushed the gangsters on the other end of the line to the point where Rodriguez thought that she might reveal her true motives, Brenda still wasn't satisfied with her performance. She grew upset, on the verge of tears. Brenda desperately wanted Rodriguez to believe her.

"Calm down, Brenda," Rodriguez told her, trying to get her to relax after she hung up. "Just calm down. I'm the one you're talking about here. And I'm okay. I appreciate what you're doing. I'm not sure why you're doing it, but I appreciate it," Rodriguez said. Brenda's face remained twisted in a scowl. She was still upset, but had composed herself somewhat. The tears were gone. "The fact that they're not talking to you is okay. I believe that you're telling the truth," Rodriguez offered.

"When I set my mind on something, I want it done," Brenda responded in a huff. "There is no waiting," she said, still scowling.

After his discussion with Brenda, Rodriguez was convinced she was right about at least one piece of information: he was a target. But he still had his doubts. Rodriguez continued to ponder his situation as he left the interview room and headed for his office in Arlington. Against his better judgment, he couldn't help but like the girl. He thought about what Porter had told him before he left, about Brenda's knowledge and her group of friends, but he just couldn't imagine how she ended up running with the real bad boys of the MS.

"On one hand," Rodriguez said to a colleague at the office after spending some time thinking about the young MS informant, "Brenda Paz could probably sell an Eskimo a block of ice. And on the other hand she could be as ruthless as anybody else. She has this smile. I mean, her nickname is Smiley. She has this cute little smile, and she has a great personality," Rodriguez continued, shaking his head as if trying to clarify Brenda's confusing dual personality. "What in the world would possess her to get into this kind of crap? I mean, she's got personality, she's got spunk, people seem to just gravitate toward her— and yet she has this other side of her that frightens people."

Rodriguez was worried that Brenda's personality was so contagious that she could even convince a law enforcement person that she was doing the right thing when in truth she was setting him up for the kill.

She's that good at it, and she knows it, Rodriguez thought to himself. Brenda had earned respect to the point where she had the tattoos. And according to all accounts, the people she ran with were not wannabes or friends of members. They were hard-core.

Ten percent of MS members were the guys who give their life and soul to the gang, spending every day of their lives in gang affairs. Veto and Denis were part of this group. About half of the homies were jumped in, calling themselves MS, but spending time with the gang mostly on weekends, holding regular jobs during the week. The rest, Rodriguez often told the rookies, were simply posers.

After Rodriguez met Brenda and began spending time with her, he continued to feel that something was not right. He had to get to the bottom of why she was helping them.

"Let me ask you this, Brenda," Rodriguez said to her at a meeting at the end of July. "Why on earth are you helping us? What is your motive? What's your angle?"

Rodriguez couldn't shake the feeling that she was setting them up. Maybe she gave the cops the little things that meant nothing to the gang so they entered a comfort zone with her. Rodriguez considered that Brenda was likely well versed in the various methods of rocking the cradle, gaining confidence before the strike, and he knew cops were not immune.

During the first few weeks after Brenda decided to become an informant, she remained in constant contact with Mike Porter and Greg Hunter. By the end of July, Rick Rodriguez was also a regular presence at her interviews with other police. Whenever she called, one of them would show up. Who knew if she wouldn't call one day to lure them into a trap?

Responding to Rodriguez's question, Brenda was surprisingly frank with him. It was an important moment when Rodriguez finally realized that Brenda was genuine about wanting to help the police. He had begun to realize the truth. She was a teenage girl simply trying to get out of trouble.

"Listen, I'm tired of this life. I'm tired of running. I'm tired of watching people get hurt. I'm just tired of it all," she said with a sincerity Rodriguez found hard not to believe.

"So how is working with us going to help you?" Rodriguez countered.

"There are only two ways I can get out," Brenda replied. "One, I can help you guys dismantle MS. With the information I have, you can be rid of them quickly. You will be locking every one of them up," Brenda said with confidence. "We eradicate them all, they're all gone, and I've got nothing to go to. I have to start brand-new."

Rodriguez waited for her to offer up option number two. Brenda slowly looked up and said with a straight face: "Or they kill me."

CHAPTER 23

Addicted to the freedom she'd experienced while living on the streets, Brenda got antsy in her new role as informant. For nearly two months she had spent most of her time locked up with no hope for release or escape. Greg took her out to eat on occasion, and there were always the meetings with Porter, Ignacio, her defense lawyer Jason Rucker, Greg, and Rodriguez, but she was ready to get out of detention.

Her wish was granted. The social workers at the Landmark Juvenile Detention Facility could no longer house Brenda. She was a minor who had committed no crime in Arlington: she had to go. But Greg knew she couldn't return to the streets. She had already provided so much information, more than she originally intended, including the contents of five letters from Denis and one letter from Veto she had received during the month of June. It was simply not an option to put her back on the streets.

Greg scrambled, and with Porter's help, he managed to find a bed for her at the end of July in the Less Secure Facility in Fairfax County. As the name implied, the facility had little more security than a regular college dorm building. After they checked her into the facility, Greg arranged another meeting with Porter, Rodriguez, and one other detective. They had very specific questions about MS activity in Fairfax, but Brenda didn't have all the answers.

After saying good night to the cops and Greg, Brenda waited until lights-out, and with two girls she had met that day, she snuck out the back door. It was easy. The two attendants on duty that night were making out on a couch in the lobby. All Brenda needed to do was walk out quietly and not let the door slam shut.

Free of the Less Secure Facility, Brenda and her friends waited at a nearby bus stop for the George Mason bus to take them to the Vienna metro stop, the last stop on D.C.'s orange line. At the metro station, Brenda and the girls hopped the turnstiles and boarded the train for East Falls Church, the stop closest to Bailey's Crossroads in Fairfax County, where Brenda knew there was always an MS party. An older member of her clique held a party at the same house every weekend. Brenda didn't think that this weekend would be any different.

On her first night of freedom, Brenda took her two friends to a destroyer party, a celebration of the gang life. MS members would drink Coronas, smoke pot, and share stories, and those who had earned rank or respect would receive tattoos. They were wild parties that lasted all night.

When they arrived, Brenda fell right back into the gang life. She introduced her friends around and began partying. She had been away for close to two months, but she didn't have to make up any excuses. Most of the people there didn't question her absence. Those who did received a well-constructed lie. Since leaving Texas, Brenda had grown accustomed to lying and knew how to leverage her special position as a member of the venerable Normandie Locos clique and as Denis Rivera's girlfriend.

Brenda got high, had a few drinks, and introduced her friends to the upside of gang life. They were in awe of what they saw. The excessive partying was easily absorbed, but when one MS leader got into a shouting match with another, the party ended in a fight. One pulled a knife and stabbed the other. For Brenda it wasn't a big deal. She'd seen her fair share of knife fights and was comfortable behind the gangster façade she wore. But the other two girls were scared. They wanted to leave immediately.

Brenda arranged a ride with a homie who was headed into D.C. It was early in the morning. Making up some excuse, Brenda got the driver to drop her and the girls off at the National Mall, where they walked around the Reflecting Pool before catching the metro to Columbia Heights. Brenda picked the location because she thought it was a place where people from Colombia lived. She thought she would feel more comfortable surrounded by Latinos before she tried to call Greg again and get a ride back to the Less Secure Facility.

During the night Brenda had tried to call Greg with the disposable cell phone he had given her, but wasn't able to reach him. Greg's cell phone was on the charger and not set to ring.

The next morning Detective Porter received a call from the Less Secure Facility. Brenda and two other girls were missing. Porter called Greg, who was at home with houseguests.

It was an emergency. Porter and Greg knew if Brenda was back on the streets, she could be in serious trouble with her gang. She had been in custody for nearly two months, long enough, they thought, for her homies to note her absence. Best-case scenario, Brenda would never come back. Worst-case scenario, she was dead.

Before Greg decided what to do, he received a call from Brenda. She was at the Columbia Heights metro stop in Washington, D.C. He knew he had to go get her, but in the back of his mind, Greg wasn't sure if it was a setup or not. He thought that Brenda probably wouldn't try to harm him, but he didn't trust the men she ran with. He decided to grab his Sig Sauer P228 pistol before heading into D.C. to pick her up. But there was no threat. He found her standing in a slice of shade by a pharmacy on Fourteenth Street NW with two white girls.

Greg pulled up to the curb and got out. Brenda explained she had met the two girls at Less Secure. One girl didn't want to go anywhere with Greg. He couldn't force her to do anything, so he gave her $20 and told her to go home. The other girl wanted to go to jail, or anywhere safe. She was observably nervous. She got in the backseat and Brenda happily hopped in front. Greg thought it would be a good idea to get them something to eat.

"Where do you want to eat?" Greg asked Brenda.

"I dunno, maybe Italian?" she replied.

"How about the Olive Garden?" the other girl chimed in.

"I've never been to the Olive Garden, but I've seen those commercials," Brenda admitted, clearly interested in what she thought was a meal fit for kings.

When Greg, Brenda, and her runaway friend were seated at the Olive Garden in Tyson's Corner, back in Fairfax County, it was immediately apparent to Greg that Brenda did not know how to act in a restaurant. Brenda was embarrassed by her table manners. Greg immediately set out to teach her basic table skills—no elbows on the table, napkin in your lap, eat with your mouth closed. Greg showed her how to use a fork and twist the pasta noodles on a spoon before taking a civilized bite without slurping. Greg restrained himself the whole meal. Brenda had made a stupid decision when she left the Less Secure Facility. She had endangered both their lives. But he held back. He didn't want to get started on her with the other girl present.

Once they were back at Less Secure, Greg dropped off the runaway girl. He was burning to ask Brenda why she had escaped, but before he could begin on Brenda, they ran into Detective Porter.

"They're refusing to take her," Porter said. Great, Greg thought. What a fucking mess. The only place in Virginia that would take Brenda was now out of the question. He thought a lot of Brenda, even respected her. But she could be a real pain in the ass, he thought, as he absorbed the consequences of Porter's news.

Brenda had burned the only place they could legally keep her. There was nowhere else Greg could place Brenda, and he still hadn't managed to remove the capital murder warrant out for her in Texas. Greg knew that if they couldn't get Brenda into a safe place that night, she would most likely be extradited to Texas the next day and face a very serious charge in a state that had a long history of capital punishment.

CHAPTER 24

t was late on a Sunday. Greg was tired, and the last thing he wanted to deal with was finding Brenda a safe place to stay. He and Porter were at a loss for where to put her. They stood just inside the doors of the reception area of the Less Secure Facility with Brenda seated on the couch and talked over their options, trying to force out a solution. An idea finally formed after long minutes of back and forth. They would have Brenda charged with a crime that Porter and Greg agreed would later be dropped.

Denis Rivera had once tried to kill the father of a rival gang member, but failed when the gun misfired. Brenda had knowledge of the event. It had happened earlier that summer. Brenda was supposed to make the kill. She was in new MS turf, and despite her street credentials, she had to prove her loyalty to her new homies in Virginia through an act of violence. When the moment arrived, Brenda didn't have it in her to kill the man, so Denis took the gun, aimed, and pulled the trigger. The gun didn't fire. Denis pulled the trigger a second time. Nothing. He grabbed the barrel with one finger wrapped around the trigger guard and hit his victim repeatedly in the face with the pistol grip.

Denis had been charged with the assault, called a malicious wounding in Virginia, and Porter agreed they could charge and hold Brenda as an accessory after the fact.

It was legal fiction. Greg was certain that if Porter asked the judge to drop the charge, there would be no questions asked. It was a rare leap of faith between an arresting officer and a defense attorney, but it paid off. Porter arrested Brenda so he could legally place her in the Fairfax Juvenile Detention Facility. It was a building connected to the Less Secure Facility and considerably safer. Her new home was a place where Greg knew Brenda could remain safe until he figured out their next move.

With that troubling snag out of the way and Brenda safely checked into the detention facility, Greg picked up where he had left off. He needed to know why Brenda had snuck out.

"I went to find answers," Brenda replied, showing Greg bits and pieces of notes she had taken on separate scraps of paper. She listed the nicknames and cell phone numbers of a number of MS members and additional information Porter and other cops wanted to know.

Brenda had risked her life just to get a few answers to questions asked the day before. Greg thought that it was a stupid risk to take, but Brenda was determined to get the information. For Greg it was a sign Brenda had become more sincere about helping, but he was worried about her judgment. She obviously thought she was smart enough to get away with fooling her MS homies. Greg couldn't help but remind himself that for all her street-smart experience, Brenda was still only sixteen years old. Her importance as an informant and subsequent treatment often masked the very real fact that Brenda was still a teenage girl with all the weaknesses and vulnerabilities associated with growing through adolescence into adulthood.

After their quick chat, Greg turned Brenda over to the facility staff and headed home. He had a choice to make. In Arlington County, Greg was her guardian ad litem, but in neighboring Fairfax County, he was her defense counsel. A guardian ad litem had been assigned to her case in Fairfax, but he only did what he had to do, nothing more. The onus of responsibility for Brenda's well-being was on Greg. He had initially been uncomfortable with performing the duties of both guardian and lawyer in Arlington, and still felt a little uncomfortable with his dual role between the two counties.

It had been a long, frustrating weekend, and keeping Brenda in a secure location and out of trouble had turned out to be a real job, not just a few hours of paperwork, as he had initially thought. Greg wondered if he should remove himself entirely from Brenda's defense in Fairfax.

He could dump her case onto the Fairfax juvenile justice system and walk away, or he could stick with her. For the moment, Brenda was safely ensconced in the local Juvenile detention facility. She had an established relationship with local gang unit detectives as a reliable informant, and Greg had kept careful notes. He could easily debrief any defense counsel in Fairfax who picked up her case.

Greg continued to think about his options the next morning as he sat in the front hall at the Fairfax juvenile court, waiting to apprise the judge of Brenda's situation. He watched the faces of the Fairfax County lawyers as they passed him by. They were frustrated or bored, tired or uninterested, he observed, yet these were the men and women called upon to help children out of a tight spot. Greg could see clearly how the Fairfax County judicial system was struggling under the weight of a high caseload and a limited budget. It was depressing.

Enthusiasm and compassion were completely absent. In their place was a begrudging sense of duty, laced with some greed. Every day, the judge assigned one guardian ad litem and one defense counsel to all the cases that came through the juvenile court docket. That number swung wildly from half a dozen to well over triple that number. Two lawyers splitting an entire day's caseload could make good money, but the attention they gave each individual, each child, was almost always lacking. The strained administration of a tired old court often got in the way of delivering blind justice.

Greg thought that most of the men and women who served the kids who came through that court system were lawyers who had failed in every other area of the legal profession, from divorce law to real estate and taxes. In those halls walked men and women who functioned best in a poorly run judicial system. This was welfare for bad lawyers, Greg realized as he reached a decision. There were a few decent lawyers in the bunch, but Brenda's chances of landing one of them was slim to none.

That morning, as Greg sat on the bench waiting his turn, he ultimately decided to stick with Brenda. He had grown to like Detective Porter, and Brenda had become more than a client. She was almost like family. His first impression of Brenda as a street-savvy runaway punk had given way to a feeling of friendship. He simply couldn't leave Brenda to the mismanagement of a hack lawyer.

At his hearing that morning, Greg felt renewed enthusiasm for debriefing the court on what had transpired with her case thus far. Greg had worked Brenda's case for just under seven weeks and had earned only $117. But he didn't care about the money. Keeping Brenda safe was his priority.

At the end of the hearing, the judge assigned Greg to continue on as Brenda's defense counsel in Fairfax County. She also gave him an order that allowed him to check Brenda out of the Fairfax Juvenile Detention Facility without the presence of a Fairfax County police officer. It was a favor from a judge who realized that Brenda was in good hands. Greg planned to make every effort to break out Brenda for a meal or some mall time and talk to her about finishing high school and college, books she was reading, and other interests for a regular teenage kid.

After that day's hearing, Greg closed out the first seven-week phase of the Brenda Paz case. It had been an exciting and challenging period, but he was just getting started. The following weeks would force him to the extremes of what he was willing to do to keep his young friend and Mike Porter's most charismatic informant alive.

CHAPTER 25

The more Brenda talked, the more her notoriety grew. There were too many loose ends. Too many people were talking about Brenda. Greg's most immediate problem was not the courtroom rumor mill. It was the legal battle to keep Brenda safely out of Texas. She was a minor who had more legal reason to be set free than incarcerated. Freedom was an ultimate goal, but it was not what Brenda needed while she was talking to cops about the MS.

Greg had already considered a list of alternatives. Initially he thought that placing Brenda back with her family in California might be an option but he quickly dismissed that idea. Southern California had a very active MS-13 presence. Although Brenda's hometown of El Monte, outside of Los Angeles, was likely not MS turf, Greg couldn't take that risk.

Brenda had told him her dad was an MS gang member. While he wasn't sure this was true, Greg thought her father might be involved in some criminal activity—another reason to keep her in Virginia. Her uncle in Texas was another option, and he was considered by the Virginia courts to be Brenda's first point of contact, since her father had transferred legal guardian status to Rafael. After several attempts made by Greg and the court to get in touch with Rafael resulted in little to no action on his part, it was clear her uncle didn't want to have anything to do with her.

Greg also considered foster care, but ruled that out because he was certain the MS might harm the members of any family who agreed to house Brenda. He explored other locations. She could be placed in a rural youth ranch, the kind used to help rehabilitate criminally minded minors. Or she could be put into a girls program in Georgia. Yet none of these options were good enough to guarantee her safety. As much as Greg wanted to isolate Brenda, at least enough to keep her safe, he couldn't be sure they could find a place outside of a juvenile detention facility where the Mara Salvatrucha couldn't find her.

As time moved forward from July into early August, Greg had secured Brenda's trust, no small accomplishment, but he still faced a paradox. Brenda met dozens more people as she revealed more MS secrets about hand signals, organizational structure, and the gang's various criminal enterprises. It was impossible to maintain the secrecy of her informant status. She had become a minor celebrity with the law enforcement community in northern Virginia. Eventually the wrong people would hear she was cooperating with police. The more she spoke, the harder it was to keep her safe. Fortunately, her rising star as an important informant did give him some leverage in Texas, where Detective Oseguera's arrest warrant was still outstanding.

The Grand Prairie major crimes detective, Rick Oseguera, hadn't seen Brenda since March 2002. There were warrant posters with Brenda's mug shot in the greater Dallas area, but they had generated no leads. To him, she was gone.

In the first week of August, Flaca appeared on Oseguera's radar. She was the girl who, according to Brenda, had killed Javier and stolen his car and might pass through Dallas at some point on her way to Maryland. The detective received a call from the officer on duty at Farmers Branch Police Department who explained he had a wispy young Latina female who went by the name of Flaca in his custody. Excited about moving his case forward, Oseguera drove out to Farmers Branch to take her into custody and drive her back to Grand Prairie for questioning.

Just as he had with Brenda, he walked her to his interview room and sat her down at the table. She wasn't hardened or tough and smart like Brenda, nor was she well versed in what she could and couldn't tell the cops. Scared of the men who had killed Javier, Flaca had decided she wanted to rid herself of the gang life. She was a gangster wannabe who didn't want it anymore. She had seen and heard things that had scared her and had nearly been killed for her association with Brenda's gang. Her boyfriend at the time of Calzada's death, Little Zico, had tried to kill her in mid-July, only weeks before Flaca met Detective Oseguera.

Her best recourse had been to go to the cops. Oseguera had to be careful to nurture this potentially rewarding relationship, he thought as he sat down across from Flaca at the interview table. She was his biggest break in the case since January, when the Dallas Gang Unit cops passed him Brenda's shoebox with letters from Veto. Before Flaca began, Oseguera asked her if she would agree to give him a signed statement. She said she would and began telling the detective what she remembered. She revealed a number of details that Oseguera had no other way of learning.

"I was with Brenda when she called Javier and asked him for a ride to Grand Prairie," Flaca timidly stated. "On the way, a guy I didn't know got in the car and he placed a gun at Javier's head. Javier got out of the car and soon I heard two gunshots. Then we drove back to Dallas and tried to take off the tires," Flaca concluded.

It was a short story, but she had gotten to the point. Within five minutes, Flaca had provided the essential links to allow the rest of Oseguera's facts to fall into place, with only one discrepancy: the Dallas medical examiner had found evidence of only one bullet wound.

She went on to tell Oseguera that Little Zico was one of the gang members who beat up Javier before he was shot. She pronounced his name "psycho," like Brenda did. And after the murder, she said, Little Zico, Veto, and three others stripped Javier of his shoes.

Oseguera took careful notes as he lined up the facts in his head. He was now convinced Veto was the gunman behind the Calzada murder. He knew Veto and four of the other gang members were already locked up in the Dallas County Jail. But they were there on an aggravated-robbery charge, not for the Calzada murder. If Oseguera didn't push forward with his investigation, Veto and the others could possibly get away with killing Calzada. That was something Oseguera could not allow, especially now that he knew more about Veto's gang.

Flaca had told him important facts about Javier's death, and she had placed Brenda at the scene of the crime, possibly implicating Veto as the gunman. It was great information, but Oseguera concluded that Flaca didn't know quite enough for him to go forward with an airtight case. He still needed corroboration.

The detective wanted more than ever to talk to Brenda again. Oseguera then asked Flaca about Brenda. She told him Brenda was in Fairfax County in northern Virginia and that she had been there since early June after spending weeks drifting from one MS group to another between Texas, Nashville, and North Carolina. Oseguera fought to conceal a smile under his moustache. Flaca had just given him all the information he needed to track down Brenda.

After the interview, Flaca called her dad in Carrollton and had him pick her up and take her home. Oseguera then returned to his desk and began making phone calls to search for Brenda.

Oseguera was surprised when his police contact in northern Virginia knew exactly who he was asking about. Brenda, Oseguera's contact said, was a wealth of information. Word was, she had even helped save the life of an Arlington County detective. At the end of the phone call, Oseguera took note of Mike Porter's number. His contact explained before hanging up that any out-of-state cops who wanted to talk to Brenda had to go through Porter first. Oseguera pushed the button for a new line and immediately dialed Porter's number. He was relieved when the detective picked up.

Porter told Oseguera his informant was open to on-the-record interviews and sharing information that was verified. Oseguera was incredulous. The same girl who had comfortably lied to his face about the Calzada murder had for some reason decided to become an informant. If Porter and the rest were right, Oseguera reasoned as he listened to Porter, Brenda would speak to him about what really happened the night Calzada died. Brenda was already providing information on a number of cases, but Porter made it clear that before Oseguera could speak with her, he would have to go through her legal guardian, Greg Hunter. Porter gave Oseguera Hunter's phone number.

"Hello, this is Detective Rick Oseguera with the Grand Prairie Police Department," Oseguera started when Greg answered the phone, hopeful of some cooperation from what most cops consider the other team. "I am investigating a murder case down here in Texas and I would like to speak to your client regarding what she knows," Oseguera explained in a formal tone.

"I was expecting you," Greg said. "Brenda will tell you everything she knows about your case, but you have to agree not to prosecute her before I can allow you to walk away with any signed statements," the lawyer began.

Hunter drove a hard bargain. Oseguera thanked the lawyer for his time, and stepped out to find Sergeant Alan Patton, the detective who had initially found Javier's remains. Oseguera explained that Brenda's immunity was on the table in exchange for all the information she had on the night of Javier Calzada's murder. Through Greg, Brenda agreed to produce a statement, and based on her reputation with the cops in Virginia, Oseguera thought the information would be valid. He still wanted to arrest Brenda, but he needed her information more than he needed her in jail. Patton agreed. Now Oseguera had to get through to the Dallas County prosecutor's office before he could talk to Brenda again.

Weeks passed before Oseguera, Greg, a judge in Dallas, and an assistant district attorney ironed out the details of Brenda's immunity agreement. During this time, Oseguera renewed his efforts to tie up loose ends on the Calzada case before he traveled to Virginia to interview Brenda.

The same week Oseguera spoke with Greg, he called Warren Navidad, a friend of Javier's whom the detective had interviewed the first week he was on the case. He recalled that Warren had always been able to answer the tough questions in earlier interviews. Warren agreed to come to the station for questioning, and within hours they were seated in the interview room in Grand Prairie. Oseguera pulled out a stack of photos. He first showed Warren a photo of Flaca. He recognized her as a girl from school, but couldn't remember if he had seen her at Bachman Lake, where Javier Calzada liked to spend time with his friends. Oseguera then showed Warren a photo of Veto. Warren immediately recognized him and said he'd seen Veto before at Bachman Lake. This piece of information set Oseguera's wheels spinning.

He decided to meet again with Flaca the next day.

"I believe you know who got in the backseat with you, and maybe you're scared to identify him, but I need to know," Oseguera said once he and Flaca were again seated in the interview room. "I've been in contact with Brenda Paz's attorney and I know who the guy is," Oseguera added, thinking it might ease Flaca's mind to know Veto had already been fingered.

He then showed her a photo lineup, and she pointed to Veto's photo.

"Veto was the one in the backseat with me, and he was the one who pointed the gun at Javier's head," Flaca said in timid tones, this time revealing his identity. Oseguera pushed a little harder and found out her ex-boyfriend was also there. She said he was locked up in North Carolina for a stabbing and was wanted in Los Angeles for murder. Little Zico was the guy Brenda had fingered for Mike Porter, who then passed along the information to police in North Carolina.

Flaca said Little Zico was mean. She showed Oseguera a scar on her upper left chest where Zico had stabbed her with a piece of broken glass when she broke up with him in North Carolina. It had happened before she returned to Texas when she first spoke with Oseguera. After he concluded his second interview with Flaca, Oseguera called the Dallas County Jail to make sure Veto and the other four suspects were still in custody.

Armed with more information from Flaca and Warren, Oseguera planned to meet with all of Veto's cellmates to see if Veto had talked to any of them about Javier's murder. He was also careful enough to schedule a meeting with the Dallas district attorney to compare notes before he traveled to Virginia to interview Brenda. It was very important that he and the attorney were on the same page on this. Oseguera had struggled to get anything out of Brenda before. As far as he was concerned she was still a tough and smart gangster. He still couldn't believe that she was willing to talk to him. This third interview with Brenda would put everything on the line; either she had the information to nail down his case or he would be in a tight spot to prove that Veto had killed Javier. This interview was his last chance to get all the information he needed, and he was determined to get it right.

CHAPTER 26

The FBI is a law enforcement organization with a long history of combating organized crime. For decades, federal agents have targeted a number of gangs, including the Bloods, the Crips, and the Mexican Mafia, but in 2002, the FBI still had not registered the Mara Salvatrucha. Because MS-related cases still circulated only in local and state courts, the importance of the Mara Salvatrucha as a nationwide threat had not reached the upper levels of law enforcement.

The FBI reached out to local law enforcement by assigning its agents to Safe Streets Task Forces, created in 1992 to target violent crime and gang activity. These task forces used the FBI's investigative resources, such as a national DNA database, and the bureau's connection with federal prosecutors, who sought heavier sentences from federal-level criminal statutes.

Location alone determined federal involvement in the investigation of the Joaquin Diaz murder. Denis murdered Joaquin in a federal park, pushing the National Park police to the forefront of the investigation just five days before the attacks of September 11, 2001, forced the FBI to focus on terrorism, not organized crime or even street gangs. Joaquin Diaz's murder put the Mara Salvatrucha on the federal radar, but it was at a time when people at the federal level who cared enough to look closely at street gangs had no time for anything but terrorists.

Few at the federal level recognized the MS as a national threat.

Even at the local level, it was difficult to establish the MS as a gang problem. Because of petty politics, budgetary considerations, and bureaucracy, street gangs were often ignored in the smaller cities and towns where the MS had begun to appear. Benign neglect was the status quo in most of these local jurisdictions. Many police chiefs and mayors preferred to deny there was a gang problem, even when it was clear to many cops on the street that the MS was thriving and growing fast in immigrant communities.

With local leaders in denial, FBI agents working in the Safe Street Task Forces were unable to respond to the MS. Los Angeles alone had embraced its gang problem, while most other cities around the country had not. FBI agents in other cities may have suspected the MS presence in their area, but without local support, they were not able to focus solely on that one gang. The task forces were a cooperative effort, and the FBI could not call the shots. As local leaders looked the other way, the MS spread across the country and built a significant membership in dozens of states before there was any semblance of an organized federal response. Greg and Detective Mike Porter's growing worry for Brenda's long-term safety, in part, sparked the FBI's attention to the MS presence across the country, starting in northern Virginia.

Through the end of the summer and into early fall, Porter and Greg began to believe that Brenda might have been burned. Greg knew he was at the end of his rope after bouncing Brenda from one secure location to another. At the local level, there were no more options or legal tricks to keep her safe.

At the juvenile detention center in Fairfax, during one of the daily recreation periods in the early fall, Brenda was on the girls' side of the gym when a young MS-13 member named Boxer broke away from the boys' side. He turned and hurled a basketball at Brenda's head and missed, but it got her attention. The gym fell silent when the basketball bounced with a reverberating clamor off the wall next to Brenda.

"We know you're a rat," Boxer yelled. "You're dead," he said, pointing directly at her.

She told Greg about the incident that night. She mentioned the kid was an MS member, but she didn't know him. The basketball incident confirmed Greg's suspicions. Brenda was burned. Someone in MS knew she was talking to the cops. After his conversation with Brenda, Greg began making calls and asking questions about the people who worked at the juvenile detention facility. He had to know if someone on the facility staff might try to harm her.

Days later a custodian at the detention facility sauntered up to Brenda and said, "If you were in my old gang, you'd already be dead." Greg did a background check on the girl and found out she used to be a member of the Bloods from Chicago and had come to work with troubled youth as part of a reform program. The girl still wore her colors though, always coming to work with a red shirt under her uniform.

Despite these threats, Greg felt that the juvenile detention center was still the safest place for Brenda in Virginia; but he knew it was only a short-term solution. Brenda would require protection for months, if not years. He needed more help than the state of Virginia could afford, so he began making the necessary calls to engage the FBI.

Months before Greg had met Brenda, FBI Special Agent Laurence Alexander was assigned to a Safe Streets Task Force in northern Virginia, working out of the FBI's Washington, D.C., field office. His primary role was to investigate Latino street gangs. The former Marine embodied everything law enforcement looks for in an FBI agent. Laurence Alexander—Alex to his friends—was a straight shooter. His failsafe integrity instantly impressed everyone who worked with him. Unlike the stereotypical FBI agent in a cheap polyester suit, Alexander was well dressed. He was quick to smile or make a joke, but just as stern as the next investigator when it came time to work.

When a contact told Alexander there was a witness in Fairfax who needed FBI assistance, he didn't hesitate to act. At the time, Alexander had been attending a number of street gang–related meetings and was spending time with the one- or two-man county gang units. The Fairfax County Gang Unit was the largest in the region, and when the twelve-man team reached out for help, it got his attention.

"Look, we have a female witness," Detective Mike Porter told Alexander when they first talked about Brenda. "She has a lot of intelligence on MS-13. And she was burned. There's a threat out on the street against her, and we're at a loss as to what we can do to help protect her."

Apart from the threat that Brenda received inside the detention center, Greg and Porter believed the wrong person on the street might have seen something. Brenda had hopped in and out of a police car, laughing and talking in a friendly manner with Greg and Porter, on one too many occasions. Any MS member who saw this activity had to assume that Brenda was a rat.

Alexander agreed to meet with Greg and Brenda at the end of September in a conference room at the Massey Building, Fairfax County's unlikely police and fire department headquarters. It was a 1970s design not originally intended as police headquarters. Too tall to blend in with the Fairfax city skyline, its glass-paneled siding carried a dull brown tone that suggested boring business, not law enforcement. In the shadow of this ugly building sat one of the county's most venerable attractions of the law enforcement community, a brick-and-mortar building older than the Civil War. The Fairfax County courthouse was first used in 1800, and graced the immediate area with the aura of a national monument to justice and the rule of law. Layers of reform ensured it was still in use. The two buildings, one tall and ugly, the other old and still important, made for an odd couple in the Fairfax County judicial complex.

Seated in a conference room inside the Massey Building, Alex, Greg, and Brenda went over her complete case. The meeting lasted nearly five hours. Alexander's initial notion of Brenda was similar to that of most other law enforcement individuals—he was impressed. By now, Brenda could talk about her MS past with reservation only for Veto, Denis, and some of the friends she had made before her arrest. Brenda spoke candidly with him about MS activity in Virginia and a number of other states across the country. Alexander sat straight in his chair, didn't make jokes, and took careful notes as Brenda talked and told him her stories. Alexander considered this chance to debrief a former MS member a first for him, while Brenda considered the meeting just like any other she'd had with Greg and other cops. Brenda thought Alexander was just too professional, and soon after their first meeting, she teasingly began calling him *El Frío*, the Cold One. As his nickname suggested, Alexander took her case very seriously. He immediately thought about how she could be useful as a federal witness in an upcoming trial against the Mara Salvatrucha.

Alexander thought of Assistant U.S. Attorney Ronald Walutes, who was prosecuting the Joaquin Diaz case. It had evolved into a federal capital murder case because the primary suspect, Denis Rivera, had been arrested with Brenda. Alexander didn't know if Walutes had many witnesses for the case against Denis. He figured Brenda would be a perfect witness, and after contacting the attorney, Alexander set up a number of other meetings to get to know Brenda and her situation better.

Alexander had found Brenda intriguing. During their first meeting, he had her analyze a homicide photograph to see if she could deduce what had happened. She had not been at the crime, but was able to explain why the body was found where it was, based just on her knowledge of the gang and what she learned from looking at the photograph.

The victim was an MS member marked for punishment. He was to receive a 13, Brenda explained, which meant that, like the jumping-in process, he was to be beaten by four or five fellow members for a count of thirteen seconds. But when he was taking off his shirt, someone decided to shoot him. That was why his body was found with the shirt halfway off.

"Wow, where did she get that from?" Alexander had asked himself. He thought her insight was unprecedented. Alexander was stunned that she had pegged the situation accurately without knowing much more than what the photograph suggested.

After he learned enough about Brenda to feel confident she was telling the truth, Alexander was convinced Greg was right. She was a strong candidate for the Federal Witness Protection Program. He immediately began working on a threat assessment for Brenda. It was a critical document required for her entrance into witness protection. He listed over a dozen individuals as direct threats to Brenda's life, including Denis and Veto, and three of the men who were present with Denis at the Diaz killing.

The threat assessment was only the beginning of processing anyone into witness protection. A U.S. attorney must also sponsor the witness, providing in detail the reasons why an individual should be allowed into the program. This was where Walutes's participation was crucial. The final decision rested solely with the attorney general, a considerable bottleneck in the process, given the busy schedule of the nation's top lawyer.

Brenda and Greg met Alexander and Walutes five days after the initial meeting in the Massey Building. Walutes knew of Brenda through his FBI connections and from local police officers. All had vouched for her. At the meeting, Walutes told Greg that he was willing to sponsor Brenda's entrance into witness protection. He clarified his intention by stating that her entrance was not conditional upon her testimony against Denis Rivera in the upcoming Joaquin Diaz murder trial.

She could still be helpful. Like the icing on the cake, Brenda could take the stand and place the facts of his prosecution against Denis in a broader context. Her knowledge of the gang grounded the confessions of some of the gang members who had decided to become federal witnesses in exchange for a reduced sentence, Walutes explained. Brenda's testimony could also establish the fact that Denis was aware of his own guilt. Even the mention of taking the stand against Denis made Brenda nervous. Greg picked up on the subtle change in her attitude during the meeting, and made a mental note to revisit the issue with Brenda in private. This was a serious meeting, even Brenda wasn't kidding around. It wasn't the time or place to explore Brenda's feelings about testifying against her boyfriend.

Walutes wanted to prosecute Denis and Fiel, the clique leader who had backed him on his decision to kill Joaquin. The U.S. attorney said that as the government moved forward with other MS prosecutions, Brenda could also be very helpful. Federal prosecutors in northern Virginia believed the best way to dismantle the Mara Salvatrucha was by treating the street gang like an organized criminal group.

Walutes was thinking of the Racketeer-Influenced and Corrupt Organizations Act, or RICO. Since its inception, it had been used successfully to break apart organized criminal families like the Cosa Nostra in New York, the Hells Angels, and others. For a RICO charge, two overt criminal acts needed to be connected to a criminal organization. Homicide, a drug enterprise, or rape all qualified. Proving the overt acts was easy. Proving the actors were part of a criminal enterprise that conspired to commit those acts was much harder. As a legal tool, RICO was essential for dismantling organized crime because it allowed prosecutors to focus on the criminal organization, not necessarily the crimes committed by individuals within the organization. In any RICO case against the MS, Brenda could provide the details that would help the prosecution establish the MS-13 as a criminal enterprise that conspired to commit federal crimes.

Before the end of the meeting, Walutes made it clear to Greg that Brenda's age presented a complication. Witness protection normally only accepted adults. Kids did enter the program, but an adult, usually a parent, always accompanied them. Unaccompanied minors in witness protection were an entirely new concept, and Brenda was still sixteen.

Walutes and Greg agreed she would have to be emancipated, or legally declared an adult, before they could pass her witness protection application to the attorney general's office.

Greg felt determined after the meeting. He finally had a goal and the path was clear. He had to have Brenda emancipated, and then he could pass her over to the U.S. Marshals, who ran witness protection and had a well-known reputation for never having lost a person under their care. If accepted, Brenda would be the first minor allowed into witness protection.

Before he could focus on Brenda's emancipation process, Greg had to first finish his business with Detective Oseguera. Since the final weeks of summer, Greg had been in touch with Oseguera, and had butted heads consistently with the Dallas County prosecutor, who insisted that Brenda be extradited to Texas to answer questions about the night Javier Calzada died. Greg felt no pressure. He knew the legal fiction he signed with Porter to keep Brenda in Fairfax County would hold.

And it did. The Dallas County prosecutor finally agreed to give Brenda immunity in exchange for a signed statement. With his case nearly completed, Detective Oseguera traveled with Sergeant Patton to Virginia only days after her first meeting with Walutes.

Greg invited Alexander to the Massey Building, where they arranged to meet with Oseguera and Sergeant Patton. The two listened as Oseguera asked Brenda questions. Patton took notes. Brenda provided a detailed account of the night Javier Calzada was murdered and identified from a group of photos Little Zico, Veto, and the other three men who were all at the top of Oseguera's suspect list. Unlike the other two times she had met with Oseguera, Brenda was forthcoming with the information and was willing to sign a four-page statement.

After four hours of question and answer, she corroborated nearly everything Oseguera had learned prior to the interview. He now had enough information to take to the Dallas County prosecutor. With Brenda as a witness for the prosecution, Oseguera was confident his case was all but closed. At the end of the interview, Brenda confirmed that one of the men present when Veto shot Javier had taken Javier's shoes. She also said it was possible Veto had worn Javier's white Adidas shoes. That statement stuck in Oseguera's mind like a sliver of splintered wood. He had to get back to the Dallas County Jail to look for those shoes.

Patton walked out of the meeting slowly shaking his head, thinking

Brenda knew too much for her own good. He knew what her gang had done in Grand Prairie, and from what he'd learned, MS-13 had a much stronger presence in Virginia. Brenda could be killed if she wasn't careful, but Patton kept his thoughts to himself. They had gotten what they'd come for. With the taste of success in their mouths, Oseguera and Patton finished the meeting, then spent the evening at a baseball game in Baltimore—Baltimore Orioles versus the Texas Rangers. They might as well make use of the one night they had on the East Coast before boarding a plane for Texas at BWI Airport in the morning.

Back in Texas, Oseguera wasted no time driving to the Dallas County Jail, where he requested to see the personal effects of Veto and the four men arrested with him. He carefully searched through the belongings until he found the shoes he was looking for. It was a moment of clarity when Oseguera held in his hands the evidence he thought would finally close his case. It had been nine months since he took on the Calzada murder investigation, and in this moment he could see the end.

Oseguera immediately wrote up a request to take a DNA sample from Veto and the other four men. Within hours his request was approved and a lab technician took mouth swabs that were submitted to the Dallas County DNA lab along with the shoes. The results showed that three separate strands of DNA removed from dried sweat in the shoes matched the DNA of Javier Calzada, Veto, and the inmate who had been wearing Javier's shoes when he was arrested.

As he suspected, the DNA match was Oseguera's strongest evidence against Veto and at least one of his accomplices. There were also soil samples, fingerprints, and Brenda's affidavit. Within weeks of having interviewed Brenda a third time, Oseguera was prepared to make his case, largely due to her tip-off about the shoes.

The day after Brenda spoke with Oseguera, she agreed to speak off the record with another detective from the Dallas area. The two-day meeting stretched across Saturday and Sunday. It was held in the same conference room in the Massey Building. During the marathon interview, one with little more than an overnight break to sleep, Brenda met the detective's long list of questions head-on. There were some questions she couldn't answer, but the information she did have was detailed, as usual. Brenda talked about how a group of MS set out to rob a bank a couple of states over from Texas. They had left Dallas in a borrowed car and parked it in Arkansas. Then they stole a car, drove to another state, and robbed a bank. They stole another car before driving back to Arkansas, where they ditched it and got in the borrowed car before heading back to Dallas.

Brenda also described how her homies in Texas had stolen baby formula to sell it to undocumented immigrants. The baby formula was parceled out into smaller portions, affordable for their black market customers.

On Sunday afternoon, after three long days of interviews, Brenda finally described a murder that had haunted her for months. One night in Dallas, shortly before Calzada's murder, Brenda was with Veto and other MS members when there was a shoot-out between the MS and a rival gang. One of the rival gang members was shot but not killed. Not wanting to waste bullets, the MS members had decided to use a car to finish him off. Brenda and the others sat in the car as they repeatedly ran over the wounded *chavala* until he quit screaming.

The detective told Brenda the kid was still alive. Her eyes widened. She didn't believe it. The detective then produced a photo of the kid. Brenda took in a deep breath when she looked at the photo, and then sharply turned her head away. The sight affected her deeply. What was she thinking at the time? How crazy had she been? Greg was shocked that anyone would do such a thing. For him, it was another moment when he looked directly at the evil things some members of the MS-13 did. The kid's face was a mess. He was barely recognizable. It was a disturbing conclusion to an exhausting three-day ordeal with the detectives from Texas. On the way back to the detention center, Greg detected that Brenda was emotionally spent, but he listed the weekend as a major victory for her. Brenda probably wasn't thinking about it at that moment, but she was clean and free from the Texas murder that had been haunting her for so many months. That night, Brenda didn't sleep well. The sight of that boy's face had triggered a long list of memories she thought she had successfully forgotten.

CHAPTER 27

The most remarkable interview Brenda gave occurred days later in one of the same conference rooms where she and Greg had had so many of her previous interviews. The room was long and narrow with a blackboard on one of the end walls. On it she had once drawn a diagram of the MS organizational structure in Virginia, Texas, and across the nation. There was a conference table in the middle surrounded by surprisingly comfortable chairs, complete with padded armrests, wheels, and adjustable hydraulics. The walls were covered with a tightly woven upholstery that looked like processed straw. The room could have been in an elementary school, except for the Spartan décor.

Brenda sat cross-legged at the front of the room, in a chair between an open door and a white dry-erase marker board. She fiddled with one of the black markers in her hand. A brown hair-band was on her right arm, comfortably resting just below where she had the name VETO tattooed on her wrist. Her curly brown hair was tucked behind her ears and flowed halfway down her chest. Brenda was dressed in a loose-fitting red shirt and blue sweatpants. She looked like a teenage kid ready for an afternoon at the park or a stroll in the mall, not a taped interview where she would talk about one of the nation's most dangerous gangs.

Brenda was a little nervous seated in front of the top street gang detectives for miles around, including two federal agents. Just after Porter pressed the record button on the video camera, Brenda giggled. It was a way for her to break the tension in the room with all these serious adults.

"What do you want me to say?" she asked, flashing her trademark smile at Porter and twirling the marker between two fingers.

"Tell them . . . tell them what gang you're with," he began with a deadpan voice, all business but calm, not pushy.

Nervous, Brenda looked at the red blinking light of the video camera, then directly at the lens.

"MS-13," Brenda replied, matter-of-factly. Her Spanish accent contrasted sharply with Porter's deep southern drawl.

"What clique?" Porter asked, moving forward with the most basic questions. These were the answers she was most comfortable giving.

"Normandie Locos Salvatrucha—NLS. The first clique in MS started way back in the day in El Salvador," Brenda said with some pride. She bounced in her seat when she said it, projecting her smile across the room.

"How long have you been with MS?" Porter asked. It was a controversial question.

Brenda looked up at the ceiling and sighed before answering. "I've been affiliated since I was eleven and in the gang since I was thirteen." She had told that lie so many times, she was beginning to believe it was true. It was one of the lies she most repeated. Brenda was never affiliated with the MS before she met Veto in Texas. It was a truth she kept close—something she even kept from Greg. On film, in front of her lawyer and the entourage of detectives, it was the last place Brenda would tell them she had only been a member for less than a year before she was arrested that summer.

"And how did you get into the gang?" Porter asked, staying on familiar ground with Brenda.

"I got jumped in to the gang, and then I got jumped in to another clique, and then got jumped out and got re-jumped in to MS Normandie clique," Brenda said. It was a second lie, backing up the first. Though Brenda's lies were believable in the don't-ask-questions world of the MS, her fabrications were harder to pull off in front of experienced investigators. She could keep the false information straight but had a poor delivery in front of the cops. Fortunately her smile often came to the rescue. Yet there was some truth to her second answer.

Any MS member who wanted to leave one clique to join another had to be jumped out of a clique with a thirteen-second beating before being jumped in to the next clique with another thirteen-second beating.

"Can you . . . ah . . . do the MS hand signs? Can you spell out, can you show us the MS hand signs?" Porter jumbled out the sentence, referring to stacking, a practice among street gang members that was something akin to sign language, using both hands to spell out words in a rapid succession of finger twists, curves, and seemingly difficult feats of pinky and ring finger dexterity. Brenda had stacked for the Grand Prairie detective, Rick Oseguera, when he had first interviewed her. She had also viewed some police surveillance tapes with Greg and Porter when MS members in the video stacked in front of the camera. Brenda could read their hand signs like a book. It was a complicated and fascinating method of communication that Brenda had perfected.

She knew the hand signs, and after placing the dry-erase marker in her lap, she readily showed the camera and the men present how to spell out the name of her gang, moving forward letter by letter beginning with the Spanish word *La* and moving on to *Mara*, then *Salvatrucha*. She made the hand symbol of each letter just as fast as she was talking.

"The *L* is for *loco*. The *A* is for arsonist. The *M* is for *maldito*. The *A* for arsonist. The *R* for *robo*, which in English is translated to robbery. The *A* for arsonist. The *S* for Salvatrucha. The *A* for arsonist. The *L* for *loco*. The *V* for *violar*. That means rape. The *A* for arsonist, again. The *T* for . . . God, I forgot."

"*Trece*," Porter suggested, thinking the *T* in Salvatrucha could mean *trece*, the Spanish word for the number 13.

"*Trece*," Brenda agreed, smiling at Porter for the help.

She continued. "The *R* for *robo*. The *U* for united. The *C* for *controlador*—controlling. The *H* for Home Beat, Homeboys. And the *A* for arsonist. And the 13. That's *sureños*. We're from the south side. That's why we carry the 13; we just adopted the 13. There's also sayings in MS that it comes from the Bible. I really don't know what passage or anything, but in MS, they affiliate themselves with the Bible a lot." Brenda was starting to open up. Her extroverted nature was beginning to shake loose the grip her nerves had on her tongue. Soon, Porter thought, Brenda might tell the men in the room information they had never heard about the Mara Salvatrucha.

"There's a lot of different stacking and when you're taught how to stack people do it differently. People stack their cliques, the gang. Like I'm spelling out my whole clique," Brenda said, using her hands in fast motion to spell out Normandie Locos Salvatrucha. Each letter required a specific hand pose. She shifted her weight in her chair to accommodate inverting her arms to place her elbows above her shoulders or quickly alternate the position of her wrists. Brenda stacked equally well with both hands.

"Everyone's taught how to do it differently, but the more significant ones are always with the M and the S and the 13," Brenda explained, making an intricate sign for M before positioning her pointer finger under her middle finger and curving her thumb to make an S. She crossed her ring finger and thumb and spread her other three fingers apart to make an X and a 3 for the number 13. She stuck out her tongue a little to help concentrate. Her fingers were chubby and short, not ideal for stacking. But she never used her left hand to put errant right-hand fingers in the correct position. Her fingering was smooth and precise.

"Who teaches you to stack?" Porter asked.

"When you get jumped in your clique leader teaches you the basics and you learn from how you're always with your homeboys. They also do the M, this is M," Brenda said, slightly leaning forward and positioning both elbows above her shoulders to make the effect of an M. "And that's the S," she said, curving her arms and placing the fist of her right arm just below the elbow of the top arm, which extended over her head to make a crude S. "That's the 13—X, 1, 1, 1," Brenda said. She made a ninety-degree angle with one fist against the inside of her other elbow, alternating fist and elbow, left and right, each time she said "one."

Her pride in the Mara Salvatrucha, even after she had been away from the gang for over three months, was clear-cut. Brenda broke into a broad smile. Her confidence swelled. After showing the men some stacking, Brenda composed herself a little. She straightened her hair and picked up the dry-erase pen for more fiddling.

Porter noticed Brenda was now considerably relaxed. It would soon be time for more interesting questions. The men in the room were all seasoned gang detectives. They had known about stacking for a long time, but were also patient. They all had managed informants in the past and were content to let Porter run the show. But then Greg stepped in.

"What do they say when they do this stacking?" Greg asked. He wanted to make sure the men in the room knew the MS-13 motto.

"*La* Big Time Mara Salvatrucha *Trece,* for *mata, controla, viola,*" Brenda said, stacking again until she got to the word *viola*, Spanish for rape. It tripped her up slightly, and she momentarily looked at the ceiling before shifting her weight in the chair.

The Mara Salvatrucha's saying, "kill, control, rape," was more than just words; it was the foundation of gang members' behavior. Many members took the words to heart, forcing others, like Brenda, to watch. More than anyone else in the room, Greg knew what Brenda had seen and been through with Veto, and he knew how it had affected her. He had risked the whole interview by asking her about those three words—kill, control, rape—but it was important that the men in the room were all on the same page. There were members of the Mara Salvatrucha who meant business and were serious criminals. By showing the men Brenda's reaction to those three words, he demonstrated in a subtle way that Brenda had been close and personal with some of the gang's ugliest realities.

After the awkward pause, Porter pushed forward. "And if MS wants to attack an officer they use hand signs?" he asked. It was time to get into something more interesting and out of what the men in the room considered everyday information about the gang.

"For attacks I guess officers and other gang members, it's very significant, they take their shirts off, they always go like that," Brenda said, slightly lifting the horizontal stitching of her shirt at points on the top of her shoulders, "signifying that they're going to get into battle. They'll do this when they're going to shoot," Brenda said, rubbing her stomach side to side with her right hand. "It's different, everyone where MS is located they use different signs but these are the ones that everyone usually always knows."

"Okay," Porter said. He pushed on. "How do people get recruited into MS?"

"The most common recruitment is when you know an MS member. You hang around them, you like what they, what you, see. You like the action, so you're recruited. There's other recruitments gangs do. Drug dealers—if they sell drugs and you want them to be MS you'll keep stalking and bitching at that person until you get them to be MS. In jail they'll keep beating a person up until that person wants to be MS or *allows* themselves to be MS." Brenda didn't have much experience with recruitment. But she knew what she had heard from Veto and Denis. Recruitment was always on their mind and a constant focus of the gang.

"How about schools? How does recruitment work in the schools?" Porter asked.

"Well, teenagers seem to always want to be influenced by gangs, so they kind of recruit themselves into being in the gang."

Brenda had joined the gang this way. Most MS members like Brenda were self-selected, just floating into the periphery of the gang until one day a member makes an offer on joining. The offer Brenda received wasn't just from anyone. It was from a high-level leader, and that made her involvement with the MS intimate and intense from the beginning.

Brenda continued. "But sometimes MS will look for the people who they think are going to be more vicious, the stronger type." Brenda was referring to the young soldiers like the guys who were with Veto the night he killed Javier or with Denis the night he killed Joaquin. They were eager to prove themselves.

"Is MS recruiting in a Fairfax County school?" Porter asked.

"Yeah. MS is recruiting in every school around here. MS recruits wherever MS stays."

"High schools, middle schools, elementary schools?" Greg asked. He wanted her to get more specific.

"High schools, juvenile detentions, middle schools. I've known of MS wanting to get younger kids into getting affiliated so by the time the kid gets to high school the kid's so into MS that his whole life is MS. That's how they become the great hit men that some of them are," Brenda said.

"Who recruits? Anybody recruits? Any member . . ." one detective asked from the back of the room. Brenda cut him off.

"Any MS member. Any MS member can recruit. It's not really up to anybody to recruit. It's just the ones that are out there having more communication with everybody else. There's some MS that keep low profiles. And a few people know they're MS."

"What about prostitution? Does MS prostitute girls?" Porter asked. He wanted to complete the recruitment picture for the men in the room.

"They do," Brenda answered, looking away from Porter toward the back of the room, seemingly to nowhere before she started talking again. "They'll prostitute girls that get bumped into MS. They're not considered MS to the members. Nobody considers them anything, but somehow the girls feel they should do something for the gang."

Brenda talked about the girls who were sexed in. They become a sort of member, looked upon with little respect. As one of the few female members who decided to take a beating, Brenda occasionally talked back to the male members, something few female members got away with. In most cases it would mean instant retaliation for disrespect.

"They let them think that they're MS, but they're not," Brenda continued. "So they go out there and prostitute themselves and prostitute their friends for nothing. MS kind of pimps them."

"Does MS move these girls from state to state?" Porter asked. He wanted to establish the MS national level activities as much as possible. It wasn't just a northern Virginia problem.

"Yeah, sometimes. Sometimes they will and sometimes they won't. If it starts getting hot, if the cops are noticing that something's going on or if they've killed at that time or if they're wanted for any reason, they'll move. And they take the girls with them."

"Where do you personally know of that MS has moved the girls from Texas to?" one detective asked.

Brenda finished his sentence. "Colorado, from Idaho to Virginia, and then Virginia back to Idaho. LA to Nevada, 'cause there was a lot of LA girls that were getting prostituted in Las Vegas. Oklahoma. I know of a couple of girls that moved to Oklahoma. North Carolina, they moved from Texas to North Carolina, but they were in Virginia first," Brenda said, looking away still. She squinted when recalling the states. She never said the girls' names but knew exactly where they had been. Brenda was uncomfortable talking about other women in the gang. Maybe there was a bad memory in there Brenda didn't want to access. Porter shifted the questioning.

"So once you become a member, what are your requirements? What do you have to do?" Porter asked. It was important for him to establish these facts for those listening. Brenda had their attention now. Alexander was taking notes.

"Well, they tell you the thirteen rules when you get jumped in to MS. Your first requirement is to follow them. You follow the rules like a book. Just like anything else, okay, commandments, I guess. And then you have to put in work for the neighborhood. You always have to do that," Brenda said. She shifted her weight again in the chair.

"When you say 'put in work,' can you be more specific?" Porter asked, prying a little.

"By 'put in work' I mean you have to go out and recruit," Brenda replied. She started fidgeting again. "You have to go out and kill. You have to go out and shoot. Bring money in for the gang. You have to let everyone know you're in the gang. That's how you put in your work." Brenda didn't like talking about putting in work. Although she could play the role and keep up the mask of a hardened gangster, she didn't have what it took to be a killer, or even someone who would harm people. Her history as an MS member was peppered with instances when Brenda had revealed her sensitive side despite herself.

Remembering her interview with Detective Oseguera in Texas, it had hurt her to see him lower the pictures of his family members when she walked into his office. She didn't want him to think she was someone who would hurt children. Once she had arrived in Virginia, Denis had taken her out to do work, telling her she had to shoot the father of a *chavala*. That was the time when, moments before the hit, Brenda told him she couldn't do it. Then, when they were out shopping for Hondas, Brenda wouldn't steal a car with a baby seat in the back. This sensitivity was a weakness in the MS. Deep down, she was a caring, sensitive girl. She liked being part of all the MS parties, but like most members of the Mara Salvatrucha, she resisted doing the real work that made rank in the gang. Brenda had only made rank by dating the leaders and earning respect with her intelligence.

Porter broke the silence with a new set of questions. He was curious to know about what he heard was a growing trend for MS members to keep a low profile, especially the leaders.

"You mentioned that some MS members work. Do members tend to maintain a regular occupation?" Porter asked.

"The smart ones, the ones that are actually out there committing crimes and the ones that are out there actually wanting to look more like a citizen than anything else, those are actually the ones who probably are the hit men for MS or are actually the killers for MS, the clique leaders. They all maintain a job so they can keep a low profile," Brenda finished. Pens in the room scratched out notes.

With that comment still hanging in the air, Porter thought it was a good time to take a new direction and talk about the gang's inner workings.

"The meetings with MS," he began.

"There's different meetings," Brenda said, cutting him off. "There's clique meetings, there's leader meetings, and there's *generales*." Brenda had never been to the meetings. Girls were not allowed. After dating both Veto and Denis, she was very familiar with what happened at the meetings, down to things that had been said at a number of them. Veto and Denis had often asked her to remember information.

The clique meetings were called *misas*; the men in the room knew that. A few had heard of the *generales,* or mass meetings with any number of cliques gathering together, usually after dark in a large park. None had heard that clique leaders had meetings. They were secretive affairs, and Brenda had only heard of them happening. She never knew when or where.

Brenda continued. "You go to your clique meeting regularly every Saturday or Sunday, every week. And you take your tax money. Taxes can wind up from $10 to $200, depending on what your clique leader wants. A clique leader holds those meetings, and if he doesn't go, it's canceled or it's not. He might have someone below him do it. And in every clique there's a treasurer. And every clique has a head man, a spokesperson that talks for the clique."

"Does the treasurer keep a book, an accounting book or something that shows who's paying and who's not?" Greg asked.

"If you don't pay, you're not at the meeting. So if you're not at the meeting, you get into trouble. So either way no written files are kept because cops, I guess, they don't want no one to know how MS runs. But it's mostly a mental thing. So you know how much money you have, and you know how much money you get every meeting, so you know how much money you should wind up with."

"So who runs the meetings?" Greg continued.

"The clique leader," Brenda said matter-of-factly.

"And what about the general meeting?" Greg asked. He knew the men in the room were most interested in the *generales*.

"*Generales* are when all the cliques come. But let's say someone from LA comes, he can run the meeting. If he wants to intrude, he can run the meeting 'cause he has respect. But Bam-Bam gets to run the Virginia meetings. He's respected, he's been in MS a long time and he's from El Salvador, so that kind of makes him a little bit more of a leader. He takes leadership and runs it. The meetings are set up like this: Everybody waits for each other. Everyone has to be there. No one can be late, no matter what. So you go to the meetings, you give your thirteen seconds. That's you bow your heads and you give thanks for being alive and all that, good stuff, you know, 'Forgive me God, I have sinned'—whatever. You usually always throw the MS sign while you're doing it for the thirteen seconds. After that everybody collects the money. Then you say, you watch out to see who's not there. And then everybody who's not there is noticed at that time. After that you talk about what's going on. You talk about if anyone's got arrested, if they need money to get anybody out. Whatever's going on at that situation of that week, you talk about it. If there's anyone you've got to kill, if there's anyone you have to hit, you talk about it."

"And what are you told about dealing with your enemies?" Porter asked, taking over for Greg. There was a specific point he was driving toward, something Brenda hinted at during a previous interview.

"You kill them," Brenda replied with a serious look. It was a simple answer, but Porter wanted more. He kept silent, and as he had hoped, Brenda filled the silence with revealing information.

"Well, I mean if you're dealing with an Eighteenth—if you go to school with some guy who, let me just say for example, right? You go to school with some guy who is an Eighteenth Street leader, he's not going to be waiting for you to just kick his ass. You've got to come up with a way to kill him," Brenda said. Porter kept silent. She continued. "He's an Eighteenth Street leader, he's in your territory, he's in *your* common place. But if it's just another *chavala*, you just kick them. You fight them, you do anything to put them down and belittle them." Brenda made a clear distinction about how a leader is treated. The Mara Salvatrucha planned that kill. Porter wanted to drive home the point of discipline and organization.

"If MS-13 wants to kill somebody do they plan the attack?" Porter asked.

"Not all the time because a lot of MS people just act on reaction. But when it's a big crime that they want to do . . . they, they plan. They think about it, in meetings they bring it up. They think of how they're going to kill them. They don't just do it. But if it's just in the random street, if he just walks down the street and you walk next to him and he throws another gang sign and you have a gun on you, you just shoot and kill." The words fell out of Brenda's mouth in a nonchalant manner. Most of the officers in the room tensed, bristling at the information coming out of this sixteen-year-old girl, the most unlikely of informants. She was relaxed, having a conversation with Detective Porter, someone she grew to like over the weeks. He pushed ahead.

"How about murder for hire? If I know an MS member, even though I'm not MS, maybe we were friends from work or something, can I hire somebody from MS to kill somebody?" Porter asked.

"Yeah. They always do. Money talks in a gang. Money talks," Brenda said with a shrug. For her it was a matter of fact. For the officers in the room, the possibility that members of the Mara Salvatrucha would kill people simply for money was deeply disturbing.

One of the detectives in the room couldn't contain himself. He had to ask. "If I wanted MS to kill somebody *tomorrow,* or if I wanted somebody killed, how long would it take MS to send somebody here if I paid them?"

"How long will it take you to give us the money?" Brenda asked, looking in his direction. She was serious.

"If I gave you the money today, how long would it take MS to come up here and . . ." the detective continued.

"A couple of hours," Brenda said, still looking at him. "We'll throw a meeting like that"—Brenda snapped—"just to get a person to do it. Someone's always going to do it for the money."

"Would it be somebody local or would they send somebody from out of state?" the detective asked, still not believing what this girl was saying.

"It depends who you want to kill. If it's just a nobody just anybody local could do it. If you're talking about killing someone who people are going to give a fuck about, a cop, anybody like that, then we'd probably get other people to do it. More professionalized people and then I guess more people that know how to kill."

Another silent pause descended on the room. The weight of what Brenda just said hung in the air. The men in the room were digesting one of the most serious revelations of the Mara Salvatrucha they had ever heard. Sure, they thought, MS members extort immigrants for money, even pimp undocumented women and sell drugs from time to time. They have a violent streak, and could be hard to track down because they moved from state to state. But a street gang that was willing to kill anyone for money and one that would plan an assassination, even on a cop? That was new and very disturbing information. It was the most memorable thing Brenda said that day and spurred many in the room to consider how far down the evolutionary path the Mara Salvatrucha had gone from street gang toward true organized crime, the kind only the FBI had the resources and experience to handle.

CHAPTER 28

The interview lasted for nearly two hours. Brenda was open and honest about almost everything and left all the men present with a long list of new information and some disturbing insight into the Mara Salvatrucha. Greg and Porter were very pleased with Brenda. The taped interview would go a long way toward proving her knowledge of the gang and willingness to provide information. Porter thought any cop who wanted to know more about the MS should watch the tape. It was the perfect primer for any new gang detective. He thought it should be made into a training video.

After dropping off Brenda at the juvenile detention facility, just across the parking garage from the Massey Building, Greg returned to his thoughts on a strategy to ensure Brenda's long-term safety. She had again demonstrated how much she knew about the gang, and he was convinced there were MS members on the street who were eager to get hold of her.

Brenda's immunity from prosecution in Dallas County was the last of Greg's list of legal hurdles that he'd had to jump in order to keep Brenda out of prison and away from prosecution. He now faced down her emancipation.

Brenda's emancipation required Greg to argue that she was capable of taking care of herself, but more importantly Greg had to argue that Brenda required a high level of safety, one that could only be provided by witness protection. She was a proven informant and could only be an asset to federal investigations into the Mara Salvatrucha. The bottom line, he had to argue, was that witness protection was now Brenda's only option for guaranteed safety.

The emancipation process required numerous court appearances and took much longer than Alexander, Greg, and especially Brenda, had anticipated. October was a tough month. The mid-Atlantic states lived with a three-week reign of terror as two killers, known as the Beltway Snipers, attacked people at gas stations, leaving ten innocent men and women dead and three others critically wounded. It was not business as usual for the area. The Washington FBI field office was working overtime to unravel this top-priority domestic terrorism case. Special Agent Alexander was pulled off Brenda's case in an all-hands-on-deck effort to button down the Beltway Snipers. It was an inescapable delay in processing Brenda's paperwork. Frustration mounted.

Meanwhile, the tension and fear surrounding Brenda climbed. On one outing with Greg in mid-October, Brenda lowered herself in the seat after he pulled up to a gas station. She thought he was going to get shot. On a separate incident, Greg and Porter left the Massey Building with a coat over Brenda's head before placing her in a van for the short drive to the detention center. Throngs of press, gathered to get a glimpse of one of the Beltway Snipers, thought she was Lee Boyd Malvo. Flashbulbs popped like it was a red-carpet event.

The frustration came to a head in court at the end of October. Greg met with Brenda in one of the interview rooms the night before the court case that he thought would be her last. It was a simple space with a small window and venetian blinds. Once both were seated, Greg pulled the blinds shut and explained to Brenda that he thought she would be set free the next day. Brenda was ecstatic. With the exception of the one night she snuck out, Brenda had been incarcerated for nearly four months. She was eager to get out of detention. Before Greg left, he told her that he would see her in court the next day. He gave her a broad smile that barely masked his anticipation. It would be a big day for both of them. Brenda didn't mask anything. Her smile in return held high hopes and a clear display of trust in her guardian.

The next day, Greg stood in the very same hall where he had once contemplated leaving Brenda to her fate in the Fairfax County juvenile justice system. Just before the hearing, while he was waiting his turn to enter the courtroom, Alexander walked up to him briskly. The special agent had bad news. Because of the Beltway Sniper events that month, he was not prepared to receive Brenda. Alexander had initially agreed to place Brenda in an FBI safe house while she waited for an entrance date into witness protection, but it was still too soon. He needed more time. Alexander was shooting straight, no sugar coating on anything, and he had a point. The Beltway Sniper case had everyone in law enforcement behind on normal caseload work. Alexander was no exception. Greg frowned as the weight of this situation settled on his shoulders. He was in a tough spot. Even if he did manage to have her charges dropped and win her emancipation that afternoon, he would have nowhere to put her. Worse yet, he couldn't tell Brenda in a controlled, private atmosphere the bad news before she heard it in court.

Once the hearing started, Greg immediately realized the county prosecutor that afternoon was also going to be a pain in his ass. This guy wasn't going to let Brenda off that easily. He couldn't believe it. Everyone in the room knew Greg and Detective Porter had crossed natural boundaries between defense and prosecution to keep an important witness safe. Greg bristled and prepared his defense, but before he could put the prosecutor in his place, the judge bowled him over. Not allowing the hearing to move forward into the procedural arguments to drop the charges, the judge didn't see why Brenda should be emancipated and made that point with a certain finality at the beginning of the hearing. Greg was against a wall and had to punt. He chose to waive Brenda's right to a speedy trial. It would give him at least another twenty-one days to prepare a better defense against what he realized would be a considerably more complicated process than what he and Porter had originally thought.

During the hearing, Brenda had sat calmly, but she was paying attention. As the hearing moved forward, with conversations bouncing from Greg to the judge to the prosecutor and back, Brenda quickly put two and two together. She realized she wouldn't be set free that day. For her, it was a crushing realization. With quick whispers, Greg tried to help her keep herself together, but she stood up and with tears in her eyes asked if she could be escorted out of the courtroom. Sheriff's deputies walked Brenda out into the hall, where she lost control and began bawling before the door was completely closed. Everyone in the courtroom heard her wracking sobs. It was an extremely hard moment for Greg, who wanted to comfort her but had to remain in court to finalize the hearing. His mind burned with the memory that just the night before he had told her she would be set free, but the system was set against him that day. Damn the Fairfax juvenile court, he thought as he stood there listening to Brenda cry.

While Greg wrapped up the hearing, officers escorted Brenda back to detention, where she was placed in the general-population holding pen. Greg got over to the detention facility as soon as he could. Alexander was with him, and soon Detective Porter showed up. He had made a quick run to McDonald's to get Brenda a McFlurry.

She refused to meet with them and threatened to give up. The heavy toll levied by the bureaucracy had gotten to her. Brenda was deeply frustrated with the system and wanted out. She wanted to give up. Fuck these guys, Brenda thought. All they want is my information and don't care about what I need. Greg knew it would take a monumental effort to convince her that they were there helping her for her own safety, not just for the information she had. It was a precarious moment. Brenda was headstrong, and she was all but ready to stop cooperating.

After over an hour of coaxing and apologies, Brenda finally agreed to meet with Greg, Alexander, Porter, and a social worker to talk through what had happened. It was a tough meeting, and it took a while for her to stop crying. She finally did, but only because she ran out of tears. She had given them her all, and she felt used. She felt like she'd been punked. She'd opened herself up to them and had risked her life to tell them information that everyone knew could get her killed. Greg was in a tough position because the hearing had made him look like he was not on her side. He was desperate to convince her of just the opposite. On that frustrating day in late October, Brenda's patience for courtroom wrangling and living under lock and key expired. If she had been anywhere but in a detention center, Brenda would have walked away.

Delays were commonplace in court. Greg, Porter, and the rest were accustomed to the bureaucracy. Brenda was not. It meant much more for her to get through the process and into witness protection than Greg or Porter had realized before her breakdown. They felt guilty and redoubled their efforts to support her. Once they were able to calm her down, they embarked on a careful process to bring her back into the fold where they could trust that she understood what was going on and how long it was going to take.

For days after the explosive court case, Greg made a point of meeting with her just to hang out, not to solicit more information. He continued to bring her ice-cream shakes, and to talk to her about the books she was reading, especially *Crime and Punishment*. He also worked with her on practice GED tests. She responded well to the attention. After she passed two practice tests in just ten days of classes, she was ready to take the real one. The detention home, however, wouldn't allow it. As her legal guardian, Greg was not able to sign off on the GED permission forms. Only her real parents could do that. It was another headache and a slight setback during this delicate time of regaining Brenda's trust. Greg promised Brenda he would make sure she could take the test once she was in witness protection, but he couldn't help but feel cynicism creep in as he wondered if she would ever get there.

CHAPTER 29

The embattled emancipation process continued until the Wednesday before Thanksgiving, when Greg finally received the judge's reluctant order to declare Brenda a legal adult. At the last moment, the Fairfax County judge had tried to block the emancipation. According to colonial law in Virginia, the parents of emancipated minors had to be informed with a notification placed on the courthouse door. In Virginia's early life as a commonwealth, courthouse doors were littered with such notices. Hundreds of years later, the notices were stored in a binder kept by the court clerk. Over the due course of an emancipation process, the court was required to prepare the notification and file it with the clerk, but in an administrative snag, Brenda's emancipation notification had not been filed. Locked in a stare with the judge, Greg was absolutely livid. He wanted to strangle someone, yell, jump up and down, smash benches and chairs. He was barely able to contain his anger and frustration at this unbelievable situation.

The FBI was finally ready to receive her and this judge had slapped him with a minor technical error that was a result of the court's own failure, not Greg's lack of preparation. Greg was not surprised, given what he knew about the court's proclivities for clumsy administration. During a recess, Greg was relieved when an eleventh-hour solution presented itself. The clerk prepared the notice and amended a legal juke that allowed her to file the notice "on the door" after the dead-line. The paperwork was prepared on notebook paper. With the notice in place, the judge reluctantly issued Brenda's emancipation order before the Thanksgiving holiday.

With the order in hand, Greg ran over to the detention center and demanded that they release Brenda. Out of breath and full of excitement, he was delayed by the front-desk attendant, who wanted to double-check the order with the judge.

"If you think I'm going to ruin my career over a judge's order to let this girl out of detention, you're fucking stupid," Greg said with a self-righteous tone of voice and enough force to verbally beat the front-desk attendant into submission. Faking such an order would be the end of his career if someone found out, and he couldn't believe the attendant was brazen enough to suggest he would do such a thing.

Brenda was brought out with a broad grin. She was finally free. Greg held up her papers, weary but with a satisfied look. Brenda took one look at him and knew he'd made good on his promise. With the emancipation process out of the way, she was more than ready to be checked out of the detention center, sleep in a real bed, and wear real clothes again.

Greg felt like he was on top of the world. He had won Brenda's freedom in a hard legal battle where the system was up against him in every way. They had won that day, despite a judge who was in no mood to have a teenaged kid declared a legal adult and a county prosecutor who was unhappy about the legal fiction, that fake charge Greg and Porter wanted to have dropped.

Brenda's emancipation was just as much a legal triumph for Greg's career as it was a confidence builder for the two of them. It was also a culminating moment in the long roller-coaster ride of building trust with Brenda. He had told her he would pull it off and he had. After months of taking her out, teaching her table manners, buying her books, clothes, and toiletries, letting her cry on his shoulder, and giving her stern talks about safety and making smart decisions, Greg had become more than Brenda's lawyer. He was more than her guardian. He had become a father figure, and standing there on the street in front of the detention facility, Greg felt like the light at the end of the tunnel was shining on both their faces.

Greg finally allowed himself to believe that Brenda actually had a chance of moving on. Brenda could have a future after the Mara

Salvatrucha. She had already realized that her intelligence could get her somewhere, maybe even into a career where she could help young people like herself, kids who had been confused and had become tied up in something that they felt they couldn't get out of. Now it was time to move forward and make that future a reality.

For this moment alone, Greg had saved something special for Brenda's new future. He handed her his personal copy of *Crime and Punishment* by Fyodor Dostoevsky. It was one of her favorite books. Greg had lent her a copy a couple of weeks after having met her, hoping Brenda could find inspiration in the one book that seemed to resonate with many people who dragged themselves through a life of crime.

Brenda had surprised Greg. She had devoured the book and asked intelligent questions concerning various layers of meaning in the plot. Brenda read between the lines. This book, in so many ways, had helped bring out the real Brenda for Greg, and had solidified their relationship. It was the appropriate ending to the long battle they had fought together and the friendship that they had formed.

Greg was optimistic as he handed Brenda over to the very capable hands of Special Agent Laurence Alexander, who would drive Brenda to her new apartment. It was an apartment the FBI agent had selected personally.

Winesburg Manor, Brenda mouthed to herself as she and the agent passed the sign to her new home. As they entered the one-bedroom apartment, Brenda noted so many things. The refrigerator was stocked. She had new clothes and a prepaid cell phone. He had bought her magazines, books, and toiletries and planned on giving her about $15 a week to have some pocket cash. Brenda was ecstatic. She was within walking distance of the Silver Spring stop on the Washington Red Line, just inside Maryland. It was the perfect location for a safe house. No one coming in or out cared enough to ask questions or notice anything that seemed out of place.

Brenda was on the way to becoming a normal kid. In late November it appeared that the worst was behind her. But when Brenda called Greg the day after Thanksgiving, he realized his belief in a happy ending couldn't have been further from the truth.

"I'm so lonely," she said, between choking sobs.

MS

PART 3

When Greg transferred Brenda to FBI custody, he was no longer her lawyer or legal guardian. Brenda was now in the federal system and, legally speaking, an adult. Greg's role as her legal guardian was relevant only as long as Brenda was a minor. Once she was placed in the safe house, he was no longer bound by law or legal ethics to oversee Brenda's well-being. But he didn't stop caring.

Brenda hadn't been alone for more than forty-eight hours before she called Greg.

"I'm so alone," Brenda said, upset and crying. "They gave me this cell phone and the first thing I did was call Mom. Now I'm nearly out of minutes," she continued between sobs.

Brenda had spent all the money Alexander gave her on prepaid cell phone cards calling Honduras to speak with her mom. Greg knew Brenda had a difficult and special relationship with her mom. He wasn't sure what the problem was, but Brenda had told him her mom needed her help. Someday Brenda wanted to bring her mom back to the United States from Honduras and take care of her.

After Alexander dropped Brenda off at her safe house, he reminded her of the lessons she had learned from Greg and Porter once they knew she would eventually be on her own. They had instructed her not to write down any of their names or what they had talked about.

A paper trail could be easily followed and would lead directly from her to the police.

She was also told that if she ran into old friends with the MS, she would have to lie about where she had been. She would have to do everything possible to maintain a façade of loyalty to the gang. After her first weekend at the safe house, Brenda hadn't seen anyone. And instead of being a relief, that happened to be the most pressing problem.

"I didn't want to call you over the holiday," Brenda told Greg, a little calmer.

"But you can call me anytime, you know that," Greg said.

Brenda talked about her mom and wanting to take care of her. For Greg, Brenda's relationship with her mother was an effective fulcrum to leverage a strong argument in her mind for staying away from the gang. "If you're going to take care of your mother, you need to be able to take care of yourself. If you need a job, what would you do? You know, you need an education," Greg said.

These words were part of the repetitive lectures he used to push her to getting serious about her future. Greg had purchased GED practice books for Brenda, encouraging her to study for the test. She had already passed the practice tests before her emancipation hearings concluded, and once ensconced in witness protection, she could schedule the real exam. As far as Greg knew, Brenda's formal education had stopped at eighth grade. With the GED, she could skip over high school and head straight into college.

"Honey, so long as you're here I will do everything I can for you, you can call me anytime. I'm going to see about getting clearance to see you and meet you and take you out. I know it's tough but I know you can read. I know you can watch TV.

"Whatever you need, we're going to get it," Greg continued. "The U.S. government has all those resources and they want to help you."

Brenda was silent, listening to the only man she could trust.

"Honey, you've got to get off the phone. You've got to get some sleep. It's just like being in jail—the first day is always the worst. It's a new environment. That first day is really long. You'll remember it forever," Greg said, empathizing with her.

He could sense she was feeling a little better.

"Look, have you got food in the place?" Greg asked. He wanted to make sure she had enough to eat.

"No, no," Brenda replied. "We bought a bunch of food, so I'm going to be fine."

After he hung up, Greg realized that loneliness would be a challenge for Brenda. He made a point to call her over the weekend to give her some company. Greg genuinely thought Brenda was slowly adjusting to her new life in the safe house, but he remained worried. Brenda had struggled through the Thanksgiving holiday, a time when family and friends get together. With Christmas around the corner, Greg feared that Brenda might reach out to her old friends.

ust under six months after she was arrested in Arlington, Brenda sat in her safe house alone. She was forced to wait out the time between the closure of the emancipation process and her entrance into witness protection, the opening of a new chapter in her life. Days blended into weeks, and Brenda couldn't sit still. She had to get out of the apartment, and she knew more or less when Alexander would stop by to check on her. It was easy for her to get out during the day and return in time for Alexander to stop by. Eventually her wanderings brought her back to the Arlington County Jail, where she knew her boyfriend was still behind bars.

Brenda and Denis had stopped talking after they were separated by Arlington police, but they never stopped writing. Brenda wrote him letters and he responded, sending her mail to the Landmark Juvenile Detention Center or the Fairfax Juvenile Detention Center. Brenda agreed to share these letters with Greg and Porter, but she never agreed to stop seeing Denis. He had replaced Veto as the love of her life, and Brenda had no intention of leaving him behind, despite his leadership status with the Mara Salvatrucha.

When Denis told Brenda to take care of herself in the back of the police cruiser after they were arrested in June, he knew his arrest meant the beginning of a long legal process that would likely find him guilty of a number of crimes.

After they were separated, Denis was placed in the Arlington County Jail while he awaited his trial date in December. It was shortly after his arrival that Detectives Rodriguez and Ignacio brought in his mom and aunt for the interview. Denis didn't love Brenda, but he respected her and saw in her a way to make himself more powerful. Brenda was also known as an MS member who had been jumped in by a clique from Los Angeles, and in Virginia such history meant instant street credit.

After his arrest in June, Denis was in a tight situation. He kept his mouth shut, but as the months rolled by, the realization of state and federal charges began to sink in. He wasn't up for just a few years. He was looking at a tall stack because of his state crimes and a possible death penalty for his federal crime. Denis remained a prime suspect for the Joaquin Diaz murder, and he knew it was only a matter of time before he would be charged with that murder and possibly locked up for life.

At the end of November, when his girlfriend moved into an FBI safe house, Denis Rivera decided it was time for him to talk to the police. He broke the Mara Salvatrucha's number one rule: don't rat.

Denis's lawyer called Rodriguez to say he had knowledge of the threats against him. That phone call corroborated Brenda's claim. Officers who worked as homicide or gang unit detectives were accustomed to threats made on their lives. This situation is never comfortable, no matter how experienced the detective. Rick Rodriguez didn't live in the Arlington area, but he still had to watch his back everywhere he went after the warning went out. The fact that a gangbanging punk could pull up to a stop light and unload a clip into his car was unnerving.

As word spread that the Mara Salvatrucha was out to kill Rodriguez, his chief pulled him off the gang unit detail. This upset him more than the threat against his life. Rodriguez was determined to get to the bottom of the threats and possibly help the investigating officers make an arrest so he could get past it and back on the gang unit detail. His boss was being cautious, but Rodriguez's die-hard attitude chomped at these constraints.

"Well, okay, but what does he know?" Rodriguez asked Denis's lawyer when he called at the end of November, skeptical Denis knew anything that would be helpful.

"Well, he wants to talk," the lawyer responded. He wanted to be very careful not to give anything away prematurely.

"Does he mind being interviewed?" Rodriguez asked, pushing a little.

"No. He will talk but there have to be certain things that need to be known. He'll help you guys, but are you going to help him?" the lawyer said. He was working to pull together some sort of deal for his client.

Deal or not, Rodriguez couldn't lose. There was a chance he could gain important information about the threats against his own life. He made it clear to the lawyer it didn't matter what his client said. The information his client shared had to lead to an arrest. There had to be results.

Rodriguez was interested in any information Denis had on the *luz verde* the MS issued on him. Anything else was a fringe benefit. It would be up to the Virginia commonwealth attorney prosecuting Denis's case and Rodriguez to decide if his information was valid.

Denis had a few cards to play, but he was running out of time. He would be tried on the malicious-wounding charge in December and likely convicted for the crime that Brenda had been unwilling to commit. He was sure to do some time, but if he could throw out a few names, there was a chance he could enjoy a reduced sentence.

Rodriguez, Denis, and Denis's lawyer were seated in an interview room at the Arlington County prison with the prosecuting attorney, a hard woman. Rodriguez tried not to be hopeful. Denis was a man with a vast knowledge of local MS activity, but everyone in the room knew he would serve some time at both the state and federal level. If Denis's decision to speak with the police ever hit the street, he would have serious trouble in prison. It would likely mean his death. Rodriguez was just as likely to catch a bullet on the street from one of Denis's homies. The two were locked into a dangerous game. Rodriguez had the prosecuting attorney and Denis's long list of crimes on his side. He was holding a number of cards. Denis likely knew who was ordered to kill Rodriguez. Stringing Rodriguez along long enough to get some time shaved off his state sentence was his only play.

"The things we're interested in are the following," Rodriguez began. "We're interested in knowing about stolen cars." Rodriguez knew Denis was a master car thief, but that was an easy pitch. Denis sat on the location of any number of stolen cars. "We want to know anything about who's taking them, where they're taking them to, and any robberies or any other crimes MS is committing."

That request was already a little harder for Denis to meet. As a cel-

ebrated MS leader, he knew better than most the consequences of ratting out his homies to the cops. Many of the cars MS members stole
were almost immediately driven to MÉXICO, where MS contacts south
of the border would buy them for a decent price. These cars were long
gone. There was no sense in talking about stolen cars, and both knew
it. But Rodriguez wanted to give Denis a way to gradually work himself up to sharing the most important information. Gang members who
were willing to talk rarely, if ever, gave up critical information during
the first interview.

Rodriguez pressed on. "We want to know about weapons trafficking and who has these weapons. And any crime you get wind of between this moment and whenever, we want to know about that too."

Rodriguez put pressure on Denis to talk. He knew what Denis was
up against. The young gangster would talk if he valued his freedom.
An extended moment of silence passed.

Then Rodriguez delivered the bottom line. "And, most importantly,
we want to know about any, *any* threats you have heard, or know of,
toward me or any other police officer, including Victor Ignacio."

"My understanding," Rodriguez said, focusing solely on Denis, "is
that what's kicking this off is the fact that you have information concerning threats about me."

Denis remained silent.

"So that is your ticket," Rodriguez said. "There is the big one."

He had made his position clear. It was now Denis's turn to deliver.

"Well, I can tell you where you can find a stolen Corolla," Denis
offered.

It was a start, and something Rodriguez could use to establish
Denis's credibility, but it was far from what he needed. Rodriguez had
little confidence in the young man as a star informant and was still
convinced Denis didn't care about where he was headed. He was looking at jail time as his final rite of passage, the moment in which young
gangsters graduate from small time to the real deal. But Rodriguez
knew Denis would never get out to enjoy his newfound respect on the
street.

"He's going to start by giving you little things," Denis's attorney
told Rodriguez after two fruitless interviews in late November and
early December.

"That's fine. We'll take whatever," Rodriguez said. Any shred of
information could help solve a crime. "But time is of the essence here,"

Rodriguez reminded the attorney. Rodriguez was able to talk to Denis as long as he was under the jurisdiction of Arlington County, which would hold until he had been tried for all his Virginia state crimes.

Leads on the threats against Rodriguez were thin. So far they had little more than Brenda's initial comments to work with. It was frustrating, and Rodriguez hated to think that the only man who had information preferred to play games with stolen cars. He knew damn well that Denis had information on the guy who was planning to kill him.

"Let's talk about stolen cars and let's talk about parties and let's talk about meetings, talk about assaults, that's all fine. But somewhere along the line he needs to lead up to who and when and why there are threats against me and any other police officer," Rodriguez told the lawyer, driving home his bottom line.

Denis continued to play. Interviews ensued, sometimes dragging out for hours with little to show for the time spent. One day, though, Denis identified MS members who had been captured on a security camera stabbing a rival gang member at a local hotel. Rodriguez thought that Denis might finally be willing to do more than blow smoke. Denis went further to reveal the location of a house in Maryland where some MS members lived, though the information did little to further the investigation into the threats against Rodriguez's life.

As hard as Rodriguez pushed Denis, he was not about to give up the information. There was much more at stake than winning a few years off his prison sentence. His life was on the line. Homies on the outside knew there were very few MS members under lock and key who knew the details of the plans to kill cops in Virginia. Any hint the police had found out and he would be a dead man.

Virginia's Mara Salvatrucha cliques were under pressure to prove themselves to their West Coast homies. A rift had grown between MS cliques in Virginia and California. Cliques on the East Coast were generally considered part of the new school of MS members. The hardened, old-school MS gangsters in California, who had experience fighting to the death for their turf, thought the East Coast cliques were a bunch of punks. They didn't put in their work and couldn't spread the power and respect of the MS in Virginia, Maryland, North Carolina, and New York. Virginia especially had garnered the ire of the California cliques. Northern Virginia was considered the most important region for the new-school MS cliques. Denis did his part to spread

MS respect and power in the region, but other leaders had not pulled their weight. In the eyes of the West Coast leaders, there simply were not enough bodies. The pressure intensified into the fall. Denis wasn't even on the streets, and he could feel it. Mara Salvatrucha clique leaders from California were in Virginia to get answers. They wanted to know why the Virginia homies had not yet killed any cops.

More pressure boiled up from El Salvador when a high-ranking member of the Sailors Locos Salvatrucha, a Salvadoran clique with members in California, Virginia, and Maryland, showed up in northern Virginia demanding that every individual in his clique kill two rival gang members every fifteen days. He was there to apply pressure. The Salvadoran clique leaders had received word that the Virginia new-school homies were soft. Together with the national leadership, they wanted to know why.

While Denis played hardball with Rodriguez, he was acutely aware of the shifting sands of power within the Mara Salvatrucha, subtle changes that didn't register with the police. Pressure from both California and El Salvador pushed down on his Virginia homies. A *luz verde* was out on both Ignacio and Rodriguez, but no one had the *cojones* to pull the trigger. Denis thought plans were in place to kill both, but he was locked up and didn't know the latest. He knew better than to ask about it while talking on a prison phone. He could only hope that someone would take out Rodriguez soon so the cop would stop bothering him.

Rodriguez remained on edge at work and discouraged until Denis's court date for the malicious-wounding charge arrived on a cold day before Christmas. An hour before his case was heard by the judge, Rodriguez and the prosecutor walked down to the holding cell to confront Denis directly.

"We're going forward with this case today," the prosecutor said, visibly irritated with Denis's lack of cooperation. "And you're screwed because you've given us *nothing*," she said, emphasizing the word.

After the prosecutor left, Rodriguez remained with Denis, hoping the weight of the last moments before his case would pressure him to say something.

"Denis," Rodriguez began, shaking his head. "Nothing, you've done nothing. Thank you for trying, but you've got nothing to show for it, nothing!" He couldn't help but show his frustration with the process.

Denis turned to his lawyer. "Can I tell him what I know?"

"Why are you asking him?" Rodriguez exclaimed. He had run out of patience with Denis's games.

"If you know something more, isn't it in your best interest and mine to share?" Rodriguez asked, not believing Denis had waited until the absolute final moment before sharing some information. He had been out on the street this whole time looking over his shoulder and enduring his office work, and he longed to be back on the streets on the gang unit detail.

"Hold on a second," Rodriguez said before turning to run and ask the prosecutor to convince the judge to delay the start of the trial by a couple minutes. Rodriguez returned with the prosecutor. "Okay, what do we have?" the prosecutor asked Denis.

Denis looked at his attorney, who was visibly uncomfortable with the situation. It dawned on Rodriguez that Denis probably had scared his defense counsel.

The prosecutor finally broke the silence. She wasn't willing to wait another moment.

"I've had it," she huffed. "I'm done. I'm outta here. If anything changes, Rodriguez, get to me before I start the trial. Once it starts we're not stopping," she said, already walking back to the courtroom.

"Denis, this is it," Rodriguez said, making his final play. "She's heading to the floor. When that judge comes back to the bench it's over for you."

Denis continued to stall, looking at his lawyer.

Rodriguez had reached his limit. He was angry and convinced Denis wouldn't talk. "I don't care if you open your mouth, at this point I'm not going to listen. Even if you tell me who's doing it or when or where, it's done," Rodriguez said.

Then the lawyer spoke. "Okay, here's what he's told me. It's Porky. Porky is the one," the lawyer said.

"You mean Curly?" Rodriguez turned to ask Denis. The two street names were used for the same guy.

"Yeah," Denis said in a low voice. Rodriguez gave Denis a physical description of Porky. He agreed it was the same guy.

Once Denis confirmed they were thinking of the same guy, Rodriguez walked out of the room and into the hall, where he could think back to an arrest he had made months ago.

Porky was an MS member and rumored to be an arms trafficker who lived in Arlington. Weeks before Denis and Brenda were arrested,

Rodriguez had visited him on a regular basis just to make his life difficult. When Porky robbed a check-cashing store, Rodriguez arrested
him, and put him behind bars for a long time.

After the robbery and before the arrest, Rodriguez had called
Porky's apartment number to see if he was there. A male voice answered
the phone, and Rodriguez pretended he worked at a local garage and
wanted to make sure Porky was home because the boss would call
soon with a job offer. The guy on the phone told him Porky was home
and wouldn't leave. With the trap set, Rodriguez and his partner drove
over to the apartment and knocked on Porky's door. He answered and
they arrested him for the robbery. It was a humiliating experience—
one that Porky never forgot.

Rodriguez stood outside the holding cell where Denis and his defense counsel waited to be called to court. He was spinning his wheels.
In just a few minutes someone would arrive to escort Denis to the
holding room just outside the courtroom. He had to figure out why
Denis gave him Porky's name, and quickly. Was Denis lying? He asked
himself if Porky was actually capable of pulling off the planning and
organization to kill a cop. Did he have enough pull in the MS to put a
luz verde on Rodriguez, then order younger members to kill him?
Could Porky be part of a larger plan to bring in members from another state to kill him? Rodriguez concluded that it was a stretch.
Porky had means and motive. There was reason and history, but one
thing was missing. Porky didn't have the backbone to organize the
death of a cop.

Denis was just being clever. Rodriguez remembered that Porky and
Denis had been in jail together since the summer. At least five, maybe
six months had passed. It was possible Porky was just running his
mouth about how he wanted to kill Rodriguez. Most gangsters behind
bars at the Arlington County lockup talked tough to keep up their
hardened street attitude, but few ever did anything about it. Rodriguez
considered Porky a screwup, and even if he had the *cojones*, he doubted
the kid had enough pull in the MS to put out a hit on a cop.

Denis had likely heard Porky's complaints, Rodriguez reasoned.
Many of the MS guys in the Arlington jail complained about Rodriguez. Porky stood out, but Denis knew it was just talk. He had used
the bogus information about Porky to prompt his lawyer to begin the
interview process with Rodriguez. He had wanted to play the detective
a bit, get some free phone calls to his homies, get off the cell block for

interviews, and take a stab at reducing his sentence. Rodriguez would follow up on the Porky angle just to be absolutely sure, but now he was convinced that Denis had never sincerely wanted to help.

Rodriguez left the holding cell area disgusted with Denis. He had allowed himself to consider Denis was willing to talk. But the kid was too far gone. He was willing to tell Rodriguez about small-time crimes, but killing a cop was a big deal inside the Mara Salvatrucha. Once the order was put out, only the highest-level leaders were involved in the planning and execution, not someone like Porky, or even Denis for that matter.

There were many working parts in plans to kill a cop, and much of the discussion occurred among leadership at the highest level. MS leaders had identified Detectives Rodriguez and Ignacio as a problem. They knew both had to be removed from the scene but were well versed about what happened when a cop was killed. Police, hell-bent on vendetta, would crawl the streets until a suspect confessed the deed. MS activities across at least three states in the mid-Atlantic region would have to be put on hold. And the murder would never blow over. The cops would hunt down the assassins until they arrested someone. A sacrificial lamb had to be planted and offered in the perfect way so the cops believed their investigation had led to the arrest, not the MS's careful planning and flow of misinformation. Such a planning process took months, Rodriguez thought as he took the stairs up to the courtroom floor, rounded the corner, walking past the doors of the courtroom where Denis would have his hearing, and ran into the last person he expected to see at Denis Rivera's trial.

CHAPTER 32

Brenda Paz sat on a bench by the wall, chatting pleasantly with Denis Rivera's sister.

Forcibly closing his jaw and regaining his composure from the shock, Rodriguez immediately turned to call Greg.

The cell only rang a few times. As soon as Greg answered, Rodriguez told him: "Hey, Brenda's in the courtroom. What's up with that?"

Greg was just as surprised. He had just finished a separate case in the same building and was on his way back to the office when he took Rodriguez's call. He immediately did an about-face and rushed to the floor where Brenda had been seen. Just as Rodriguez had said, Brenda was sitting on a bench outside the courtroom next to Denis's sister. She had already spoken with Denis and was waiting for him to get out of court so she could see him again.

Greg was incredulous when he walked up to her, and she turned around, happy and excited to see him.

"I found the metro!" she exclaimed.

"Honey, you can't do this! You can't do it!" Greg hissed through pursed lips, cursing under his breath and counting the ways Brenda had seriously jeopardized her security. *Stupid, stupid, stupid!* his mind screamed as he walked with Brenda away from the bench and Denis's sister.

"I found the metro and I came here to visit Denis because I knew he was in jail and I knew the court date was here today," Brenda said, bubbling with teenage excitement and clearly happy she managed to find her way out of the safe house to see her boyfriend. She was oblivious to Greg's frustration and the danger to herself.

"And the Rivera family, you know, they're so nice. His sister, she's really nice. And the mother, she's like my mother and—"

"Honey, no, no," Greg said, cutting her off. He tried to remain calm.

"There could be MS here. Maybe they don't know about you, maybe they do, but you just can't take that chance. You just can't take that chance." Greg repeated himself, trying to impress upon Brenda the weight of the danger. Greg could only assume the MS had already marked her for death.

CHAPTER 33

Greg was wrong: Brenda was safe. Even if local MS leaders knew Brenda was cooperating with the police, there would be no immediate order to kill her. Denis was protecting her.

Once Brenda was free, Denis was one of the first people she had decided to visit. It took her some time to figure out how to find him, but within days of his trial, she was able to visit him in prison. She told him about what had happened since they were separated, skipping over many of the details but not holding back the fact that she had talked to the police. Denis could have reacted with promises of death, but he had a reason to stay calm. He needed Brenda.

Through the winter, Denis had diligently doused any rumors of Brenda's treason within the local leadership ranks of the Mara Salvatrucha in Virginia. Days before his trial, Denis had to consider his future: he was looking at a heavy stack of time in Red Onion, a Virginia state prison with a nasty reputation for murder, gang rape, daily beatings, and other horrible stories. He had to make sure a hard reputation would precede him before he arrived. Brenda was part of that insurance plan.

After his first of many trials in Virginia, the reality of countless years behind bars spread before Denis like an endless highway. He was resigned to his fate and needed all the help he could muster to stay alive and out of the hands of prison predators. And that was only at the state level. The Joaquin Diaz murder case would be tried in federal court, which meant federal prison time—maybe life. He needed Brenda to tell as many people as possible of his horrible misdeeds and penchant for violence—to paint a picture more menacing than the reality Denis's pretty face relayed.

When Alexander found out Brenda had left the safe house to visit Denis in prison and at court, he instructed Greg to have another chat with her about the dangers of associating with MS members. Alexander wanted to remain nonconfrontational with Brenda and saw Greg as her primary disciplinarian. He hoped Brenda looked up to and respected Greg enough to listen to him.

After Greg's admonition at court, he took Brenda to dinner before dropping her off at the Farragut North metro station in D.C. She took the Red Line back to the safe house. When she opened the door on a cold, empty apartment, Brenda felt an emptiness in the pit of her stomach. No one was there to welcome her. There were no hugs, no inquisitive looks or questions about where she had been or what she wanted for dinner. She was alone. The kitchen was cold. So was her bed. It was so quiet she could hear the refrigerator hum. The phone never rang. Her magazines, books, and GED practice books were piled up on the table in the living room. Her recent conversation with Denis's sister made the stark silence of her apartment even more glaring. She desperately wanted companionship, a reason to laugh, or something to keep her from descending into past memories and the thoughts that clawed at her consciousness.

Brenda's loneliness gnawed at her logic and reason. She had a complex, deeply rooted emotional response to solitude. Alone in the safe house, there was far too much time to think about what she was doing, what she had done, and where she was headed. She alternated between wanting to return to the streets and embrace her homies' love or brace herself for what could be months of loneliness before she left the dark path she had started down when she met Veto in Texas. Surrounded by silence, she had trouble envisioning a brighter future when she could go home to California with something to show for all this time she had been away.

Brenda was scared and longed to reach out to someone who could just give her a smothering hug and tell her everything would be all right. She wanted to be someone's little girl. She wanted to be someone's best friend. She wanted to be part of a long conversation about anything. In that apartment, Brenda had no one but herself to keep company, and her mind refused to stop spinning out memories from her recent past.

Memories of violence bubbled to the surface of her consciousness. The blood, the screams, the rapes and abuse, and the images of pain were all cataloged in her head—as organized and neat as all the information she had recounted for the police. Her memory was photographic, and when she was forced to observe the violence perpetrated by her especially dedicated Mara Salvatrucha boyfriends and their followers, the scenes repeated in her mind's eye like a horror film. Except it was real. These things had happened to her and to people she knew—stabbings, cigarette burnings, rape, vicious beatings, murder. Brenda had seen much more than the average MS recruit, and when she was alone, those images swirled in her mind.

She kept those demons at bay around other people. She pushed the images and memories out of her mind with conversation, laughter, and the warmth she felt from the attention and companionship of friends and loud groups. Once under her control, the images didn't bother her, and she could talk about what she had seen and done with her usual bubbly charisma, despite the grim nature of her stories and the reality she described.

Brenda was a federal witness, waiting on the U.S. Marshals to enter the Witness Protection Program. She had graduated from local police informant to something much more important. But the price she paid for that status increased with every day she spent alone. Brenda knew she had to stay away from her MS friends, but the long hours of solitude defeated her better judgment. She needed company, if only to distract her from herself and her demons.

Greg and Alexander were not always around, and calling her mom was too expensive. Fatefully, the cell phone that kept her in touch with Greg and Alexander, the men who would escort her to a better future, was an ever-present liaison to her past. Between visits from Greg and Alexander's weekly checkup, Brenda commanded her own time for the first time since her arrest in June. She realized she could do whatever she wanted with no reprisal from Greg, Porter, Alexander, or anyone else. She could get away with just about anything. Solitude pushed her out the door. Her newfound freedom pulled her back to the streets.

With the taste of laughter on her tongue, Brenda made a decision. Almost as soon as she got home from Denis's first trial, she decided to call her friends. The only real friends she had—the Mara Salvatrucha.

CHAPTER 34

Brenda called her friends from the Centrales Locos Salvatrucha clique, the same group of guys she had hung out with when she first arrived in Virginia. She had been off the streets for a long time, though. There were questions. Explanations were required.

She remembered the things Greg and Porter had taught her. She lied about where she had been, what she was doing for the past six months, and why she was suddenly back. Brenda told them she was arrested and then held for questioning for a number of crimes they tried to pin on her, but she never told the cops anything. They kept her in juvenile detention and only recently let her out when her lawyer, some gringo, got her off the hook. When she got together enough money to call, she did. And now she was back. It was a lie delivered with enough truth to make it plausible. The respect she had earned held, as it had the night she snuck out from the Less Secure Facility in late July, and the Centrales members welcomed her back with open arms and little suspicion.

The clique's leaders, Oscar Grande, known as Pantera, and Cabro, got in touch with Denis to ask about Brenda. When Denis confirmed that Brenda was legitimate, they accepted it as truth. What was between Denis and Brenda was not their business. No one knew Denis was protecting Brenda to save his own skin.

Respected by Pantera and Cabro, Brenda was accepted as an honorary member by the rest of the Centrales members in Virginia. Apart from Pantera and Cabro, she reconnected with the men she liked the most during those summer days before she was arrested with Denis. Two of her favorites were Ismael Cisneros, known as Arana, the spider, and Pantera's little brother, Joaquin Grande, known as Diablito, "little devil."

Araña was an older MS member with a violent past. He grew up in Mexico City, where he was beaten as a child, so much so, a neurologist would later testify that it was the likely cause of his severe brain damage. His decision-making ability was severely inhibited. Abusing PVC pipe glue was thought to be another cause.

Araña had a small head, too small for a man his size, and it tilted to the right. He was slight of build and moved with a jerky motion. He kept his hair closely cropped, so it did little to cover up the scars on his forehead and the back of his head, where his dad had beaten him with a beer bottle. Araña was an experienced MS member, and, like many others, he considered it his only family. He also knew the reality of deportation. In 1999, he was arrested for a malicious wounding in Virginia and was deported to Mexico. Within three days he had worked through Mara Salvatrucha contacts to illegally cross the border and get back to Virginia.

When Brenda fell in with the Centrales, Araña had already earned a comfortable position of respect and power within his clique. In late 2001 he preferred to work hard, spend time with his kids, and hang out with the gang mostly on weekends. But he was still as dedicated as any other member of the Centrales.

Slowly, with some care at first but with more vigor after the first couple of calls, Brenda arranged to meet up with Diablito, Araña, and Pantera at destroyer parties. At the first party she immediately had to explain her long absence. But it wasn't a big deal. She had Denis's backing, and the clique leaders weren't asking the questions. They were satisfied.

Once she fell back into the gang life, Brenda tried to keep her street life separate from her life at the safe house, but it didn't last long. Before Christmas, some of the more suspicious guys from the Centrales followed her from a fast-food restaurant by her apartment building where she normally broke off from them to walk home. When they realized she had an apartment, she had to open it to them. Another quick lie settled all doubt. She told them her dad had sent her money to rent the place. Again, there was some truth to the lie. Someone else did pay for the apartment and food, but Special Agent Alexander was not her dad.

Back within the gang's embrace, Brenda fell into the same routine of dating the leader. Just as Rodriguez told Denis during their first interview days after his summertime arrest, his girlfriend wouldn't wait around for him forever. Once Centrales members started hanging out at the FBI safe house, it wasn't long before Brenda was sleeping with Pantera. He was considered the clique's second in command. It was a position he had earned over the years of doing work for his clique.

Cliques within the MS generally had two leaders, sometimes called the *primera palabra* and *segunda palabra,* meaning "first word" and "second word." When the clique leader could not attend a meeting, the second word would lead the meeting and make decisions. The power carried by the *segunda palabra* in larger cliques sometimes extended beyond the members immediately below his position. Larger, more respected cliques like the Centrales had some influence over smaller cliques in the local area. Because many of them mixed at destroyer parties and other MS functions, the *segunda palabra* of a larger clique garnered power and respect in an entire region. And then there was the promise that one day the *segunda palabra* would be first.

Pantera carried a number of tattoos above his neck, including a teardrop just below the outer corner of his left eye—indelible evidence of murder for the gang. His long eyelashes did little to cover his dark, penetrating stare. His eyes were like orbs with no distinction between pupil and iris. Pantera kept his head shaved but maintained an unshaven look on his jowls, chin, and moustache. His skin was a living parchment, full of amateur tattoos that told a story of a heart and soul given to the Mara Salvatrucha, a choice he had made long ago. Despite the numerous tattoos, Pantera was an attractive man. Dressed in tattoos and his preferred outfit of Dickies pants slung low on his hips, a white muscle shirt, white Adidas shoes, and a blue bandanna hanging out his back pocket to show color, Pantera was the embodiment of Hollywood's version of a Latino gangster.

Pantera had arrived from El Salvador at a young age. His parents were both forced to work, leaving Pantera, his brother, and his sister alone to take care of themselves. When he was old enough, Pantera joined the MS and didn't look back. There was no other life. He would not hesitate to kill for the gang or die for his homies.

Through Christmas and the New Year, Pantera continued to ask

Brenda where she got the money for an apartment. He still thought something was up. She repeatedly told him and her other homies that her dad put her up. Brenda added that he would come by from time to time to check on her, which was why sometimes she was out of touch for a few hours or even the whole day. But this was a thin lie, and one she did not deliver well.

Yet Brenda managed to live a double life. She was the perfect informant and teenager with a future to Greg, Alexander, and the other cops. She took practice GED tests and had polite conversations with lawyers, cops, and FBI agents. It wasn't hard and they were eager for anything she told them.

For her homies, she was Smiley, having a good time at parties at night and by day supporting her homies when she could in any money-making scheme they had going.

For many weeks Brenda's double life was harmless. Together with her homies, it was like old times, hanging out drinking Corona beer, telling stories of conquest and crime, and roaming the streets looking for excitement and avoiding the cops. With the newly found freedom legal adulthood allowed, the Mara Salvatrucha lifestyle flowed back into her life. She was living a dangerous lie, but it kept the loneliness at bay. Through her young and impatient eyes, it was worth the risk.

Greg and Alexander, as much as they wanted to keep her safe, were limited in what they could do. The FBI was not a babysitting service, and Brenda was legally released from Greg's care. He was still there for her as much as he was able, but he had to get on with his own life. The decision to stay safe and focus on the path to a bright future was ultimately Brenda's alone. It was her dangerous game to play.

CHAPTER 35

On one of his routine visits to Brenda's apartment not long after the New Year, Alexander noticed something was wrong. Brenda's refrigerator was empty. He zeroed in on the ice cream. The last time he'd checked her fridge, the ice-cream container had been full. Days later it was completely empty. He doubted Brenda could eat that much ice cream in such a short amount of time.

He was suspicious, so he confronted Brenda directly. For the first time since meeting him, Brenda lied to Special Agent Alexander. She told him she had met her neighbors down the hall, and sometimes they came over to hang out. The last time they came over, she had offered them ice cream. He didn't believe her, but realized there was little he could do about it, so he restocked the kitchen, then left, taking his worries with him. Then he began to put the pieces together. She had already been to visit Denis. It wasn't a stretch to assume she had probably reconnected with her friends in the Mara Salvatrucha too. He was very nervous for her safety. On his way back to Washington, Alexander made a mental note to see if he could hasten Brenda's induction into witness protection.

As soon as he arrived in Washington, Alexander visited Ronald Walutes, the attorney who wanted to use Brenda as a material witness for the government's case prosecuting Denis for killing Joaquin Diaz. "This process is taking way too long," Alexander told Walutes. By his count, Brenda had been in the FBI safe house for five or six weeks. She was restless, and he was convinced she had slipped back into the gang life despite the shroud of secrecy he tried to keep about her. They had nowhere else to keep Brenda. The safe house was her last option.

The courts had made her an adult, but she was still every bit a teenager in need of social interaction and attention, which neither he nor Greg could fulfill. Alexander feared the worst. If they didn't get her into witness protection soon, they might lose her.

There were disturbing signs, he told Walutes. Once when Alexander recharged Brenda's phone with prepaid minutes, he checked her outgoing calls. There were always numbers he didn't recognize. Every time he asked, Brenda had an excuse. Their hands were tied, and if Brenda wanted to play with her life and risk hanging out with the MS, it had to be her choice. No one was in a position to constantly watch over her.

Teenagers think they're invincible, important, and smart. Brenda was no exception. She walked a tightrope between the promise of a bright future and the possibility of falling into her past. But she thought no harm could come to her. She trusted Denis not to say anything and thought she had outsmarted Pantera and the rest. Brenda was hanging out with a bunch of guys who believed every word she said. Pantera's questioning eventually stopped, and Brenda was easily able to avoid Alexander's questions. He chose not to become confrontational with her. It wouldn't help to alienate her, he thought.

Brenda was always aware of when he was coming. Alexander had to let her know before he came by. He had his own key, but respected Brenda's privacy. For many weeks, Brenda lived the good life. The government paid her room and board and her gangster friends gave her company with no questions asked.

On a cold morning in mid-January, Brenda received a call from Alexander. He was coming over to check on her. She hung up the phone and began running around the apartment waking everyone up. She told the gangsters that her dad had called. He would arrive at any minute and she had to clean up the place before he got there. They had partied all night. The place was a mess, and there were people everywhere, curled up in sleeping balls across the living room floor and squeezed into every corner of the bedroom. Brenda woke everyone up and told them to leave. It was strange behavior. She was not the usual, laid-back Smiley. Brenda was barely able to cover her fear. Her two worlds were about to crash.

Maria Gomez was one of the girls sleeping on the floor. She had been hanging out with Brenda for some weeks. They had met at a Virginia Inn when the Centrales clique threw a birthday party for Maria and Pantera just after New Year's. Maria was not an MS member, but she was the mother of Araña's daughter and the sister of another Centrales member.

As Brenda ran around kicking people awake, Maria saw that someone had slipped a letter under the front door next to where she slept. She couldn't help but notice that the letter was from Denis Rivera.

Despite Greg's warnings, Brenda kept in touch with Denis from the first time she visited him in prison before Christmas. She wrote him constantly from the safe house, using her new apartment as the return address. Maria knew of Denis Rivera, and thought if Brenda received letters from him, it was something normal, not out of the ordinary.

But before leaving Brenda's apartment that morning, Maria saw what she thought was an undercover police car in the parking lot. It immediately made her suspicious, but she kept her thoughts to herself, knowing rumors were not appreciated with the Centrales clique. Besides, it was just a car with tinted windows, a flat paint color, and one spotlight on the driver's side.

Alexander arrived moments after Brenda cleared out the apartment. He ran through the routine questions. Did she need anything? Was she okay? Did she have enough food? Satisfied that Brenda's needs were met, Alexander left.

Maria's suspicions were confirmed less than a month later. When she was cleaning out a purse Brenda had borrowed from her weeks before, she found three business cards stuffed into the small inside pocket. Brenda had memorized the numbers and stored them in a safe spot—but then had forgotten that they were there. All the cards belonged to local police, including Rick Rodriguez, one of the cops the MS was trying to kill. It was a paper trail that led from Brenda directly to the Arlington police.

Maria grew worried for Araña. They had not been together for some time, but he continued to support her after he moved out of her parents' house five months after their daughter was born. If Brenda was talking to police, then at least Araña needed to know.

Like Pantera, Araña wore a tattooed teardrop at the corner of his left eye. He had killed for MS and would likely do it again. Yet there was more to Araña's life than the gang. He was older and more responsible, often working two jobs to send money back to his mom in Mexico. He regularly traveled back and forth across the border to visit his family, returning illegally to the United States to work. Sometimes it took him weeks to return.

Araña also gave money to Maria to help raise their daughter. If Brenda was talking to the cops, he could be deported, meaning a certain disruption in the monthly payments Maria relied upon to take care of their daughter. She was more worried about the money than whether Brenda had betrayed the Mara Salvatrucha.

She told Araña about the business cards, but he didn't want to believe Brenda was actually talking to the police. They were close. She was his homie, and he was her best friend in the clique. Sure, she could have cards, but he reasoned it was probably just some game she was playing with them. Brenda was smart. Maybe she was playing that cop Rodriguez. If she could get him to trust her, she could help set up his murder. There was no way she was ratting out MS homies. Besides, he hadn't heard anything from any other gang members he trusted about Brenda's possible treason. He told Maria to keep it to herself. Maria did as she was told and soon left the country to visit the father of her second child, who was living in El Salvador.

Not long after Brenda returned to the street scene, rumors began circulating on the street that Brenda was talking to the cops. Members of another MS clique in the northern Virginia area, the Silvas Locos Salvatrucha, were talking about how she had been seen with cops in the fall. No one in the Centrales clique wanted to believe them.

There were always rumors about this or that MS homie talking to the cops, and they always flared up right after an MS member was arrested and then set free. The paranoia was normal but not by itself a cause for alarm. Until there was concrete evidence, the Centrales could ignore what the Silvas said.

Brenda was still safe, but both Denis and Araña knew something. Denis protected her for selfish reasons. Araña was confused about what the cards meant. He was not at all convinced his homie Smiley would betray the MS, and he decided to keep his own council on what Maria had shown him. But he couldn't shake a need to know why she had cop business cards, especially Rodriguez's.

While Araña considered the possibility of Brenda ratting out her homies, Alexander and Greg worried about Brenda's seemingly flippant attitude toward her security. All the men could do was wait and hope that every time they called she would pick up, or when they came by to visit, she would answer the door.

The day she didn't answer was on the Monday before Valentine's Day nearly three months after Alexander had moved her into the safe house.

CHAPTER 36

Alexander arrived at the safe house with his partner and knocked on the door. There was no response. Alexander used his key to unlock the bolt and with the other hand slowly opened the door, calling out for Brenda. He was enraged by what he found inside. The whole apartment was torn apart. Cigarette butts and empty Corona bottles were strewn about. Furniture was ripped and broken. There was food smeared on the floor and walls.

But there was no Brenda. The apartment was empty.

His first reaction was to call Greg and tell him Brenda was missing. She had disappeared and Alexander had no idea where she was or how long she had been gone. He was upset and angry and didn't try to hide it from Greg.

Worried, but not surprised with Brenda's behavior, Greg began working the phones, calling everyone he knew on a short list of people connected to Brenda to try to get a lead on her. He told them he was her lawyer and had some money in an escrow account he needed to get to her. It was a common excuse he had used in the past, and it normally worked.

After he spoke with Greg, Alexander and his partner picked through the mess, trying to make some sense of what had happened. Then there was a knock on the door. Alexander looked through the peephole and saw that it was a kid with tattoos snaking up his neck.

Alexander flung open the door, grabbed the kid, jerked him inside, and slammed the door shut. He got in the kid's face and demanded answers. The luckless kid at the other end of Alexander's wrath was a young MS member. He quickly told Alexander there had been a party on Saturday, two nights before. He was there but ran when the cops showed up.

"Who owns this apartment and where are they?" Alexander asked, interested to see what the kid knew.

The kid replied the owner wasn't around and left just before the cops showed up. Alexander then told the kid to get lost and immediately got in touch with the Montgomery County Police Department, which had jurisdiction over the area. Within a couple of hours, Alexander had the police report and a better idea of what had happened.

The police had responded to calls from Brenda's neighbors who were complaining about the noise. Kids were running up and down the halls shouting. The apartment had become the center of a high level of rambunctious activity. When the police arrived, they found the place mostly empty. The apartment still smelled of weed and cigarettes. Whoever was there left only minutes before the police arrived. There was one girl left who said three guys had raped her. The police interviewed her, but she didn't remember much.

Alexander's anger returned. He couldn't believe what had happened. In one fell swoop, Brenda had burned a safe house, ruined a perfectly good apartment, endangered her life, been involved in underage drinking and drug use, and possibly been complicit in the gang rape of a runaway girl. He was in a bind. If they found Brenda, he couldn't put her in another FBI safe house. If they didn't find her, he didn't want to think about what might happen.

Frustrated, he called Greg a second time to try to figure out what they would do.

"Greg, look, we've got to do something here," Alexander began. "If she stays on the street, she's putting her life at risk."

A full-scale manhunt involving the police or the FBI was not prudent, because it brings more attention to the individual. Luckily, when Greg took Alexander's second call, he already knew Brenda was safe for the time being. Brenda had called him, but she was not interested in being found and didn't tell Greg where she was.

"But that's what she wants to do. She wants to stay on the streets,"

Greg told Alexander, clearly not happy with Brenda's decision, but not in a position to force her to do anything.

"She doesn't want to go back to the safe house, and she does not want to go to a hotel," Greg said. He felt obligated to respect Brenda's rights even if he knew her judgment was clouded and might get her killed. Brenda had told him she'd found a place to squat in a garage at a friend's house. Anything, she said, was better than hanging out alone at the FBI safe house.

"She feels like she's okay to stay on the streets until the government is ready to physically relocate her," Greg concluded. He was frustrated but determined to remain calm and collected about Brenda's extremely poor judgment. He had to remember she was an adolescent, despite the gravity of her current situation and what she had already experienced.

Greg was also just beginning to understand the real depth of her loneliness. Brenda could not deal with being alone. That was why she chose to risk a safe environment by inviting MS members to stay with her. Their partying forced her to flee local police and live in an unheated garage in the middle of winter. Rather than be alone and safe, she chose to run around with men who would not hesitate to kill her if they knew she was talking to the cops.

Brenda had made her decision. She told Greg she would live the street life as long as she could before entering the Witness Protection Program, but that didn't stop Alexander, Rodriguez, and Porter from looking for her, or Greg from doing everything he could to convince her to come back into custody and assured safety. His contact with her was limited. Brenda had left everything at the safe house when she ran away with the MS. She had even left her cell phone, severing the only way Greg had to contact her. He could only wait for her to call.

CHAPTER 37

Days passed packed with tension, worry, and frustration. Then she called.

"Honey, you've got to come in." It had been a little over a week since Brenda had hit the streets.

"No, maybe not," she responded, clearly not liking the idea of protective custody. "Maybe I can just get a job," she said optimistically. She tried to get a job at Chuck E. Cheese's but Greg later found out from the manager that Brenda was not hired because of her excessive gang tattoos.

Brenda was high on the street life, but Greg was worried about something much more sinister than her difficulties with getting a job. He thought the MS was babysitting her, gaining her confidence so they could easily kill her when she least expected it. He didn't have any hard evidence, but he told Brenda his concerns. He kept to himself the fact that it was a feeling that kept him awake every night Brenda was on the streets.

As long as Brenda's with her homies, Greg thought, they're not in a rush to kill her. As they had done with so many other fellow members who had to be killed, Brenda's MS homies were content not to show their hand. If the rumors of her betrayal were true, the best place for her was near them so they could deal with her if necessary. If the rumors were just lies, there was no sense in disrupting the peace. Greg thought her homies in Centrales would babysit her and let her believe that everything was cool until they heard otherwise. This was standard procedure.

He couldn't shake the feeling that Brenda did not have much time. Greg was constantly worried about Brenda. She was on the streets and her safety was completely up to her. He felt helpless and it ate at him. This big man, who could barrel over any presence in a courtroom, couldn't get a sixteen-year-old girl to listen to sense. Worse yet, a sixteen-year-old girl he cared about. So this is what dads must feel like, he thought.

Alexander, Rodriguez, and Porter all agreed: Brenda could be killed any day. They were all determined not to let the MS kill her, but they had no way to get in touch with her. She would call to chat with Greg, but rarely let him know where she was hanging out.

There was little percentage in looking for her, but they continued to try. After a long day at work, Alexander would go home, have dinner with his wife and kids, and then call Greg to see if he wanted to go look for her again.

Rodriguez and others reluctantly contacted Denis to ask him if he knew Brenda's whereabouts. Denis did everything he could to help them locate her. He worried she might let something slip about their conversations, especially that Denis had not reacted when she told him she was cooperating with the cops. Any MS member who wanted to know what Brenda was up to would go first to Denis. She was easier to protect if he knew she was off the streets. He passed along the names of restaurants, identified corners, fast-food restaurants, and other locations where he thought Brenda could be hanging out.

Brenda had been missing for over two weeks at the end of February when Alexander called Greg to tell him there was an opening in the Witness Protection Program coming up in mid-March. If they had Brenda, she could enter the program. If not, the window would close. They had roughly two weeks to bring her in.

Everyone involved redoubled their efforts to find her. Alexander printed out a list of phone numbers he had taken from Brenda's cell phone and passed them to Greg. With the list in hand, Greg called every number, telling whoever answered he had some money for her. He hoped the allure of money would get the message out.

Eventually, Greg's phone rang.

Brenda called him from a pay phone at Fairfax Circle and asked if she could see him. He immediately got in his car and drove to the Dunkin' Donuts where she said she would be waiting. When he arrived, Brenda sat inside the store with another female friend. Greg assumed it was just another runaway Brenda was so fond of mothering and paid her no attention. He only had time for Brenda.

Greg left the runaway at Fairfax Circle and drove Brenda to a nearby restaurant where they could have dinner and not worry about running into MS members. He tried to reason with her. He used every argument he had to convince her to come back, but it was nothing new. Brenda had heard it all before.

After dinner, Greg took Brenda back to their meeting spot. Brenda said she could walk back to where she was staying. Before they parted, she showed Greg a new tattoo on her arm. Denis had drawn the stencil used to needle the ink into her skin. The tattoo was of an evil clown smoking a cigarette with MS and 13 on its hat.

"You know you can come to my house, and we'll get you set up with a temporary place to live," Greg said with a stern voice, standing outside the Dunkin' Donuts before Brenda turned to walk away. "But you know the rules. If you come over, you're turning yourself in. I can't support your lawless lifestyle. I just can't," Greg said, warming up for another lecture. It was heartfelt.

"There are a lot of people putting out for you and we'll do a lot for you, but there are conditions. And you don't actually have to testify. The fact that everybody thinks you are going to testify is enough to get you the protection. If you don't want to testify, you don't have to. They will extend the same protection, because at this point they have to," Greg argued, knowing Brenda's greatest fear was testifying against Denis and Veto. "But at this point, you've got to come in." Greg knew he had her attention. "There are conditions, but they're all good for you. They are conditions you asked for. You asked me, you agreed with me that this needs to be done, and I went out and I did it. And Alexander did it. And Rodriguez did it."

Brenda deeply wanted to find a new future but not one where she had to spend long periods of time alone. Greg reminded her of the people who were invested in helping her find a new future. But the conditions were her entry into witness protection and complete severance from MS.

"Go on down the list of people," Greg pushed on, wanting her to think of all the people working to help keep her safe and pointed toward a better future. "And you know it's the best thing for you. You know if you stay out here, even if nobody in MS does know and you completely get away with it and you talk your way back in the gang, there's still a chance you'll wind up . . . But he couldn't finish. Greg didn't want to admit out loud the fate he knew could be hers if she didn't seek the safety of a new identity and a physical relocation. Brenda was also aware of this possible fate, but unlike Greg she saw the situation as one she could control. She had the boys all fooled. They would never hurt her.

With that, they parted. Greg wasn't sure if he would ever see her again. He had done his best to convince her to come in, but she had resisted. Her fear of loneliness continued to win over logic and the promise of a better future.

Before Brenda could walk away, Greg grabbed her hand and showed her the tattoo between her thumb and index finger of three dots that signaled the three destinations of the gangster life, and used Brenda's own gang reality to make his point.

"In the hospital, in the jailhouse, or in the grave."

CHAPTER 38

When Brenda called Greg from a pay phone outside a McDonald's a couple of days later she was tense and speaking quickly in a low voice. It was the first time Greg had heard fear in her voice.

"I really think I'm in trouble," Brenda said, nearly whispering. Her voice was shaky. "I've figured out they're babysitting me, and I may be in real trouble with some of these guys." Brenda forced the words out, triggering Greg's immediate alarm and concern.

"Okay, do you know where you are," he began.

"No."

"Do you know what road you're on?"

"No."

"Can you tell me some of the places you see?" Greg asked, desperate.

"Well, there's a Marshalls nearby." Brenda made no effort to hide her fear. "And there's a Total Beverage." There was only once place in the area where Brenda could be. She was at the McDonald's on Little River Turnpike in Fairfax County.

"Honey, I'm coming," Greg said. He hung up and rushed out the door to his car. With one hand he steered the racing vehicle to the McDonald's where Brenda was hanging out with the men who had scared her. With the other hand, Greg worked his cell phone, paging a number of cops. There was no time to wait for them to respond. He had to get to her as fast as possible, but if anything went down, he wanted them to know there was an emergency.

Greg was so nervous, he cursed when he mistakenly took a slightly longer route. He ended up on the opposite side of the highway from the McDonald's where Brenda was anxiously awaiting her rescue. It was a four-lane road in a busy section of the northern Virginia metropolis.

The fast-food restaurant sat up off the road on an embankment supported with a two-foot concrete retaining wall. In the left-turn lane with his blinker flashing just past the McDonald's, Greg willed the light to change. It couldn't turn green fast enough.

Greg was looking over his left shoulder at the fast-food restaurant when the glass-paneled door at the far side entrance flew open. He saw Brenda taking off at top speed. Four MS members sprang out of the slowly closing door, just paces behind her.

Brenda slid down the loose gravel embankment, leaped down the retaining wall, and sprinted across two lanes of traffic before jumping over the concrete median and skidding around the back of Greg's car.

As she got to his car, the men chasing her were in the middle of traffic, just a lane away.

"Drive, drive, drive!" Brenda shouted as she jerked open the door and jumped in, wide eyes staring at her narrowly averted fate. Boxer, the same guy who had thrown the basketball at Brenda's head when she was in juvenile detention and a member of Denis's clique, led a group of tattooed gangbangers. He was only feet away. If they caught her, Brenda's smile would not get her out of trouble.

Greg didn't hesitate. He stomped on the gas and ran the red light. As he took off, one of the guys chasing Brenda got so close he smacked the back of Greg's car with his fist. Greg raced at top speed to the Arlington Police Department, breaking half a dozen traffic laws on the way. He wasn't worried about the cops. If they stopped him, that would be great.

PART 4

reg came to a screeching stop in front of the police department. He didn't care if he was illegally parked. He forgot the emergency blinkers and just focused on getting Brenda inside to safety. They got out of the car, and as Brenda rounded the front of the car to join him on the sidewalk, Greg turned to lead her into the building. He was anxious, sweaty, and nervous. Looking around for any sign that MS had followed them to the police department, he pressured her to go in. She wouldn't budge.

"I can't," Brenda said matter-of-factly.

Stunned, his heart pounding in his chest, Greg demanded, "Why? What's the problem?" Safety was just steps away and she didn't want to move.

"Just a second," Brenda said, beginning to unbutton her pants.

Greg stood there, at a loss as to what would happen next. They were standing in front of the Arlington County Police Department main entrance in broad daylight. What the hell was in her pants?

Before he could open his mouth and insist they go inside, no matter what she had in her pants, she pulled out a switchblade with a narrow sharpened blade that was nearly three inches long.

"I picked it up this morning. If any of them tried anything on me, I was going to stick them," Brenda said.

She handed him the knife. He fingered the knife in his hand, wondering if the day could get any weirder, then put it in his pocket. He planned to get rid of it before they headed past security.

As they entered the building, Greg asked the guard to hold on to the knife, feeling a sense of relief at having finally achieved safety. He led Brenda upstairs to Detective Rodriguez's office, where he called Porter and Alexander. Both men had spent long hours looking for Brenda. They would be relieved to know she was back in custody.

Once Greg reached Alexander, he received news he'd been waiting to hear. "I've heard from the Witness Protection Program. They'll take her in two days," Alexander explained.

"But do you have a safe place to keep her until then?" Greg asked, looking over at his precocious ward, who was sitting in a nearby chair, flipping through a magazine. He was still concerned Brenda might act like a teenager again and try to make it on her own.

"Yeah, I've got a place far out in the country," Alexander said. "Stay put. I'm on my way over."

Greg heaved a huge sigh of relief. This was it. She would go with Alexander, wait a couple days, and then formally enter the program. No more shenanigans, no more bullshit. He approached Brenda with the news.

If she behaved, she would be moved out of the state, given a false name, and placed under the protection of the U.S. Marshals. Greg wouldn't be able to see her, and she wouldn't be able to speak to anyone from her past.

Brenda agreed to everything, but she had one last request. She wanted to speak to Denis. Greg couldn't say no. Rodriguez, who was listening in on their conversation, also did not have a problem with letting her make the call. Rodriguez still held out hope that something about the plot to kill him would come up in this last conversation with Brenda.

Rodriguez arranged the phone call. With Brenda on one line and Denis on the other, Greg and Rodriguez were able to listen to the recorded conversation.

Brenda was understandably emotional. She had just been chased by a group of men who would have beaten and tortured her if she'd been caught. It was only an hour later, and she had to say good-bye to Denis, someone she considered a real friend, someone she loved and trusted.

Greg was surprised when Denis began to cry.

"This was a good thing for you," Denis said, sharing with Brenda what both already knew. They were both cooperating with the police. "Go do this," Denis continued, clearly emotional. "I'm fucked. I'm in prison. I'm done. I love you."

Brenda was crying and still upset when she said her last good-bye and hung up. It was painful for Greg to watch, but he knew it was a necessary step for Brenda.

Alexander arrived soon after Brenda's phone call and took Brenda to a hotel more than two hours away. There was little risk of her meeting up with her friends. Brenda spent that night and the next day alone before Alexander picked her up. It was her last night before she entered witness protection, and her last dinner with Alexander and Greg. They decided on an Italian restaurant near Quantico. When Greg arrived, Brenda was bouncy and excited. He was so pleased to see her happy. At dinner, she even showed off the pasta-eating skills that Greg had taught her months ago. They both laughed fondly, remembering the night he took her out after she had snuck out of the Fairfax County Less Secure Facility. Dinner was relaxing and fun. Brenda was surrounded by men who cared about her. Just as in the MS, Brenda loved being the center of attention. The one difference was, these powerful, engaging men meant to keep her safe.

Of all the men and women invested in Brenda's future, Greg knew Brenda best; he knew that her only option for survival was witness protection. Perhaps better than the rest, he also recognized the challenges the program created for someone like Brenda. Witness protection was a tough decision for her. Loneliness would be her only companion for many months while she worked to create a new life. They both knew too well that Brenda did not deal well with being alone. It had been their biggest trial during their journey together. Greg hid his concerns amid the happy faces at dinner and decided to hope for the best.

Before they parted, Greg took the books he'd loaned her, and gave Brenda her own copy of *Crime and Punishment*, another book on how to handle worst-case scenarios, and *Catcher in the Rye*.

After a big bear hug, Greg watched Brenda walk out of the restaurant with Alexander and drive away a second time to safety and into a bright new future.

CHAPTER 40

Brenda's "new future" would begin with orientation meetings, lectures, rules, and explanations. Not a very bright start. In fact, she hadn't known that she'd have to spend the next couple of weeks learning the structure of her new life, bogged down in the minutiae and paperwork as she separated the new Brenda from her old name and past.

Brenda wasn't the only one unhappy. After waiting out the two days between her McDonald's near miss and her delivery to the federal marshals, Alexander had discovered that Brenda had called gang members from her hotel and cell phone. Alexander had given back her safe house cell phone, and in only two days, she certainly had made use of it. Some of the same numbers on the phone before she took off with the gang were back on the registry. She had called her friends from the hotel.

Alexander liked Brenda and was 100 percent dedicated to her protection, but he was a straight shooter, and he was realistic. She was a constant frustration. He knew from her previous behaviors that it was likely that she would do something immature again, like run off. Her calls to her gang buddies only confirmed his worries. He'd spent many a long night looking for her in just about every corner of northern Virginia. She had been missing for weeks before Greg had rescued her from the McDonald's. For all he knew at the time, she could have been dead.

Plus, he fumed inwardly, she had trashed the FBI safe house. Alexander had to take responsibility for acquiring new furniture and getting the carpet cleaned. Truthfully, the safe house was just an annoyance. He acknowledged that she was young and simply needed protection, not only from the gang but from her own youthful desires. He was truly worried about her safety. She just wasn't getting the message that she had to *stay away from the gang or she would be killed*.

Alexander continued to deal with Brenda's tendency to do whatever she wanted despite the potential harm to herself. He didn't empathize with Brenda's problems with loneliness. From his perspective, her conduct at the hotel was simply a breech of security. He decided to use the drive to her dropoff point as an opportunity for a lecture.

"If you start playing these games with the U.S. Marshals, they're not going to be as forgiving," Alexander began. "They're going to take note of it, and they're going to kick you out. And any chance of you starting a new life away from the gang is going to be lost forever." Brenda sat in silence, hoping he would drop the subject, but he was just warming up.

"Look, you know every time you reach out to them, you know it doesn't take much for them to do the callback and have the hotel number and find out what hotel you're staying in. I'm saying your caller ID is out there and readily available," he explained, sounding frustrated.

Not only was she putting her life in danger, but she was endangering his and his partner's lives. As they made their way down the road, Alexander kept lecturing. Brenda was quiet. She had heard it all before, but from Greg. Alexander had never used such strong admonition. She was about to enter witness protection. There was no room for half listening and then doing whatever she wanted. This time it was for real. She was in a car with an FBI agent who had every intention of turning her over to the marshals. For any teenager this was serious business.

As Alexander talked, Brenda's focus turned inward, to her own thoughts. This is it. There is no return. You break the rules and you're out, on your own. There was no turning back to her life in Texas, or the life she had had with her family in California. Brenda Paz as the world knew her would have to disappear. She was not happy about going into witness protection, but she was resolved. She knew it was the right thing to do. If she ever wanted to see her family again, her only option was to push forward through witness protection and hopefully come out years later with enough distance from her past to risk doing so, but the thought of so much time away from her family put her stomach in knots.

When the car stopped, Brenda roused herself from her deep thoughts and realized that they finally had arrived at the dropoff point. Alexander checked her to make sure Brenda was not carrying anything that could harm the marshals. The last thing he wanted to do was to hand over a potentially dangerous individual. This treatment, though, reminded Brenda that although these men protected her, they were not family, nor were they her friends. For them, especially the marshals, she was a job.

Satisfied that Brenda was clean, Alexander told her to grow up. It was a strange mix of demand, annoyance, and caring. Brenda looked at him gravely, sensing the seriousness of the moment, then gave him and his partner a hug. She got into the car that would escort her to her new reality without a backward glance. It was last time Alexander ever saw her.

CHAPTER 41

Over the following days and weeks, Brenda's life completely changed. She was in a new world, one sequestered from normal life on many levels. Secrecy was paramount. Along with a number of other federal witnesses, Brenda moved into a hotel in Philadelphia where she went through weeks of background checking. Her past was combed for details that had to be scrubbed out of existence. New papers were fabricated. At first, she thought it was actually kind of cool when they handed her the new driver's license and a new name.

The end of March came and it was her birthday again. Brenda was in a hotel room in Philadelphia, alone. It was the second birthday she had spent by herself. The loneliness was an ache in her heart, but she knew it was a very sensitive stage of the Witness Protection Program and she was forbidden to call anyone. Brenda turned on the TV and reflected on being seventeen. She sighed and flipped through the stations. The television was her only company for the night.

Brenda was, in fact, fascinated with the process of creating a new past. She had done a good job of creating stories herself while in the MS. Now, thanks to the marshals, she was from Ohio. Texas and California were completely erased. Her past life in Virginia disappeared, and the pieces that couldn't be removed were buried under secrecy and protection. It sure is easier changing your story on the streets, she often thought, as the weeks went by. All documents relating to her past life were altered or erased, and a new identity was created. It was one thing to make up a story that people believed; it was altogether another to make that story true on government papers. Like many of the other witnesses, Brenda also enjoyed the first opportunity in a long time to sleep the deep sleep of someone who is truly safe. She was surrounded by protection twenty-four hours a day, fed and housed, and given any amenity she required, within reason and the law. Once Brenda was settled into the routine of the marshals' orientation program, she did what was most natural to her and reached out to someone who would talk to her.

She befriended a Latino boy who was not a member of MS-13 but was under similar circumstances. He was in her cohort of witness protection entries. He had entered the program at roughly the same time she did and was staying in the same hotel as Brenda during the orientation process. Over the weeks they spent together, it was easy to grow close. Around him, in this new world, she could be anyone. They were young, in a completely novel environment, and safe. Where some teens would be at camp or headed off to college, these two were holed up in a hotel, running from a strange and scary past, with no one else to turn to. They spent every moment together, and he quickly became her new best friend and lover.

reg heard from Brenda just as spring broke in northern Virginia, weeks after he had dinner with Alexander and her in Quantico. She called from Philadelphia to say she had lost her purse and needed him to wire her some money.

He didn't believe she'd lost her purse, but he knew that whatever the real story was, if she was asking for money, she probably needed it. She asked for $200, but he wired $300. This was when he learned her new identity.

Brenda Paz was now Ellysia Gonzalez.

What Greg didn't know was that the marshals had placed Ellysia Gonzalez in Kansas City, not Philadelphia. Brenda's new apartment was on a nondescript street. Her days consisted of reading and studying for her GED and sometimes going out to look for temporary work with the help of the marshals. Anyone who knew Brenda would have foreseen that she'd grow bored. All she could think about was seeing her new boyfriend from Philadelphia. He was the only person she knew in her new life.

Fed up and bored, Brenda had taken all of the money that the marshals had given her and bought a one-way ticket from Kansas City to Philadelphia. After a couple of days in Philadelphia, reality dawned. She realized in a tense moment that she needed to get back to Kansas City before the marshals found out she was missing. There was one man that she knew she could count on. Greg was the person she called.

With her new Ellysia license, Brenda picked up the $300 from a convenience store a block away from Philadelphia's Ninth Street Italian market. She booked a flight back to Kansas City and again disappeared into the secret world of witness protection.

She surfaced weeks later when she called Rick Rodriguez's cell phone. "Whatcha doing, Rodriguez, you barbecuing?" she asked in a bubbly, nonchalant manner.

Brenda was still in Kansas City, and Rodriguez's cell phone was one of the numbers she had memorized. Out of boredom she just called him. When he answered, she had made a lucky guess about what he was doing. It was during the afternoon on the weekend. Chances were he was barbecuing.

Rodriguez was spooked. The detective assigned to discovering who had put the *luz verde* on Rodriguez had not yet closed the case, and Rodriguez thought maybe Brenda was spying on him. But it didn't make sense. He knew she was in witness protection. He chatted with her for a bit, then got off the phone and tried to forget she had even called. How weird, he thought.

When Brenda called again less than a week later, describing exactly what Rodriguez was wearing when he had exited the Arlington County police building, he got mad. Brenda had obviously been in town— that's how she knew what he'd been wearing. His worries intensified when he realized she had been watching him, even possibly spying on him. Perhaps she was setting him up for some type of ambush. He focused considerable effort on figuring out what was going on, where Brenda was staying, and, most importantly, if she was back in Virginia to help pull off the *luz verde* on his head. But that wasn't the case. Brenda had flown from Kansas City to Baltimore and taken a bus into Arlington not to spy on Rodriguez, but to see Denis.

Kansas City was boring. She didn't like the program and needed her friends. Of all the people Brenda thought she could reach out to, Denis was her first pick. She still loved him. And she felt very comfortable around his family.

While in Arlington, Brenda stayed with Denis's parents. When she went to see Denis, she saw Rodriguez as he was leaving the Arlington County prison where Denis was awaiting trial for the murder of Joaquin Diaz.

Rodriguez was on fire. It was spring, and through the entire summer, fall, and winter of the previous year he'd lived with the threat on his life. The pressure was getting to him. Denis still hadn't given him any information, and the detectives working his case hadn't found any solid leads. As far as he knew, Brenda was in witness protection, but suddenly she was back in town and knew what he was wearing. This was the last thing he needed. He put out an all-points bulletin on Brenda and then called Greg.

Greg was alarmed by the news. Dammit, he thought, I should've known it. He started making phone calls and eventually learned Brenda was staying with Denis's parents. Not good. He looked up the address and immediately went to the Riveras' house, where he found Brenda and took her to a restaurant. He wanted to shake some sense into the girl, but he knew the way to win her over was to appeal to her intelligence and convince her to go back to witness protection. She obviously had no clue what she was doing.

Brenda was sullen at the restaurant, picking at her food with her fork as she explained her frustration with the marshals. She told him she was in Kansas City and lived in a bad neighborhood. It was full of methamphetamine addicts, whom she called "tweakers." Greg pointed out that though the situation wasn't ideal, it was a hell of a lot better than being here, where there were many people who wanted to harm her. She needed to stay in witness protection. Brenda countered that Denis was protecting her from the MS. He would make sure no one knew she was talking to the cops, and she could handle Denis. She trusted him.

Greg didn't trust Denis. Brenda looked at Denis through rose-colored glasses, but Greg saw something entirely different. Any kid who could do what Denis did to Joaquin Diaz could not be trusted, ever. Why didn't Brenda see that? Greg knew Denis couldn't protect her forever, if protecting her was even his intention. His house was the last place she should be hiding out. She was playing a dangerous game. Bottom line, she needed to get back to Kansas City, and fast. Greg's arguments were clear. He appealed to her logical side. He used every bit of his persuasive nature and southern charm to win Brenda over. He pointed out that Kansas City wasn't that bad. She had met a few people, and, as Greg reminded her, she even liked the federal marshal assigned to her case. He worked on her slowly, winning her over to good sense.

By dessert Brenda had agreed to return. After all, Greg wasn't a lawyer for nothing. If anyone could change her mind, he knew he had the power, and he'd done his best to wield it for her sake. However, she wanted to spend one more night before going back to the program. Greg knew it was risky because when Brenda was thinking on her own, she tended to follow her impulses, not her head. Right now he had her thinking objectively, just as he wanted. However, it was her life and he had to respect her need to make her own choices. He went home and eased his concerns by booking her a flight back to Kansas City for the following day. The next morning, just after breakfast, he drove over to Denis's parents' house to get her. Thank God she's still here, he thought when he arrived.

Greg made a day of it for Brenda before the flight, taking her to see some movies at the Lockheed Martin IMAX National Air & Space Museum. When it was time to drive her to the airport, he parked and escorted her inside, determined not to let her out of his sight. He couldn't get her back to Kansas City fast enough for his peace of mind. After spending many hours killing time before her flight, Greg finally saw Brenda off with a sigh of relief.

Brenda's trip to Virginia was actually the fourth time Brenda had voluntarily left protective custody. First, she had run away from the Less Secure Facility in Fairfax. Then she had abandoned the FBI safe house to live on the street. Recently she'd snuck away from the marshals in Kansas City to fly to Philadelphia. Now she had slipped away again to visit Denis in Arlington. All four times Greg was there to bail her out of trouble, possibly saving her life on every occasion. He couldn't, and wouldn't, always be there for her. Brenda had to make her own decision to stay put, to stay safe.

Witness protection, formally known as the Witness Security Program, was not designed for teenagers. It was created to provide a safe living space for middle-aged federal witnesses who were willing to testify against organized-crime bosses in New York and Chicago. It was a program mostly for men who needed to disappear with their families. Essential informants in ongoing federal investigations into organized crime, these men had a reason to stay out of sight and mind. They sought to protect their families. By placing Brenda under witness protection, the government acknowledged the importance of her cooperation and the value of her knowledge of the inner workings of the Mara Salvatrucha on a national level. Such a young, naïve girl, with so very much power. Her placement in witness protection also reflected the government's acknowledgment that the Mara Salvatrucha was an organized criminal group, one able to reach out and get to Brenda from many places within the United States. The marshals took Brenda's security very seriously, as with any top-level informant. The long stretches of solitude required for security, though, were undoubtedly Brenda's Achilles' heel.

Before Brenda had boarded the plane, Greg snapped her picture, proof she had boarded her flight. He took the photo at a memorable moment in both their lives. It was May 10, 2003. Walking out of the terminal, Greg couldn't help but wonder if he would ever see her again.

CHAPTER 43

Brenda wasn't back in Kansas long before the unthinkable happened. She spotted an MS member and was afraid that he had
recognized her. The marshals didn't take any chances. They moved
Brenda to Rosemount, Minnesota.

The process of moving Brenda from Kansas City to Rosemount was
not pleasant. She was very confrontational. The marshals wanted to
restrict her movements; Brenda wanted freedom. She had a long, serious conversation with her handlers. She told them she needed a social
outlet in Minnesota, but they told her it was not possible. She needed
to keep a very low profile at the outset. After some time they would
review her security situation and see if they could allow her more freedom. They gave her the same ultimatum as Alexander: follow the rules
or you're out.

Brenda called Greg from her new home in Minnesota, distraught.
She couldn't stand her restricted situation and was afraid of spending
time alone. She reached out to him from hundreds of miles away for
reassurances that everything would be all right. Brenda the needy teenager pleaded for help, but Greg had no leverage. She was out of the
state and in a federal system. As much as he wanted to help her, he simply couldn't. They were not even supposed to be talking on the phone.

Greg explained that she had to make a life-or-death choice. She
needed to find a way to follow the rules and move forward, or she

could leave the program but face a life of probable squalor and possible death. For the duration of a very difficult conversation, Greg tried to keep Brenda focused on her future and how her sacrifice and distance from her friends could pay off. When the conversation ended, Greg hung up the phone with a heavy heart. Brenda was a young girl in an extremely difficult situation. She was in a secret federal program not designed to accommodate teens without at least one parental figure. He was not even supposed to talk to her and could do nothing to create change in her daily activities. Greg wanted to believe Brenda had some sort of social outlet. He had no idea she had been told to stay in a hotel room by herself. There was no way the marshals could know how much Brenda hated solitude.

Greg was torn. He knew contacting the marshals about Brenda's past misbehavior and possible future problems was the right thing to do. They should know that she was calling him and had been sneaking out. But if he blew the whistle on her it would only jeopardize her safety. She could lose her place in witness protection. Above anything, he wanted her to remain in the program. Calling the marshals to debrief them on Brenda's wayward behavior and problems with loneliness, Greg decided, could only do more harm than good. He kept her trips to Philadelphia and Virginia to himself.

It was late spring, and Minnesota was still cold and dark. Brenda was housed in a hotel room under relatively loose supervision. She thought over her situation. Her handler with the marshals would come by once a day to check in on her, stay for only a moment, and leave. He was strict, not a friendly man, and he was there to do a job, not become Brenda's best friend or offer any consolation or empathy for her situation. Every day he told her not to leave the hotel premises. She hated that. She spent most of her time alone, waiting for the day she would be called back to Virginia to take the witness stand. There was nothing else to do.

Sometimes she flipped her new license over in her hand. She recognized her face in the photograph, but she wasn't from Ohio. Her name wasn't Ellysia. The novelty of it had worn off, and she began to resent her weird new name and fabricated past. The marshals told her she could never again be Brenda Paz. But she *was* Brenda Paz. Brenda Paz had more personality and life in her pinky finger than most people had in their whole bodies. No new name could rob her of her identity and spirit. It was a confusing mess of personality crossdressing in a moment in her life when most teens are still stumbling over who they are and what their own name means to them as an individual. The reality of never again being Brenda Paz was unreal. Brenda Paz was someone she liked and was comfortable with, and having to deny her self was a heavy weight on her young psyche. Brenda chucked the annoying license on the floor, only to pick it up again many times while holed up in her room.

Other times, Brenda couldn't stop thinking about her future. She wanted an education and a job. She longed for the time when she could be through with all of this and put the MS permanently in her past. She cursed Veto. She cursed the damned situation in Texas that forced her to choose between her uncle's house and the street. She cried and missed her family. Brenda was also terrified of testifying in court. How could she sit on the stand in front of Denis and say the words that would put him in prison for life? Could she even face Veto again? They were frightening thoughts. What worried her more than testifying had nothing to do with the MS, school, or a job. It had everything to do with the boy she had met in Philadelphia.

One thought above all others reverberated in her head like a ringing tower bell. Brenda Paz was pregnant.

CHAPTER 44

Hormones coursed through Brenda, out of control. Three months into it, and her body was changing. Everything was changing. She cried herself to sleep. She was in a new place, with a new name, and would soon be a mom. Her pregnancy distorted her perception of reality and her situation. It amplified every worry and stressor in her life. The constant drone of the inner voice in her head became a shouting match she had with herself. Besides, who else was there to argue with? The angel on one shoulder shouted through her head to tell the devil on the other side to be quiet. She was emotional and weepy for seemingly no reason. She needed to be away from this place, away from the hotel, away from the marshals. She needed to be with someone, but not just anyone. Brenda desperately needed to be with her baby's father.

They still kept in touch. She knew he was still in Philadelphia. She longed to see him, hoping he would help her feel joy for the growing life inside her, and longing for someone who would share the burden of her doubts and fears about being a mother. Her need to be with the father of her child rose above all her other problems, doubts, fears, and logical reasoning. The marshals handling her in Minnesota were either oblivious to her need or simply didn't care.

CHAPTER 45

With little interaction in her immediate surroundings, Brenda thought through every angle possible. How could she get back to Philadelphia? She didn't have much money, certainly not enough to get far. And she knew Greg wouldn't support her plans to run away. As much as she didn't want to admit it to herself, her best option was to go back to Virginia, get back in touch with her homies there, if only for a short while.

Brenda knew it would be only a matter of time before someone found out about her betrayal, but it was a calculated risk. She was still considered someone important, and as long as Veto and Denis didn't say otherwise, Brenda was still a respected member. Even if someone suspected her as a traitor and wanted to kill her, there would be an investigation. It would take time before anyone could put a *luz verde* on her. She sat on the edge of her bed, alone, emotional, and resolute. She could get to Philadelphia from Virginia; she'd just have to be smart about it.

When Brenda finally did reach out to her homies in Virginia, she had to go through Denis's two trusted men on the outside. She couldn't call him directly in jail. He had to make a call out to a preauthorized number and then wait on the line while the person he called made a separate call to a third party. Only through these three-way calls was Denis able to speak with Brenda.

Boxer and Filosofo were the only two men in constant contact with Denis. Boxer was one of the members chasing her when Greg rescued her from the McDonald's. He was also Denis's eyes and ears on the outside. Denis managed to rein in Boxer, but he couldn't control the young MS member's contempt for someone he considered a rat. Boxer hated Brenda and didn't understand why Denis still wanted to keep her alive. Filosofo was a young member in Denis's clique. He was an errand boy and did as he was told, mostly passing messages from Denis to other gang members on the outside. He asked no questions but agreed with Boxer that Brenda should be killed.

When she finally got in touch with Denis, they had a long talk to catch up on everything. Brenda explained that she had been moved to Minnesota and how much she hated it there. Better than prison, Denis thought. He explained how he planned to escape custody during a transfer from the prison to the police headquarters where he had his interviews with Detective Rodriguez.

Denis thought about getting the police to drive him from the jail in Arlington to an interview room in Alexandria so Boxer and Filosofo could set up an ambush, kill the cops in the car, and set him free. But then he quickly backed away from that plan. Boxer was hesitant about killing two cops at once, and Denis expected serious repercussions within the MS leadership if he tried to pull off such a stunt. Another idea was to break out of his cell through the window and climb down a rope thrown up to him from below by Boxer or Filosofo. But Denis needed information. He had to know if people had tried it before and what would happen once his homies arrived at the side of the building where they would throw him the rope.

Denis's planning process lasted for a number of days and occupied the better part of at least half a dozen phone calls with Boxer, Filosofo, and Brenda. Once Denis settled on his escape plan, he told Brenda he needed more information and wanted to call Greg. Brenda thought it was a stupid idea, but she gave him the number anyway. Boys will be boys, she thought. Anyway, Greg would talk some sense into him.

Denis told Filosofo to anonymously call Greg on a three-way call so he could listen on the other line. Denis instructed Filosofo to get information out of Greg by asking random questions about prison breakouts, what the cops would do, and what happens in escape investigations and prosecutions.

When he called Greg, Filosofo didn't tell Greg who he was, but Greg correctly assumed it was Denis's clique member and one of his main connections from prison to the real world. He was curious about why this kid would be calling him and decided to play along.

As Brenda suspected, Greg thought any idea for a breakout was stupid. There was a thick glass pane in all prison cell windows, and even if someone managed to rope down three stories from the window, he wouldn't get far from the prison before all the cops in northern Virginia would be out looking for him. It was absurd.

Denis didn't care. "Fuck it," he said in one of his last phone conversations with Brenda. "Yeah, fuck it," she replied, but it was the gangster in her talking. Despite her words, she grew worried. Brenda knew if he tried to escape, his chances were slim, and after he was captured, it would be impossible for her to see him. She couldn't let Denis try to escape. Greg could fix it. She called him from her hotel room and told him she had talked to Denis and that he was planning on breaking out. Greg immediately linked her confession with the phone call he had received from Filosofo. He was stupefied. Denis was the last person Brenda should be calling. But Greg kept calm. She may be back in touch with her MS friends, he thought, but at least she was still in Minnesota, a far distance from Virginia.

When he ran into Detective Rodriguez at court soon after his phone call with Brenda, Greg told him he had credible information on a possible breakout organized by a guy named Joker. Greg didn't want to mention Denis's name because he knew it would implicate Brenda. If he simply alerted Rodriguez to an escape plan, then the prison deputies would turn over every cell in the building to figure out who was behind the caper. That was good enough for Greg.

Any escape plan normally involved knocking out or otherwise harming a policeman. Rodriguez wanted to prevent anyone from being hurt and immediately notified the deputies at the prison that he had information on an escape plan. Rodriguez didn't think it could be Joker. The only Joker he knew was an MS member who had been released just two days before Rodriguez learned of the escape plan from Greg. He suspected it might have something to do with Brenda, and knew Greg wouldn't do or say anything to implicate her, so he took Greg's warning at face value and didn't press for the truth.

Rodriguez asked the deputies to look into another inmate named Joker. The deputies asked around and quickly found themselves in Denis's cell. They searched it and found the map he had drawn indicating his plans for escape. His chances of breaking out were over. Denis was furious. When he got on the phone with Filosofo in mid-May, he was determined to find out if Brenda had tipped the cops to his plans.

Denis called Filosofo and immediately asked him to call Brenda so he could listen to their conversation without Brenda knowing he was on the line.

"I will cover the phone now, and you call her now, talk to her for seven minutes," Denis told Filosofo. He was very specific with Filosofo. There were high stakes here. The woman he had protected for so long might have betrayed him. He didn't know how much longer Brenda would be at the hotel or room number she had given them, so it was likely a one-time shot to confirm if she ratted on him.

"Okay," Filosofo responded, obedient as ever.

"Seven, eight minutes, but try to get all the information that you can, about the lawyer, everything," Denis said. He wanted to know if she had spoken with Greg.

"Okay," Filosofo responded, taking orders.

"And chatter with her, throw her some chatter," Denis suggested. He knew Brenda was talkative. If Filosofo could get her to relax and talk, maybe she would slip and say something wrong.

Denis instructed Filosofo to relay the message that he was going to break out in two months, since his earlier plans had been foiled. When he broke out, he would come looking for Brenda first.

Filosofo started dialing Brenda's number in Minnesota. Denis pressed the palm of his hand against the microphone on his end of the line and listened.

When the Marriot hotel clerk answered, Filosofo asked for room 111. He hoped Brenda was still in the same room where she had told them she was staying.

"Hello," Brenda answered.

"Hello," Filosofo began.

"Wait," Brenda interrupted.

When she came back on the line, Filosofo started the chatter.

"Let's see, so are you going to send me the money then?" he asked. Brenda had previously agreed to send him money to share with Denis. It was part of the money the marshals had given her as allowance.

"Yes," Brenda said.

"But through Western Union?" Filosofo asked.

"I don't know. I will send it somehow," she responded.

"So what's up?" Filosofo asked. His time was running out. And Denis was listening. He needed to get her to say something.

"Nothing, you say something or put on that song."

"Which one?"

"The one that goes . . ." And Brenda began singing a love song.

"I don't have that one," Filosofo said, laughing as Brenda continued to sing.

"Does it remind you of Denis?" he asked.

"I don't think so," she said flippantly

"And you love him? Do you miss him?" Filosofo pried

"We hardly even talk," Brenda lamented.

"Who, you and him?" Filosofo asked.

"Yeah. But we used to speak all the time. I miss him," Brenda admitted.

"He will be out soon, like in two months," Filosofo said, delivering Denis's message.

"As long as they don't kill him," Brenda corrected. She was worried any escape plan might lead to ruin.

"No, they will not kill him. Who told you that? Did he tell you?" Filosofo asked. Denis was surely interested to know the answer.

"No, his lawyer and mine," Brenda stated.

"They told you he was going to get that? Who knows. But he's going to get out. He's going to be looking for you, eh?" Filosofo said, dutifully delivering his boss's message.

"Yeah, right." Brenda wasn't so sure. "I asked my lawyer a lot of questions, but I didn't tell him it is for Denis but that it was for another homeboy. And he tells me that others have tried, but they could not [get out]. So, just for trying they give them one year. From Alexandria they have tried and almost got out, but they did not, because the federals are there in the building. In Fairfax when they are there it is a little bit easier because they have docks, where clothes are brought in. Over there [it] is easier, but you have to plan and know the building," Brenda explained.

"What a problem. Do you think he will do it now?" Filosofo wanted more information.

"The thing is that the homeboy . . . he can do it from anywhere, but that's because I have a lot of faith. You know what I mean?" Brenda did believe Denis was crazy enough to try an escape. "My lawyer told me, he said: 'Tell your friend that if he is planning to go back to his country, he better not do it, because when he escapes, then it will be federal, it will be all the police,' " she concluded.

Hearing all he needed to know, Filosofo told Brenda he had another call and hung up. Back on the line with Denis, Filosofo went over his conversation.

"Well, she told me all I wanted to know, yeah?" he asked Denis, seeking approval.

"More or less, homes, but she is a big, super," Denis said, using gang slang to describe Brenda as a big traitor, finally beginning to believe that Brenda had betrayed him. "Yeah, homes, she is a big, and I'm a stupid fuck for trusting, homes." He was seething and felt like Brenda had played him for a fool.

"Do you think it was her? I think it was her," Filosofo responded. He believed Brenda ratted out Denis's plans to Greg.

"Because, why on earth did she have to tell the lawyer, homes?" Denis asked, clearly frustrated with Brenda.

"She messed up there," Filosofo agreed.

"Stupid fucking bitch, homes." Denis began cursing and didn't stop for minutes.

Denis was convinced Brenda had ruined his best chance to escape. He had other ideas, but the plans he'd been working on for weeks were ruined by the very girl he protected, the girl who he thought loved him and would never betray him. Brenda was now dead to him. She was no longer someone special, and if he could, Denis would kill her.

CHAPTER 46

Once the cops were on to Denis's plans for escape, they gave him special "escape risk" status. The police doubled his guard during all his movements from court to prison, and after his last attempt to soften Denis, Rodriguez completely gave up on him as an informant. He no longer had any chance of escape or reducing his sentence. All he had left on his hands was time. Time to think on his life, time to stew over Brenda's betrayal. Time to plan her death.

The calls to Brenda began. During the second week of May, Brenda took a call from Filosofo. It was simply a reminder that Denis was the top dog. It was a veiled threat, but Brenda decided to ignore it. Filosofo was probably just mouthing off.

The next day, Denis asked Filosofo to call Brenda again, this time to convince her to have an abortion. Through Boxer and Filosofo, word had spread through the MS that Brenda was pregnant. This complicated Denis's plan.

"If I arrive one day and I make her like that and both of them leave, it's better for only one to leave." Denis was using a thinly veiled code. If he had the chance to kill her himself, he wanted not to have to worry about killing a fetus.

Once Denis believed that Brenda had ratted about his prison escape plans, larger possibilities loomed. He had to assume that Brenda had told Greg and the police what he had told her about killing Diaz. He was right. But he didn't know that three of his homies who were there the night he killed Joaquin had also betrayed him. They were all cooperating with the prosecution to reduce their sentences. Nearly everyone involved that night had betrayed Denis, but his focus was Brenda.

The next day, Denis called Filosofo again.

"If she wants to play games, then we'll play games," Denis told his subordinate.

"In a park, you know, we have to *pisarla*, such a big *pisada* that you won't even be able to get up after that," he instructed.

Filosofo got the message. Denis used the word *pisar* to veil what he wanted to say: kill.

CHAPTER 47

As events unfolded in Virginia, Brenda remained in her own prison in Minnesota. Filosofo stopped calling her, and now the phone never rang. Her only connection to Virginia at the time was dependent on Denis. Brenda never considered that Filosofo had stopped calling because Denis had told him to. Since Denis planned on killing Brenda, the last thing he wanted to do was tip her off. He knew how to rock the cradle as well as any gangster, but he also knew Brenda's Achilles' heel. She was at rock bottom in Minnesota, alone and desperate for attention. If he waited long enough, he was sure she would make her own way back to Virginia.

Days in Minnesota passed into weeks of unbearable solitude. Her belly grew. Her need to see the father of her baby loomed over her. As much as she reasoned through it, Virginia continued to be her best bet for getting back to Philadelphia. Days passed in increments of moments that dragged into unbearable periods of time. By late May, Brenda had resolved to take a chance at reaching out to other friends in Virginia. She used most of the allowance the marshals provided to make regular calls back to her homies with the Centrales clique in Virginia. At least on the phone she could pass the time and forget for a moment the images, emotions, hormones, and boredom that saturated her mind.

Brenda's list of phone contacts grew and grew. She called Maria

Gomez, the girl who had found the police business cards in the purse that she had lent Brenda. Brenda had tried to get in touch with Araña, the father of Maria's daughter, and Brenda's friend from the safe-house days. She had called the clique leader Pantera, the man who embraced her as his girl at the beginning of the year, when she fell back in with the Centrales. And she called Pantera's little brother, Diablito. He was someone else to chat with. Sometimes, when no one she asked for was home, she simply tried to talk to whoever was on the phone. Brenda was beyond desperate. She was borderline depressed and not thinking clearly. She seriously considered just walking away, leaving witness protection to go out on her own and somehow find her way back to her baby's father. But it was still cold and rainy in Minnesota—not the best place for her to wander the streets with no place to sleep or eat.

Long weeks of more hotel time stretched far into her future, beyond the horizon line of her tolerance. She could no longer see those inspirational images of the future when she was back in California with all her family around her, or with her mother and her baby. She was restless and needed to do something to speed up this process. She knew safety was necessary, but it was unbearable.

CHAPTER 48

In early June, Brenda called Greg. He was long overdue for some vacation and was on the way to Baltimore-Washington Airport to catch a flight to Russia.

He spoke with Brenda right up until his flight took off. He went over all the things she needed: an education, tattoo removal, psychological care, prenatal care, protection, and new friends who were not sociopathic felons. She could provide none of these items for herself unless she stayed in witness protection. He tried to reason with her and again help her to see a path to her future. It was a heartfelt conversation, but Greg wasn't sure he'd gotten through. He hung up with a sigh. Brenda was in trouble and he was on a flight to Russia. He reminded himself that he had done everything he could. She was in the hands of the marshals now.

Not long after her conversation with Greg, Brenda stared at the phone for a long time before she called Pantera's little brother, Diablito, and asked if he would come visit her. He hesitated.

"I've got a way for you to earn money up here," Brenda told him. It was a ruse to get him to visit her. He agreed but didn't have much money. Brenda made two more phone calls that day to arrange a Western Union wire. With the $150 Brenda sent him, Diablito got in touch with two other Centrales members. One had a car and was willing to make the drive.

The day Brenda asked them to drive from Virginia to Minnesota was an acute moment in time when she could have said no to herself, but something else inside her won out. She wanted to party and hang out with her friends for a little while, thinking she could lie to them about her current situation like she did when she was at the FBI safe house, and then let them leave. If she was careful, the marshals would never know. It was one precarious step back into the gangster life.

The day the three members of the Centrales got up to make the fourteen-hour drive to Brenda's hotel in Rosemount, they told no one and simply headed out. When Brenda eagerly opened the door for her visitors, Diablito's mouth dropped open.

"Wow, nice digs," he said as he entered the room, eyes wide, marveling at the lush furnishings and fancy décor. The three homies walked through, checking out the room and bouncing on the bed, as Brenda chattered excitedly. They were obviously overwhelmed by the hotel's luxury. It was much nicer than the hotels they usually partied in.

Brenda's room was luxurious and obviously expensive. She quickly improvised that her dad paid the bills, building on the lies she had started while living in the safe house. As Diablito made himself at home by stretching out on the bed, she told them her dad was a successful drug dealer and had tons of money. And he was around, so they would have to be careful when he came by to visit. Diablito nodded his understanding at this, then held out his arms to Brenda. She gave him that famous smile and fell into his hug, telling him, "As long as you're quiet when my dad comes by, you can stay a little while."

She was thrilled to have people she cared about back with her again. They'd just have to be careful of her "dad"—this time it was her marshal handler, the guy who rarely invested more than a minute or two on Brenda. It shouldn't be too difficult, she thought.

Her handler arrived that very day. Brenda hushed the boys and told them to hide, then stepped into the hall to speak to him. It wasn't a big deal at all. No sweat, she thought. She dispatched him quickly, and after that, every time the marshal came by, Brenda gave the word and they hid.

Between visits from her "dad," Brenda and her Centrales homies partied. One of them called El Salvador from the hotel phone with Brenda's cards. They charged drinks from the hotel bar to the room. They collected hotel bath products in bags to bring home to Virginia. It was a vacation for Diablito and his homies, Brenda thought with a smile. Her ruse had worked. She felt like she was back in the gang life, but more importantly, she had a distraction from the pressing weight of her reality and future. The partying lasted for days, but eventually Brenda's lies began to crack.

One of the last mornings the Centrales members were in Minnesota, Brenda told them they would have to head out to beg for money. Diablito was curious.

"If your dad has so much money, then why do we have to beg for more? We can call room service for food and get drinks from the bar," he argued.

"My dad is tired of paying for all this partying," she explained. They needed to go out and get more money if they wanted to party, she said.

Diablito refused. He stayed alone in the room while the rest walked to a nearby mall where they could beg for change. Something didn't add up. Brenda was acting a little funny, raising Diablito's suspicions.

As soon as she left, he started rummaging through the dresser drawers. Nothing. Then he attacked the bedside table. Nothing. Running his hand through his hair, he thought, maybe it's nothing. As he poked aimlessly through her things in the closet, he saw some bags tucked toward the back.

Diablito immediately dragged them out and quickly ripped them open. A blue spiral notebook caught his eye, then a diary and a billfold. Jackpot. Reading through the notebook, he came across references from months ago when Brenda had talked to the police. Holy shit, he thought. His mind raced. He found more of the same information in her diary, and in her billfold he found police business cards.

Diablito didn't know what to do. He was stunned. Evidence spread out on the floor before him. He looked away and looked back at the floor. It was unbelievable. Here was hard-core proof that Brenda had lied to them for months. She's a rat! his mind screamed. Smiley's a traitor! He still couldn't believe it. She was so cool, so respected. She had fooled all of them, even Denis, maybe even Veto.

Brenda was as good as dead. He was completely shocked. His mind ran through questions. Would they kill Smiley? Everyone loved Smiley. Denis will be furious when he finds out, Diablito thought. He would certainly want to put a *luz verde* on her. That was serious. Diablito didn't like the thought of Brenda being killed. She was pregnant! His mind raced ahead. There would be meetings, maybe even an investigation. Brenda wasn't just any low-level homie. As far as he knew, she had backing from Denis and Veto. This was over his head. *Mierda, mierda*, he inwardly cursed.

Diablito didn't know what to do, so he decided to play it cool. He took a second to think it out, then decided his brother would know what to do. He knew he needed to show the evidence to Pantera and Brenda's friend Araña. Let them make the decisions. He would be the messenger.

Diablito gathered up the damning evidence and stashed it away deep in his bags, planning on showing it to his brother as soon as he got back to Virginia. He told no one and focused on calming down so he could act normal when Brenda returned to the room. He shook out his hands and took some calming breaths before double-checking to make sure everything looked normal. This was the most important moment in his life as an MS member. He had to act cool and not tip Brenda. She was smart. If he was anything but completely cool, she would know something was up. If he messed up, they wouldn't just kill Brenda, they'd kill him too.

The next night, Brenda, Diablito, and their two other homies were all kicked out of the hotel. Excessive partying and unruly behavior was to blame. Diablito and the others said they would just leave. They stood in the parking lot near the car and invited her to come with them. Brenda was in the worst possible place imaginable. The last thing she needed was instability and forced decision making. She was not level-headed. After days of partying, a variety show of thoughts, memories, and worries had driven her just short of madness. It was too much for a seventeen-year-old pregnant kid, straddling two worlds: her gang life and her reality as a protected witness who had betrayed the Mara Salvatrucha.

Brenda stood in the hotel parking lot looking at the three MS members. They were silent, packed and ready to go, just waiting for her decision. This is it, she thought. This is my free ride out of here, and a real chance to make it to Philadelphia. She paused a moment to weigh her other option: watch her Centrales homies drive off to Virginia and face the wrath of the marshals in the morning. Without a backward glance, Brenda walked toward the car and closed the door. It was the path of least resistance, despite all the ugly possibilities that awaited her back in Virginia.

For Brenda, there was a strong force pulling her back to the East

Coast that overrode the inherent risks she was taking. For most women her age, pregnancy is something foreign, scary even. Not for Brenda. She had had plenty of time to think in her little hotel room and had grown accustomed to the idea of being a mom. Brenda's pregnancy made her happy, even ecstatic at times. It was a whole new reason to live and move ahead with her life. If only she could share this joy with the baby's father, she knew her happiness would be complete. She would be complete. Brenda didn't think twice in that moment about hopping the ride to Virginia with three MS members. Her sights were set on Philadelphia.

As Brenda rode along silently in the car, she calculated. If she could hang out with the Centrales long enough to pull together the money to get back to Philadelphia, she could track down her baby's father. It shouldn't take long. Before anyone knew the truth, she would be gone, and with her new identity in place, she could slip into her new life with her baby and her man. She knew she could do it.

CHAPTER 49

The day Brenda left witness protection, Greg was in St. Petersburg, Russia, walking the murder tour organized around the plot to *Crime and Punishment*. Dostoevsky's story reminded him of Brenda's struggle on her own walk through life as she tried to figure out what she truly wanted—a better future or the instant gratification of the gang life? In the early days of their relationship, Greg and Brenda had discussed the book at great length. It was one of his favorite novels and he was pleased Brenda liked it so much.

Greg recalled a scene in *Crime and Punishment* when Raskolnikov, the protagonist, stands by a canal looking at his reflection. In an introspective moment, he tries to decide whether to commit a murder or not, resign himself to a life of crime or not. At about the time that Brenda left the Witness Protection Program, Greg was standing by the canal where Raskolnikov made his ultimate decision to abandon a future of prosperity and enter a life of crime.

On the way back to Virginia, Brenda called Greg from a pay phone. She wanted him to know she was headed back to her old life. But Greg didn't get the message for another day. After the long drive, Diablito, Brenda, and the others arrived at Maria Gomez's house. Diablito got his things out of the car and walked straight into Maria's room, where he handed her the evidence of Brenda's betrayal for safekeeping. She didn't know what it was; she just agreed to keep it for him and not look at it. Diablito then called his brother. He had to get this off his chest. He had managed to fool Brenda so far but was barely able to contain his message. When Pantera arrived, Diablito showed him the information. Now he could finally relax. Pantera would know what to do.

As Diablito watched, his brother looked over Brenda's things. He was silent, carefully reading the evidence. Pantera finally looked up and acknowledged that there was no doubt about it, Brenda was talking to the cops. Araña and Maria had never said a word about the police business cards Maria had found in Brenda's purse—but they didn't have to. Brenda was careless with her belongings too many times for her homies to ignore the truth. The paper trail had burned her. When Araña found out about the information Diablito had uncovered, he was furious. How could Brenda betray them? They were a family. She had played them for fools for months. She had betrayed him personally, and now all their lives were in danger. They had to stop Brenda from talking to the police. Pantera agreed. Both knew Brenda had to die. When Pantera received the evidence from his little brother, he already knew Denis wanted her dead, but Denis had only said she had betrayed him. Pantera didn't have any hard proof until Diablito and Brenda returned from Minnesota.

His first move was to take Brenda back into the clique with welcoming arms. From the first day she returned in Virginia, Pantera maneuvered himself to once again be her man. He showered her with attention and acted like everything was cool. Brenda was convinced she had him fooled, but Pantera let her play her game. He was babysitting her, and she had no idea.

Unaware of Diablito's discovery and Denis's change of heart, Brenda was very happy to be home and around friends. She felt safe and complete. She couldn't know that Filosofo had already spread Denis's message among the Virginia clique leaders. It was clear he wanted her dead.

Giving a *luz verde* to a respected gang member was no light matter. Denis wanted her dead but that in itself was not enough to permit the Centrales clique, the group babysitting her, to put out a *luz verde* on Brenda. For all they knew, he was just a bitter boyfriend. They needed someone higher up to give the order, or at least come up with more proof of her betrayal. Pantera, Araña, and the others were convinced Brenda had no idea they were on to her. They knew they had some time. Pantera and Araña started an internal investigation to determine the depth of Brenda's betrayal. It was a very serious matter. Everyone loved Brenda. She was Smiley. She had respect, and it was painful to think that someone so close to many of the gang's top leaders had betrayed them. No one was going to take killing her lightly.

Greg spoke with Brenda only days after she arrived in Virginia. "I had problems with the program," Brenda started. Once she began, her emotions spilled out like water over a dam. She thought the marshal assigned to her case was a jerk. She couldn't stand to be alone *and* pregnant. The pregnancy triggered mood swings, from extreme sadness to extreme joy. She swung wildly from happy to depressed, excited to frightened, optimistic to desperate. She would laugh—and then abruptly start crying. She couldn't sleep at night, but she couldn't stay awake during the day. Minnesota was horrible. She had missed her friends in Virginia. In all the talk, all the confession to Greg, however, Brenda never mentioned her secret plans to be with her child's father in Philadelphia.

Greg listened to Brenda with patience. Rather than give another one of the same lectures that didn't seem to work, he asked her about the pregnancy and the progress of removing tattoos. Brenda wanted to get rid of some of her more visible tattoos so she could eventually get a decent job, but that project was on hold, along with her other future plans. That first conversation ended on a somber note. Brenda promised she would call again, and Greg urged her to be safe.

Brenda had finally quelled the screaming loneliness of her life. Surrounded by her homies, she could easily cork the demons, ignore her desire to see her family, and put on hold her plans to get an education and a job. She had a single focus: pull together some money and head straight for Philadelphia. She was nearly four months pregnant and couldn't hide her belly. Her baby was the only positive force in her life. Her joy about motherhood was something she shared with everyone, dampened only slightly by the absence of her child's father.

Brenda took care of herself, taking prenatal vitamins and reading maternity magazines to learn more about what was happening inside her. She spent time with Maria Gomez, who had two children, and asked her questions about child care and giving birth. Maria was happy to talk to her, but she suspected Brenda was in trouble and wasn't comfortable with spending too much time with her. All the men in the Centrales clique suspected that Brenda was marked for death. They were playing it cool, but Maria had inside information from Araña. She knew it was only a matter of time before the Centrales killed Brenda. She didn't want to get too close.

Victoria Amaya, known as Sabrosa among the Centrales members, was another one of the girls hanging out when Brenda returned to Virginia. She had known Pantera for five years, hooking up with him off and on, and she had met his children. She was friends with his sister and younger brother, Diablito. In early 2003, while Brenda was still living in the safe house, Sabrosa had been arrested for embezzlement. While Sabrosa was out on bail and awaiting her trial, she thought she would have some fun before she was locked up. She dropped out of high school, left her two children with her parents, and began hanging out with Pantera's clique. Sabrosa was never jumped in to the MS, but the allure of the street life and her connection with Pantera was enough to make her welcome in the Centrales' social periphery.

Sabrosa met Brenda at a party at the Quality Inn soon after Brenda returned from Minnesota. Pantera, Araña, Diablito, and a number of other Centrales members and girls were at the party. After learning that Sabrosa had two kids of her own, Brenda spent long stretches of time seeking advice and tips about pregnancy, childbirth, and mothering from Sabrosa. The two became loose friends.

Pantera saw an opportunity to give Sabrosa orders to keep Brenda in her sight, never let her use the phone, and never let her get into any other car that was not hers. Sabrosa knew it was an odd request. But she was too far removed from the core of the gang's communications to know Pantera's true intentions. Sabrosa was the perfect person to babysit Brenda during the day, when Pantera was taking care of gang-related business. She didn't know enough to make Brenda suspicious, and she would keep Brenda company while the men continued the investigation to figure out if they could kill her.

Soon after they met, Brenda transferred all of her belongings to Sabrosa's SUV, a white Mazda Navaho. She lived out of the car, sleeping there or in the hotel rooms their group rented for the night. Sabrosa's car was the clique's primary vehicle. She and Pantera were the only two who could drive it. Because Sabrosa had a legitimate driver's license, she became the clique's official chauffer that summer, and her name was put on hotel rooms the clique rented.

They stayed in a number of hotels, always opting for the cheapest rooms at Virginia Lodge, Holiday Inn, or other low-priced hotel chains.

The group moved around because the Centrales often partied too hard and were kicked out. Once they were kicked out, it was nearly impossible to return. Managers and local police remembered too well.

After a couple of weeks on the street with Sabrosa, Brenda confided in her and told her of her plans to gather enough money to head for Philadelphia and be with the father of her child. She wasn't leaving the gang; she just wanted to take care of her baby. Sabrosa shrugged off the information. She thought it was just girl talk and told no one. By sheer luck, Brenda had stumbled on someone she could truly confide in. Sabrosa didn't seek to protect Brenda's secret—she simply didn't care. With a couple of girlfriends and her place at Pantera's side all organized, Brenda felt like she had never left the street life.

CHAPTER 50

News of Brenda's decision to leave witness protection was delayed. Brenda left Minnesota in early June 2003, but it was at least two weeks later before Special Agent Alexander received word that Brenda was gone. A week later, her discharge from witness protection was official. The news weighed on Alexander. He knew there was nothing he could do to help her now. Brenda had made her decision. He hated that she was back on the street and likely in danger, but he couldn't force her to do what he thought was right. Brenda gambled with her own life and he was no longer in a position to help. Alexander could only call Greg to make sure he knew she was back on the streets and possibly in the Virginia area.

Greg already knew, but when he spoke with Alexander, he told the FBI agent he was focused on getting Brenda to come in off the streets. She could even stay at his place. With Brenda's new identity, they could find a program for teen mothers in another state, Greg offered. Alexander agreed it might be a good idea, but hung up with little hope. He wasn't sure what they could do for Brenda if she didn't want to help herself.

Greg remained focused. He would do anything to get Brenda away from the MS, and she continued to reach out. Greg and Brenda spoke a number of times that summer. In one phone call, they focused on Brenda's identity crisis, just one of her many problems. Her past was scrubbed. She couldn't be Brenda Paz anymore, but she didn't know who Ellysia Gonzalez was. She didn't have any of her old papers, but she couldn't go around with Ellysia's driver's license and background. Ellysia was from Ohio. She was from California. She was Brenda Paz and she wanted her old life back.

"Let's go talk to the Marshal Service," Greg pleaded with her during one of their last phone conversations.

"Maybe later, but I think I've screwed up," Brenda said. At least she admitted some fault. But despite Greg's best arguments, Brenda still stuck to her original plan. She absolutely did not want to go back to Minnesota. From her point of view, her plan was still on track. She was making money and had a decent stash built up. She only needed a little more time, and she thought she had it. She believed Denis was still protecting her.

CHAPTER 51

"Do you know the situation with Paz?" Filosofo asked.

"No. What situation?" Denis responded. He had not heard anything.

"About the light." Filosofo was again using a simple code for *luz verde*.

"Oh! What about it?" Denis asked, excited by the news. He was pleased his homies had decided to kill Brenda.

"That she already has it. In a while they are going to do it," Filosofo said.

In early July, the men surrounding Brenda were serious about killing her. She was oblivious. Sabrosa was babysitting her, but not privy to the plans to kill her. She was just there for fun, and the rest of the girls, apart from Maria, had no idea what was going on. There was no way they could inadvertently tip her off. They were mired in their own lives.

Between her old life with the gang and a future she thought she could have in Philadelphia, part of Brenda reached out to Greg and the safety he could offer. But the growing baby inside of her forced her to stick to her decision to sneak away to Philadelphia. She knew if Greg got her to come back in, he might convince the marshals to take her back, but Brenda held out hope that she could get in touch with her baby's father.

Greg spoke to Brenda on a busy Friday in mid-July just after he finished a trial at the Arlington courthouse. He stepped into a nearby office and talked to Brenda until the battery on his phone ran out.

"Just tell me where you are and we'll come get you," Greg told her. He knew there wasn't a cop or federal agent in a thirty-mile radius who wouldn't drop what they were doing to bring Brenda to safety. She resisted, though she'd become wary. Brenda felt like she might be in trouble with the gang. Maybe the Centrales were babysitting her, but she thought she would work her way out of it.

"I talked my way into this, so I can talk my way out," Brenda told Greg in a resolute tone. After they hung up, Greg returned to work, thinking about what he could say to convince her to come into protective custody. There had to be something he could tell her to make logic in her click. He held on to the hope that Brenda would wise up. It was clear, though, that Brenda continued to make the wrong decisions. And his lecturing didn't help. She had to convince herself of the right decision or it just wasn't going to stick. He'd been through this with her so many times before. No amount of argument from Greg could change her mind before she was ready.

The next day, Sabrosa checked in to room 318 at the Holiday Inn next to the Fairfax mall. It was one of the clique's choice hotels. An MS member known as Little Boy worked behind the desk and gave Sabrosa a discount on the room. With Little Boy at the front desk, the Centrales members could party hard, knowing they were covered. But serious business had to be concluded before the party could begin. The men in the Centrales clique had a meeting, a *misa*. Cabro, the clique leader, and Pantera were present, along with Araña, Diablito, and a few others. As usual, there were no women present. After roll was taken and thirteen seconds of silent reflection were allowed to pass, Cabro opened the meeting with a letter in his hands.

He claimed it was a letter from a high-ranking MS member in another state, but refused to say where. Diablito suspected it might have been a letter from Veto in Texas. After Cabro had read sections of the letter out loud, everyone in the room knew what had to be done. A *luz verde* was handed down on Brenda Paz's head. A number of high-ranking and well-respected MS members agreed she was a rat. Pantera was the first to volunteer for the job. He had been the one closest to her since she came back from Minnesota, and they were sleeping together. She trusted him the most.

Araña also volunteered for the job. He was still furious with Brenda. He didn't want to believe she was a rat back in February when Maria had shown him the police business cards from the purse. He didn't want to believe now that a woman he grew to love like a sister could betray their family. But he had to own up to the truth. Brenda had to die.

That night was just like any other Saturday night in the gang life. Centrales members crammed into room 318 to tell jokes and stories, get high and drunk, finish up some tattoos for members who had earned rank, and stay up into the early morning hours reveling in the freedom of gang life. For Brenda it was just another destroyer party. She hung out, but she didn't party that hard. Her mind was on her baby and her future.

CHAPTER 52

Sabrosa woke up the next morning to catch a glimpse of Brenda, dressed and putting on her shoes. Pantera, Araña, Mousey, and one other Centrales member had just left the room. Sabrosa did not see the men leave and thought Brenda was making good on her escape to Philadelphia. She pretended to still be asleep and just watched Brenda put on her shoes and quietly leave the room.

As Brenda walked out, she mused that it would be the last time she would ever see that particular room, maybe even her last destroyer party. The time for her to leave was near—maybe even in a few days. But on this day, a beautiful Sunday morning, Brenda was determined to spend some quality time with some of her closest friends in the MS: her boyfriend at the time, Pantera, and her good friend Araña. She might be in trouble with the MS, but these guys wouldn't do anything to harm her. Today will be a good day, she thought as she walked out of the elevator to meet up with the others. Araña loved to fish and had always told Brenda he would invite her to go with him. Her chance had finally arrived.

The friends left the hotel and drove east to the Shenandoah River valley. They planned to drop off Mousey before heading to the river to fish and hang out. The drive to the mountains was uneventful. The ride along Interstate 66 was a straight shot to the small town where they dropped off Mousey. From there, the fishing expedition turned south on Interstate 81 and headed toward Meem's Bottom Bridge, a single-lane bridge that had sat in a quiet corner of eastern Virginia for over a hundred years.

With a 204-foot span of solid Burr arch truss construction, the old wooden bridge stretched across the north fork of the lazy, slow-moving Shenandoah. The spot was a favorite of fishermen seeking quiet and solitude away from major highways and commercial centers. The lush vegetation along the banks of the river was broken in places by small granite boulders that spread apart the forest just enough to provide room to cast a baited hook into the lazy ripples.

Pantera pulled the Mazda off the road just in front of the bridge. They all got out of the car and walked across the bridge, laughing and joking about the night before. They headed down to the river along a narrow muddy path. Spring and early summer rains had swollen the river beyond its banks, saturating and softening the ground as it receded. The old fisherman's path lay inside the small flood plane, twisting and turning through the forest, bending with the contours of the riverbank. Pantera was first, with Brenda following behind. Araña was behind her, and the fourth MS member followed some distance behind him.

Picking their way through the forest, the small group slowly made progress toward one of Araña's favorite fishing spots, next to some tall granite boulders that sat on the riverbank. They had to walk away from the river to get to higher ground and double back to a point where they could get on top of the rock formation and then climb down to the river. Pantera jumped off the small ledge first, landing on the riverbank. He then turned around to help Brenda. She was five months pregnant and couldn't jump down alone. She landed off balance and slipped and fell in the mud. Her hands and knees made indentions in the soft silt.

Araña jumped down as Pantera helped Brenda up. Pantera then positioned himself behind her. Araña stood in front of Brenda, facing the river, before he turned around and slowly removed the knife he had hidden under his shirt. He quickly approached her. Standing behind Brenda, Pantera slowly removed a rope and a knife from the backpack he wore.

Before Brenda saw the knife in Araña's hands, he reached forward and stabbed her in the inner thigh. Shocked by his sudden action, Brenda looked up at him.

"What happened, *homito*?" Brenda asked with love and concern in her voice.

But Araña didn't answer.

Pantera then reached over her head with the rope and pulled it tight across her neck. Brenda screamed and began struggling with the rope. Then she was silent.

She needed air.

Pantera held the rope tight with one hand and with a knife in the other, he reached over Brenda's shoulder and began stabbing her in the chest. Araña attacked a second time. He began repeatedly stabbing her stomach, sinking the knife in before pulling it out to stab her again.

The men worked with determination. No one spoke or yelled. Brenda had no air to fill her lungs for a second scream. The men breathed heavily. Both were resigned to their task. But Brenda didn't fight. Even if she had managed to defend herself or her attackers had had a sudden change of heart, it was already too late. The first stab in her inner thigh was enough to kill her. It had hit a main artery.

In the seconds between Araña's first cut and when Pantera attacked her from behind, a flood of realities hit Brenda with the full force of unavoidable certainty. Denis had betrayed her. She would never again see the father of her child. Her baby was dead. She would die alone.

They had all completely fooled her. She knew of so many schemes to babysit an MS target, but blinded by her love for Denis and the trust she felt for the two men wielding the knives, Brenda failed to see they were babysitting her.

"Why are you doing this?" Brenda struggled to get out.

Before Pantera cut deeply across Brenda's throat from behind, nearly decapitating her, Araña answered her question.

"This is for the Mara Salvatrucha."

Then Pantera let her go. Brenda's body fell lifelessly to the ground. The two left Brenda's body just feet from the riverbank behind the largest rock in the group of boulders by the river. The job was done. The traitor was dead.

The other MS member had no idea what had happened. Some distance away, he was throwing rocks into the river when he had heard Brenda scream. He looked downriver to see Araña and Pantera stabbing her. Frenzied and confused, he broke into a run and headed back to the car to await his fate. He didn't know if he'd be next. When the other two arrived, they chastised him for running away. What kind of gang member did that? On the way back to Virginia, the boy rode in the backseat, sick to his stomach. The other two chatted idly, but mostly rode in silence. Brenda's death, it seemed, weighed heavily on all of them.

CHAPTER 53

Brenda's body was not discovered for three days. Like Javier Calzada, fishermen who called the local cops found her remains. Lieutenant John Thomas, with the Shenandoah County sheriff's office, was one of the first local police to respond. Right away, he could tell it was a murder, but there was no identification on the body. He had a Jane Doe on his hands and needed to act fast to solve the mystery.

Eyeing the horrific scene, Thomas was sickened. He knew it had been a while since the murder had happened, and with a heavy sigh realized the visible tattoos were his best bet for identifying the victim. After making it through the long day of initiating the investigation, Thomas left the tragic scene and set about faxing the photos of the tattoos to a number of police departments around Virginia. He wondered if anyone would recognize them. Detective Mike Porter was the first to call—he'd lost track of a federal witness with similar tattoos.

After he got off the phone with Thomas, Porter immediately called Alexander.

"It looks like Brenda was killed in Shenandoah County," Porter said, with a mixture of remorse and frustration in his voice. He tried to be professional, as did Alexander, but both were considerably disturbed by Brenda's murder. They had worked hard to keep her safe and alive and were ultimately perplexed by her own decisions. What was going on in her head? Why did she go back to Virginia when she was perfectly safe in Minnesota? It was a mystery to them, but the murder itself was not. They knew there were a limited number of people who could have killed Brenda, and it was likely that those men were in their region. They were determined to find out what happened and catch her killers.

Later that night, Greg's phone rang. Before he began working Brenda's case, he had missed most calls that came in while he was sleeping. But during the long months of his relationship with Brenda, he had grown accustomed to her random calls at any hour. When his phone rang, he thought it might be her. It was Porter.

There is only one reason why Porter is calling at this hour, Greg thought. Brenda was dead.

Many thoughts simultaneously wove together through Greg's head. He was very disappointed, but not surprised. For weeks, Greg had steeled himself to Brenda's probable death. He'd always known it was a possible outcome to her story. His hope drained away and turned to dust. Up to that moment, Greg had held out a small amount of hope that somehow Brenda would pull out of her free fall. She would call someone or do something. He didn't know what, but somehow she would make it. He wondered about Denis. Wasn't he trying to protect her, or did he order her death?

Greg was grateful it was Porter who told him first. He knew the detective would give him the information in a genuine way and give him the space to work through it on his own. That night Greg didn't fall back asleep. His thoughts were focused on all the questions surrounding Brenda's murder—who, how, when, why?

The next day, Porter and Alexander drove out to meet with Thomas to make a positive match. After viewing the body they were all but positive it was Brenda Paz. The DNA and fingerprint reports confirmed it. A day later, it was official: the Jane Doe was Brenda Paz.

Alexander and the other detectives suspected that local MS members had killed Brenda. They scouted the area in Shenandoah County, but found little evidence to support that theory. The killers were long gone.

Before Brenda's body was identified, state troopers found Sabrosa, Pantera, Diablito, and others sitting in Sabrosa's car, parked in the emergency lane on the New Jersey Turnpike. They were driving to New York when Sabrosa's car broke down. With no other way to get around it, they accepted the help offered by the officers and made their way back to Virginia.

Sabrosa meant to get back to her car, but she never did. The New Jersey police impounded it, still muddy from the day Pantera and Araña took Brenda fishing. But the numerous members of law enforcement working on Brenda's case had not yet made that connection.

On the first day of August, a little under a year since Brenda had first met with Alexander and decided to become a federal witness, Porter hosted an interagency meeting to talk about the Brenda Paz murder case. All involved needed to get coordinated and figure out who did it.

A federal witness had been murdered, and a number of cops wanted in on the case. The National Park police claimed a lead role on the investigation because Brenda agreed to be a witness for the Joaquin Diaz murder on Daingerfield Island. Alexander offered to help coordinate all the information coming in from the various phone calls and interviews that police in Fairfax and Arlington conducted with Denis Rivera, who as the suspect in the Joaquin Diaz murder was seen as their primary suspect in Brenda Paz's murder. By now, all the cops involved were well apprised of the Mara Salvatrucha's willingness to intimidate and, if necessary, kill witnesses. It was Brenda who had told them.

Rick Rodriguez, Victor Ignacio, and Mike Porter offered support, and after the meeting went to their offices to immediately begin combing through their files and the interviews with Denis to track down the hit men. They knew Denis was in prison when Brenda was killed. Maybe he'd given the order, but someone else had carried it out.

Lieutenant Thomas in Shenandoah continued to receive calls from Porter and Rodriguez, who updated him on their work on the case. They were scouting bars, corners, and other popular MS hangouts in their areas, trying to find someone they could question about Brenda's murder.

Another interagency meeting was held five days later to go over all the information everyone had collected so far. They reviewed interview notes with Denis and other gang members. They went over transcripts of recorded conversations. The group generated a number of leads, but nothing was yet concrete.

Brenda's murder investigation proved difficult. There were so many individuals involved in the investigation that initially coordination was very challenging. Issues of jurisdiction arose. Lines of friction had to be ironed out before smooth progress could be made. Whether Denis and Pantera planned for this to happen or not, the networked nature of the Mara Salvatrucha took its toll on law enforcement.

A month after the second meeting among all the men working on Brenda's murder case, Rodriguez obtained critical information during an interview of a suspect in Arlington. There was a white Mazda SUV in New Jersey that Brenda might have ridden in during the weeks before she was killed. He called Alexander to tell him the news, and the FBI agent offered to follow up on the information. The car was searched four days later, and a significant amount of evidence was recovered.

In an unrelated event, Mousey, the MS member Pantera and Araña took home the day they killed Brenda, was interviewed in early October about criminal street gangs in northern Virginia. He was a random pickup and not initially considered part of the Brenda Paz murder investigation. During that interview Mousey revealed his connection to the Centrales clique and was placed on the growing list of suspects.

With information from Mousey's interview and the evidence found in Sabrosa's SUV, Porter, Rodriguez, and Alexander tightened the noose around a number of Centrales members in northern Virginia. It was only a matter of time before they arrested Pantera, Diablito, and Araña, all suspected of Brenda Paz's murder. But no indictment had yet been handed down.

Before his arrest, Pantera cornered Sabrosa.

"You'd better not say anything or else your kids will grow up without a mother or you'll get old without them," he told her. She knew it was not a hollow threat.

Enough evidence was found in Sabrosa's car and gleaned from a number of interviews to implicate Araña as a primary suspect. When his arrest warrant was served in Arlington, he went quietly, remorseful.

It wasn't long before he agreed to talk. By the end of the year, Rodriguez, Ignacio, and others had interviewed dozens of leads and put many people before a grand jury, trying to pull together all the angles in Brenda Paz's murder. They were close to an indictment, but obtaining one for a capital murder case took time, witnesses, cooperation from informed individuals, and undeniable evidence. Araña's confession would give them the additional information they needed.

Ignacio, Rodriguez, and another FBI agent had the opportunity to interview Araña in Alexandria. Nearly a year had passed since Brenda was killed, and they were finally close to bringing the investigation to court. Araña's own demons had worked on him for eleven months. He was prepared to talk.

Araña was mostly worried about his kids and Maria Gomez, the mother of his daughter. He knew the rules. If he told the cops about what happened, the MS might not be able to get to him, but they could get to Maria and the kids. Before talking about what happened that day on the north fork of the Shenandoah River, he asked for protection for his family.

Rodriguez couldn't offer him anything. Ignacio told Araña he should just do the right thing. Brenda had died a horrible death, and he was in a position to give her justice. Apparently that was enough. During two interviews, Araña told the police everything that had happened. He began by working around the edges, slowly moving toward the center of the investigators' concern.

Araña told them about his clique, the Centrales. He identified Diablito, Cabro, and Veto, but initially, Araña would not implicate himself, Pantera, or the other MS member present that day by the river. When he spoke of Denis, he told the police Denis loved Brenda.

"The guy loves her, you understand," Araña said.

"Brenda never suspected what was going to happen," Araña said, saddened by his own words. When he finally began telling the truth, Araña placed himself at the crime.

"We walked calmly through the woods to the river's edge and helped Brenda jump down from the rock." Araña described how Brenda was too pregnant to jump down by herself. After some pressure from Rodriguez, Araña admitted he was the first to stab her. He never implicated Pantera or the other MS member present and refused to testify on the stand.

After concluding the interviews with Araña, enough evidence was in place to issue an indictment and begin the capital murder case against Denis Rivera, Pantera, Araña, and the fourth MS member present that day.

CHAPTER 54

W hen Diablito, Pantera's little brother, agreed to testify, the lead attorney prosecuting Brenda's murder case, Ron Walutes, had obtained a compelling witness. Diablito was not at the scene of the crime, but he knew what his older brother had done and couldn't live with it. Diablito had joined the MS when he was fifteen. Pantera had told him not to, but Diablito didn't listen. His older brother, a cousin, and a number of friends were all in the Centrales clique. Diablito regretted speaking out against his brother and former friends once he was on the stand.

Ignacio, Rodriguez, Alexander, and Greg all testified in federal court for Walutes. Walutes also put Maria Gomez and Sabrosa on the witness stand. Each told the jury a specific side of the story and chain of events leading from when Brenda arrived in Virginia from Minnesota to the morning before she died.

Greg and all the investigators thought Denis would be found guilty of ordering Brenda's death. Rodriguez and others considered that Pantera and Araña might get off, but not Denis. They had him on numerous phone conversations, in letters, and from the mouths of the witnesses as the principle driver behind the *luz verde* issued on Brenda Paz.

The jury finally delivered the verdict on May 18, 2005. Pantera and Araña stood before the judge during the final minutes of what had been a yearlong criminal court trial. They were given the opportunity to speak to the court before the federal judge handed down the verdict, decided upon by twelve members of the jury.

Pantera offered no remorse. He thanked the judge for fair treatment and asked to have his visitation rights reinstated. He stated that he would seek no reprisal against those who testified against him.

Speaking to the judge, Araña was overcome with emotion, though many in the room thought his tears were crocodile tears.

"I want to apologize for my actions, for the harm I did to the families, to Brenda's family. I have not only hurt them, but I also hurt my family. I am very sorry, remorseful about everything. I apologize for all I've done in the past," he said.

"I would like to ask the government to establish programs so more young people are not killed or are committing these type of mistakes. Give more attention to the young people and families. As you have heard here, we have come from very modest, very poor families. All we have suffered is because we grew up without any support."

The two men sat down before the judge spoke.

"Brenda Paz was murdered because the rule of the gang was that if you cooperated with the police or law enforcement authorities, a green light would be placed on you and you would be murdered or retaliated against. Brenda Paz was an active participant in gangs. She was a young person, too, and it seems to me that the U.S. Marshals Service and the Witness Protection Program did not protect Brenda Paz. They were not prepared to handle someone so young, and they did a really poor job in managing her as a witness. I think everyone who heard this trial heard it. You don't take a fifteen- or sixteen-year-old gang member and drop her off in Minnesota, leave her in a hotel by herself without any supervision. What happened to her is unforgivable. The fact is that this murder was horrible. It was brutal. It was vicious."

The judge then asked Pantera and Araña to stand.

He began again in more somber tones, "As I said a moment ago, the murder of Brenda Paz was heinous. It was cruel. It was vicious." He paused here with solemn effect. "She was a pregnant woman, nearly decapitated and murdered and left out in the woods. This grievous act warrants the most grievous punishment the law allows.

"To be clear, the sentence I impose is one of life. What you do with it is up to you, but the jury has given you clear clues of what they hope and what they expect. The court joins that jury."

Denis was acquitted of all charges for Brenda's murder. He still had to serve time for the malicious-wounding charge, and he received a life sentence without parole for the death of Joaquin Diaz, but the jury found him not guilty of Brenda Paz's death.

Weeks after Brenda's murder trial, Denis received an indictment for his escape attempt. Rodriguez asked to serve the papers to Denis because he wanted to have a last one-on-one with the kid. During the investigation into Brenda's murder, Rodriguez remained vigilant for his possible killer. His persistence paid off around the same time police arrested Araña, when Rodriguez pulled over a car with Dallas plates. The guy driving the car was the hit man. If Brenda had never alerted him to the *luz verde*, the man he pulled over that day might have killed him. Rodriguez was convinced Brenda had saved his life, and now, rounding the corner to Denis's cell, he had a chance to share some final words with the guy he knew had ordered Brenda's death.

"I hope you burn in hell for what you've done," Rodriguez said, seething, only inches from Denis's face. "You had a pregnant girl killed for doing the exact same thing you did, you son of a bitch."

Denis ordered Brenda's death because of her betrayal, but Rodriguez knew better than anyone that Denis had also cooperated with the police. Denis did not provide nearly the amount of information Brenda offered, but any leader in the MS who knew Denis was talking to the cops would have had him killed.

Rodriguez had said his piece. He felt like partial justice had been served, but remained frustrated with the system for allowing Denis to have that victory. But Denis's efforts to kill Brenda did not silence her voice.

For her own reasons, Brenda had decided to speak out against a gang that became her family since running away from her uncle in Texas. The gang had grown into something she resented. She saw deeper into the workings of the Mara Salvatrucha, likely far deeper than any other female who came before her. She saw beyond the allure of the gang life. She saw the pointless nature of the gang, and she saw past her time with the gang into a future where she could have made something of her life.

Her knowledge of the Mara Salvatrucha opened the minds and eyes of law enforcement officers across a number of counties and states. The video Mike Porter made the day he taped her talking about stacking and other truths of the Mara Salvatrucha at the Massey Building was converted into a training video. Since her death, hundreds of young officers have seen that tape and learned in a little over one hour the basics of possibly the most dangerous gang in the United States today.

Brenda opened eyes in the federal government. Since her death, the FBI has organized a national MS-13 gang task force, dedicated solely to dismantling the organization from the top down. The Bureau of Alcohol, Tobacco, and Firearms, a federal law enforcement agency that has a long history of tackling violent organized crime, has set up its own regional task forces around the country to target the MS-13. Its task force in Langley Park, Maryland, has had much success in containing the spread of the Mara Salvatrucha from the suburbs of Washington, D.C., to smaller communities in the north.

Brenda's unfortunate death galvanized a group of law enforcement individuals at both the state and federal levels who in one way or another were touched by her glowing smile and addictive personality. When asked, those who remember Brenda first mention her smile, then her intelligence and her vast knowledge of the MS-13. What she told them is still in use today, and since Brenda's death, the MS-13 has been largely removed from northern Virginia, in great part owing to the investigative work and drive of Porter, Ignacio, Rodriguez, and others.

Some of Brenda's predictions have come true. Since Brenda's death, MS members have begun using tattoos less, and high-ranking individuals keep a low profile. Many suspect the gang is today more organized than it was when Brenda died, though most who try to understand the Mara Salvatrucha are not sure how far the gang has gone toward becoming a criminal family. There is evidence, however, that younger members take classes in business administration and finance. Older members may have developed business ties with the criminal community in Mexico and at major border crossings.

In the years to come, the FBI and state-level law enforcement will largely deal with an invisible enemy, one that will continue to blend in and thrive in the country's Latino communities unless law enforcement authorities pierce the fear and prejudice in these communities and coerce information from the men and women who are today more afraid of being deported than of reprisals from the members of the MS that live among them.

Since Brenda's death, Latino communities in northern Virginia at least have benefitted from more attention from local policymakers.

Once leaders in Arlington and Fairfax counties were willing to admit they had a gang problem, solutions poured in. Latino youths in these counties enjoy after-school options. There are more prevention programs in place, and most are working.

Yet the migratory nature of the MS-13 has carried the gang to the north, into regions as far afield as Long Island, Boston, and even Maine. Counties that have small police budgets, where towns barely warrant a zip code, have reported the presence of the MS-13.

Brenda's bravery prompted federal alertness to a problem that goes much further than the violence associated with one Latino gang. The Salvadorans that first formed the Mara Salvatrucha arrived in the United States to flee certain death in their home country. For many of the same reasons, Salvadorans and other Central Americans stream into the United States every day. They seek economic opportunity, freedom from fear, and some aspect of a better life.

After more than fifty witnesses and a year of questioning and cross-examination during the murder trial of Brenda Paz, one salient point surfaced beyond all others. Latino communities around the country are full of at-risk youths with little parental supervision and a lack of love and acceptance at home. Turning to the street, these children find the love and acceptance they seek in a street gang—until they wind up in prison, in a hospital, or dead. The truth is, they're able to leave the gang just as easily as they arrived. The path from jumping in to the moment they gain the courage to remove themselves from the gang, however, is fraught with criminal behavior. The strict code of conduct promotes violence, precluding an easy departure.

A jury found both Pantera and Araña guilty of the murder of Brenda Paz. Another jury found Denis guilty of murdering Joaquin Diaz. All three will likely spend the rest of their lives in prison because of deeds they committed in the name of the Mara Salvatrucha.

Brenda spent less than two years as a fully indoctrinated and respected member of the Mara Salvatrucha. During that time, her charisma and intelligence were enough to earn her more respect than most any other females in her gang. She became one of the best sources of information on the gang anyone had come across at that time. She endeared herself to all those in law enforcement who met her, learned from her, and ultimately realized how serious the Mara Salvatrucha was about dominating the gang subculture inside the United States.

Wherever Brenda went, she left dozens of friends and memories. It is uncommon for such a spirited and gifted woman to fall into the ranks of the Mara Salvatrucha, but such is the allure of gang life. The freedom and unconditional acceptance is intoxicating. Like so many others her age, she quickly became addicted to being a gangster only to find out some time later that the high came at too steep a price. Brenda's homies told her never to look back, never to dwell on what she'd done or seen. But she did. And her demons were most intimate when she was alone.